EIGHT YEARS WITH WILSON'S CABINET

Photo from Underwood & Underwood

President Wilson reading his war message to the Congress on April 2nd, 1917

EIGHT YEARS WITH WILSON'S CABINET

1913 to 1920

With a Personal Estimate of the President

by

DAVID F. HOUSTON

In Two Volumes

VOLUME II

GARDEN CITY   NEW YORK

DOUBLEDAY, PAGE & COMPANY

1926

CONTENTS

VOLUME II

APPENDICES

LIST OF ILLUSTRATIONS

EIGHT YEARS WITH
WILSON'S CABINET

EIGHT YEARS WITH WILSON'S CABINET

CHAPTER XXI

THE ATTACK ON THE TREATY

The Round Robin—The President's Discussions with Lodge, Borah, and Harding

ON THE 5th of March, the President again left New York for Paris. On the day preceding, immediately following the President's conferences with the members of the Foreign Relations Committee, Senator Lodge rose in the Senate and offered the following resolution for the immediate consideration of which he asked unanimous consent:

"Mr. President, I desire to take only a moment of the time of the Senate. I wish to offer the resolution which I hold in my hand, a very brief one:

"Whereas under the Constitution it is a function of the Senate to advise and consent to, or dissent from, the ratification of any treaty of the United States, and no such treaty can become operative without the consent of the Senate expressed by the affirmative vote of two thirds of the Senators present; and

"Whereas owing to the victory of the arms of the United States and of the nations with whom it is associated, a

[1]

Peace Conference was convened and is now in session at Paris for the purpose of settling the terms of peace; and

"Whereas a committee of the Conference has proposed a constitution for the League of Nations and the proposal is now before the Peace Conference for its consideration; Now, therefore, be it

"Resolved by the Senate of the United States in the discharge of its constitutional duty of advice in regard to treaties, That it is the sense of the Senate that while it is their sincere desire that the nations of the world should unite to promote peace and general disarmament, the constitution of the League of Nations in the form now proposed to the Peace Conference should not be accepted by the United States; and be it

"Resolved further, That it is the sense of the Senate that the negotiations on the part of the United States should immediately be directed to the utmost expedition of the urgent business of negotiating peace terms with Germany satisfactory to the United States and the nations with whom the United States is associated in the war against the German Government, and that the proposal for a league of nations to insure the permanent peace of the world should be then taken up for careful and serious consideration."

Senator Swanson objected to the introduction of the resolution. Further record is as follows:

"*Mr. Lodge:* Objection being made, of course I recognize the objection. I merely wish to add, by way of explanation, the following:

"The undersigned Senators of the United States, Members and Members-Elect of the Sixty-sixth Congress, hereby declare that, if they had had the opportunity, they would have voted for the foregoing resolution:

"Henry Cabot Lodge   James E. Watson
Philander C. Knox   Thomas Sterling
Lawrence Y. Sherman   J. S. Frelinghuysen
Harry S. New   W. G. Harding
George H. Moses   Frederick Hale
J. W. Wadsworth, Jr.   William E. Borah
Bert M. Fernald   Walter E. Edge
Albert B. Cummins   Reed Smoot
F. E. Warren   Asle J. Gronna
Frank B. Brandegee   Lawrence C. Phipps
William M. Calder   Selden P. Spencer
Henry W. Keyes   Hiram W. Johnson
Boies Penrose   Charles E. Townsend
Carroll S. Page   William P. Dillingham
George P. McLean   I. L. Lenroot
Joseph Irwin France   Miles Poindexter
Medill McCormick   Howard Sutherland
Charles Curtis   Truman H. Newberry
L. Heisler Ball."

It will be remembered that this action was taken when the draft of the League was in its preliminary form. A full report of the action of the Republican Senators was cabled to Europe and confronted the President when he arrived in Paris on March 14th. It was eagerly seized upon by those whom the President had to fight and greatly complicated his task, which was already more than sufficiently heavy.

While the President was still in Paris, Ex-President

[3]

Taft took steps to ascertain whether it would be agreeable to the President for him to cable certain suggestions affecting the League plan over which he had been thinking since the President's departure. The President cabled that he appreciated Mr. Taft's offer, and that he would welcome his suggestions. Mr. Taft offered suggestions concerning the Monroe Doctrine, the fixing of a term for the duration of the League, the limitation of armament, unanimity of action in the executive council, and safeguards against the League's action in domestic matters.

Attacks by Senators continued during the President's absence in France. On June 9th Senator Borah inserted in the *Congressional Record* a copy of the Treaty which he reported had been brought by newspapermen. This was scarcely a seemly thing for a Senator to do when he knew that the President of the United States, charged with negotiating treaties, would soon report the completed work of the Conference. On June 10th, Senator Knox served notice that the Covenant would have to be separated from the Treaty.

The President had left Paris on June 28th and immediately after his return to Washington, that is, on July 10th, he presented the Treaty to the Senate, and then the fight was out in the open.

The Senate Committee took the matter under advisement and began its study of the Treaty, including the Covenant.

I was in the West when the President landed on his second return from Europe. Both in Washington and through my contacts with the people in various sections on this Western trip, I had become fully aware of the efforts of the opposition to create antagonism to the

[4]

Treaty and particularly to the Covenant. I had the impression that certain Republican leaders were determined, not so much to bring about the rejection of the Treaty, as to destroy the President's prestige, to pull him down, and to make such modifications of the Treaty, whether necessary or not, as would enable them to say that the final outcome was their accomplishment, and that they had saved the nation from the ills which the Treaty would have brought upon it. They were continuing to play politics, having the election of 1920 particularly in view. I felt it to be a matter of great importance, before their views and representations made headway, that the President should at once give the people an authoritative statement of the meaning of the Treaty and of the Covenant, a review of the proceedings in Paris to show the temper and spirit of the Conference, and particularly to clarify such important parts of the Covenant as Article I, Section 3, the withdrawal article; Article X; Article XXI, dealing with the Monroe Doctrine; Article XV, Section 8, covering domestic affairs; and the section of the Treaty bearing on Shantung. I, therefore, sent the President a telegram, suggesting that he make a very clear and full statement of the meaning of the Treaty, of the Covenant, and of these debatable articles, and especially that he explain the function of the Council and the bearing of the Covenant on the constitutional powers of Congress.

The President did not at the time see fit to make a statement, and, in my judgment, he lost a great opportunity. He gave his opponents time to fix their interpretations in the minds of the people and to picture him as arrogant and uncompromising. Apparently, at the time, the President was over-confident. He is likely to be when a

[5]

question involving a moral issue and good faith is before the people. He is a firm believer in the doctrine that truth is mighty and will prevail. He firmly trusts the people to perceive the moral quality of a problem and to pass the right judgment upon it. Seeing an issue very clearly himself, he trusts the masses of the people too implicitly also to see it clearly and to see it as he does, in the short run as well as in the long run. He relies too much on the simple merit and goodness of a cause, and on the capacity of the people quickly to form a right judgment, even when confronted with many issues and confused by skilful partisan arguments. Furthermore, I think the President did not adequately sense the change which had taken place in the minds of the people since the Armistice and the headway which his opponents had made in impressing their view upon the public. He felt confident that he could successfully appeal to the people over the heads of the Senatorial opposition. He underestimated the difficulty of controlling, by an appeal to the people, Senators from two to four years away from reëlection.

On Tuesday, August 19th, however, at the White House, he met in conference the members of the Senate Committee on Foreign Relations, including Senators Lodge (chairman), McCumber, Borah, Brandegee, Fall, Knox, Harding, Johnson, of California, New, Moses, Hitchcock, Williams, Swanson, Pomerene, Smith, and Pittman.

The President opened the conference by reading a summary statement. He said:

"Mr. Chairman, I have taken the liberty of writing out a little statement in the hope that it might facilitate discussion by speaking directly on some points that I know have been points of controversy and upon which I thought an expression of opinion would not be unwelcome. I am absolutely glad that the committee should have responded in this way to my intimation that I would like to be of service to it. I welcome the opportunity for a frank and full interchange of views.

"I hope, too, that this conference will serve to expedite your consideration of the Treaty of Peace. I beg that you will pardon and indulge me if I again urge that practically the whole task of bringing the country back to normal conditions of life and industry waits upon the decision of the Senate with regard to the terms of the peace.

"I venture thus again to urge my advice that the action of the Senate with regard to the Treaty be taken at the earliest practicable moment because the problems with which we are face to face in the readjustment of our national life are of the most pressing and critical character, will require for their proper solution the most intimate and disinterested coöperation of all parties and all interests, and cannot be postponed without manifest peril to our people and to all the national advantages we hold most dear. . . .

"Our military plans of course wait upon it. We cannot intelligently or wisely decide how large a naval or military force we shall maintain, or what our policy with regard to military training is to be until we have peace not only, but also until we know how peace is to be sustained, whether by the arms of single nations or by the concert of all the great peoples. And there is more than that difficulty involved. The vast surplus properties of the army include not food and clothing merely, whose sale will affect normal production, but great manufacturing establishments also which should be restored to their former

[7]

uses, great stores of machine tools, and all sorts of merchandise which must lie idle until peace and military
policy are definitely determined. By the same token,
there can be no properly studied national budget until
then.

"The nations that ratify the Treaty, such as Great
Britain, Belgium, and France, will be in a position to lay
their plans for controlling the markets of central Europe
without competition from us if we do not presently act.
We have no consular agents, no trade representatives
there to look after our interests.

"There are large areas of Europe whose future will lie
uncertain and questionable until their people know the
final settlements of peace and the forces which are to administer and sustain it. Without determinate markets
our production cannot proceed with intelligence or confidence. There can be no stabilization of wages, because
there can be no settled conditions of employment. There
can be no easy or normal industrial credits because there
can be no confident or permanent revival of business.

"But I will not weary you with obvious examples. I
will only venture to repeat that every element of normal
life amongst us depends upon and awaits the ratification
of the Treaty of Peace; and also that we cannot afford to
lose a single summer's day by not doing all that we can
to mitigate the winter's suffering, which, unless we find
means to prevent it, may prove disastrous to a large portion of the world, and may, at its worst, bring upon Europe
conditions even more terrible than those wrought by the
war itself.

"Nothing, I am led to believe, stands in the way of
the ratification of the Treaty except certain doubts with

[8]

regard to the meaning and implication of certain articles of the Covenant of the League of Nations; and I must frankly say that I am unable to understand why such doubts should be entertained. You will recall that when I had the pleasure of a conference with your committee and with the Committee of the House of Representatives on Foreign Affairs at the White House in March last, the questions now most frequently asked about the League of Nations were all canvassed with a view to their immediate clarification. The Covenant of the League was then in its first draft and subject to revision. It was pointed out that no express recognition was given to the Monroe Doctrine; that it was not expressly provided that the League should have no authority to act or to express a judgment on matters of domestic policy; that the right to withdraw from the League was not expressly recognized; and that the constitutional right of the Congress to determine all questions of peace and war was not sufficiently safeguarded. On my return to Paris, all these matters were taken up again by the Commission on the League of Nations, and every suggestion of the United States was accepted.

"The views of the United States with regard to the questions I have mentioned had, in fact, already been accepted by the Commission, and there was supposed to be nothing inconsistent with them in the draft of the Covenant first adopted—the draft which was the subject of our discussion in March—but no objection was made to saying explicitly in the text what all had supposed to be implicit in it. There was absolutely no doubt as to the meaning of any one of the resulting provisions of the Covenant in the minds of those who participated in draft-

[9]

ing them, and I respectfully submit that there is nothing vague or doubtful in their wording.

"The Monroe Doctrine is expressly mentioned as an understanding which is in no way to be impaired or interfered with by anything contained in the Covenant, and the expression 'regional understandings like the Monroe Doctrine' was used, not because any one of the conferees thought there was any comparable agreement anywhere else in existence or in contemplation, but only because it was thought best to avoid the appearance of dealing in such a document with the policy of a single nation. Absolutely nothing is concealed in the phrase.

"With regard to domestic questions, Article XV of the Covenant expressly provides that, if, in case of any dispute arising between members of the League, the matter involved is claimed by one of the parties 'and is found by the council to arise out of a matter which by international law is solely within the domestic jurisdiction of that party, the council shall so report, and shall make no recommendation as to its settlement.' The United States was by no means the only government interested in the explicit adoption of this provision, and there is no doubt in the mind of any authoritative student of international law that such matters as immigration, tariffs, and naturalization are incontestably domestic questions with which no international body could deal without express authority to do so. No enumeration of domestic questions was undertaken because, to undertake it, even by sample, would have involved the danger of seeming to exclude those not mentioned.

"The right of any sovereign state to withdraw had been taken for granted, but no objection was made to making

[10]

it explicit. Indeed, so soon as the views expressed at the White House conference were laid before the Commission, it was at once conceded that it was best not to leave the answer to so important a question to inference. No proposal was made to set up any tribunal to pass judgment upon the question whether a withdrawing nation had in fact fulfilled 'all its international obligations and all its obligations under the Covenant.' It was recognized that that question must be left to be resolved by the conscience of the nation proposing to withdraw; and I must say that it did not seem to me worth while to propose that the article be made more explicit, because I knew that the United States would never itself propose to withdraw from the League if its conscience was not entirely clear as to the fulfilment of all its international obligations. It has never failed to fulfil them and never will.

"Article X is in no respect of doubtful meaning when read in the light of the Covenant as a whole. The Council of the League can only 'advise upon' the means by which the obligations of that great article are to be given effect to. Unless the United States is a party to the policy or action in question, her own affirmative vote in the Council is necessary before any advice can be given, for a unanimous vote of the council is required. If she is a party, the trouble is hers anyhow. And the unanimous vote of the council is only advice in any case. Each government is free to reject it if it pleases. Nothing could have been made more clear to the Conference than the right of our Congress under our Constitution to exercise its independent judgment in all matters of peace and war. No attempt was made to question or limit that right. The United States will, indeed, undertake under Article X

[11]

to 'respect and preserve as against external aggression the territorial integrity and existing political independence of all members of the League,' and that engagement constitutes a very grave and solemn moral obligation. But it is a moral, not a legal, obligation, and leaves our Congress absolutely free to put its own interpretation upon it in all cases that call for action. It is binding in conscience only, not in law.

"Article X seems to me to constitute the very backbone of the whole Covenant. Without it, the League would be hardly more than an influential debating society.

"It has several times been suggested, in public debate and in private conference, that interpretations of the sense in which the United States accepts the engagements of the Covenant should be embodied in the instrument of ratification. There can be no reasonable objection to such interpretations accompanying the act of ratification provided they do not form a part of the formal ratification itself. Most of the interpretations which have been suggested to me embody what seems to me the plain meaning of the instrument itself. But if such interpretations should constitute a part of the formal resolution of ratification, long delays would be the inevitable consequence, inasmuch as all the many governments concerned would have to accept, in effect, the language of the Senate as the language of the Treaty before ratification would be complete. The assent of the German Assembly at Weimar would have to be obtained, among the rest, and I must frankly say that I could only with the greatest reluctance approach that assembly for permission to read the Treaty as we understand it and as those who framed it quite certainly understood it. If the United States were to qualify

[12]

the document in any way, moreover, I am confident from what I know of the many conferences and debates which accompanied the formulation of the Treaty that our example would immediately be followed in many quarters, in some instances with very serious reservations, and that the meaning and operative force of the Treaty would presently be clouded from one end of its clauses to the other.

"Pardon me, Mr. Chairman, if I have been entirely unreserved and plain-spoken in speaking of the great matters we all have so much at heart. If excuse is needed, I trust that the critical situation of affairs may serve as my justification. The issues that manifestly hang upon the conclusions of the Senate with regard to peace and upon the time of its action are so grave and so clearly insusceptible of being thrust on one side or postponed that I have felt it necessary in the public interest to make this urgent plea, and to make it as simply and as unreservedly as possible.

"I thought that the simplest way, Mr. Chairman, to cover the points that I knew to be points of interest."

There are several points in the foregoing statement of the President which may well be emphasized. The first is his reminder to the Committee that in a former conference with the members of the Foreign Affairs Committee of the House and the Senate, the questions which were being most frequently raised had all been canvassed, that the Covenant was then in its first draft, and that all the suggestions made had been incorporated. The second point is that Article X could not commit the United States to any policy without her own consent, because, in the first place, the vote of the Council, on which the United States would have a representative, had to be unanimous, that the vote of the United States would, therefore, be

[13]

necessary, and that she would be in effect advising herself. He pointed out also that the Council could only give advice, and that each government, exercising its judgment in the circumstances, would be free to follow or to reject the advice if it pleased.

Even more interesting were his remarks on interpretations or reservations. He did not object to interpretative reservations of the Covenant, saying:

"There can be no reasonable objection to such interpretations accompanying the active ratification provided they do not form a part of the formal ratification itself. Most of the interpretations which have been suggested to me embody what seems to me the plain meaning of the instrument itself. But if such interpretations should constitute a part of the formal resolution of ratification, long delays would be the inevitable consequence, inasmuch as all the many governments concerned would have to accept, in effect, the language of the Senate as the language of the Treaty before ratification would be complete." He pointed out that the assent of Germany, itself, would have to be obtained.

This seemed to me to be a reasonable position to take. Reservations accompanying the Treaty, but not forming a part of the act of ratification, would have put the world on notice as to the attitude of the United States and would have served every purpose. It is obvious that amendments or reservations, affecting the structure of the League itself, not simply interpreting it, would require action.

The matter was then open for discussion. Many questions were asked, but Senator Lodge, the chairman, did not seem to take much interest in the proceedings. He spoke only once or twice.

In answer to questions, the President again and again said that he did not object to interpretative reservations accompanying the act of ratification, but that he would regard amendments affecting the structure, or reservations made a part of the act of ratification, as objectionable for the reasons he had indicated, particularly as such action would cause delay. Answering Senator McCumber he said:

"We differ, Senator, only as to the form of action. I think it would be a very serious practical mistake to put it in the resolution of ratification; but I do hope that we are at liberty, contemporaneously with our acceptance of the Treaty, to interpret our moral obligation under that article."

As to the matter of withdrawal, in answer to a question from Senator Borah, the President answered flatly that, if a country should give notice of withdrawal, it would be the sole judge of whether or not it had fulfilled its obligations. "The only restraining influence," he added, "would be the public opinion of the world."

Many times he answered questions regarding Article X. He stated emphatically that the obligation assumed under Article X to respect and preserve as against external aggression the territorial integrities of the members of the League was not a legal but a moral obligation, and that the United States would interpret this obligation. When Senators Borah and Knox asked the President specifically this question: "Suppose that it is perfectly obvious and accepted that there is an external aggression against some power, and suppose that it is perfectly obvious and accepted that it cannot be repelled except by force of arms, would we be under any legal obligation to participate?"

[15]

the President answered: "No, sir; but we would be under an absolutely impelling moral obligation."

Senator Harding then asked whether or not, if there were only a moral obligation and each nation was to judge of this obligation, the whole thing would amount to nothing. The President, in effect, answered that it would amount to a great deal, since every nation with a conscience would be called upon seriously to consider her moral obligation and to decide solemnly whether, in her judgment, the circumstances required that she participate. The President had great difficulty in getting this into the minds of his hearers. Senator Borah wished to know whether, under Article X, there would not be a transfer of the power of decision from the Congress of the United States to our representative on the Council. The President answered in the negative, pointing out that our representative would act only on the advice of his government and that the government in advising him would pursue the same course that it would otherwise pursue in similar circumstances. Senator Harding, at a later stage, again asked the President whether, if the obligation under Article X was only a moral obligation, we should get anything out of the compact. The President again replied that there would be centred upon the problem the definite opinion of the world. Mr. Harding replied, "That is surrendering the suggestion of a moral obligation for this Republic to the prejudices or necessities of the nations of the Old World, is it not?" The President replied that there would be no surrender. He tried again to explain that any decision of the Council would require our assent and that, in any event, its action would be only in the way of advice which we would seriously consider and

[16]

act upon in the light of our best judgment in the circumstances.

Questions as to other points were asked, and the President patiently repeated his explanations. A few days after the Conference, he remarked at a Cabinet meeting that Senator Harding had a disturbingly dull mind, and that it seemed impossible to get any explanation to lodge in it.

CHAPTER XXII

THE PRESIDENT GOES WEST

Discusses Article X, Shantung, and the Effect of the Treaty on Domestic Affairs and the Monroe Doctrine—Again Agrees to Reservations, if Attached to Treaty as Explanation of Our Position

ABOUT a week after this conference, the Senate Committee began to vote amendments to the Treaty of a very essential character, such as that China should be substituted for Japan as the nation which was to receive Shantung, and that the United States should have as many votes in the assembly as Great Britain and her self-governing colonies. On September 10th the majority of the Senate Committee reported a number of amendments and reservations, all of which were to be made a part of the act of ratification. Among the more important of the amendments were the one dealing with the votes of Great Britain and the one transferring to China the rights given by the Treaty to Japan. The most important of the reservations was the one stating that the United States declined to assume any obligation under Article X to preserve the territorial integrity of any nation, except by action of the Congress of the United States. Senator Lodge rejected these proposals.

In the meantime, such outstanding leaders of thought in the nation as former President Taft, Mr. Henry W.

[18]

Taft, Mr. George W. Wickersham, and President Lowell of Harvard, were advocating the ratification of the Treaty, including the Covenant, and were giving explanations of the debatable provisions substantially similar to some of those given by the President. On the contention that the League created a superstate, and that the freedom of the Congress of the United States would be limited, President Lowell said:

"Vigorous objection has been made in the United States to a super-sovereign league that would have authority to order this country what to do in case of an attack against another member of the League. The objection is not without cogency; but it does not apply to the Covenant of Paris, either in its original or its amended form, for that Covenant has adopted as its basic principle the automatic type of league, fixing the obligations of the members and the sanctions for violation in the pact itself, instead of leaving them to be determined by a representative body. The Council of the League is, indeed, at liberty, and even enjoined, to advise or recommend further action by the members, but no member assumes any obligation to follow the advice unless it chooses so to do. The language is in that respect perfectly clear and consistent, unless we are to construe such words as 'advise,' 'propose,' and 'recommend' in a sense quite contrary to their ordinary meaning. How completely this is true will be clearly seen when we examine in detail the articles of the Covenant."

As to Article X, former President Taft said that it was the embodiment of a principle which we had entered the war to maintain, that it answered the German doctrine that might makes right, and that it would lessen the prob-

[19]

ability of war and of our being drawn into one. "Article X," he said, "is one of the great steps forward provided in the League for the securing of general peace."

Just before the beginning of September, the President, recognizing the strength of the opposition and that the people were not getting a true picture of the Treaty and of the Covenant, decided that he ought to make an appeal to the people, and, therefore, to take a trip through the nation. A number of his friends, including his physician, warned him that, after all he had been through, he would probably endanger his life. At one of the Cabinet meetings, it was intimated to him that he had better not take the trip as it might kill him. He promptly replied that he would be willing to give his life for the cause. It was obvious that he would not be dissuaded from the undertaking.

On his Western trip, from September 4th to September 25th, the President travelled ten thousand miles, going as far to the northwest as Seattle and as far to the southwest as San Diego. He made in all thirty-seven speeches, at times as many as three in one day. His chief thought was to emphasize the need of immediate peace, the fact that the Treaty was the best that could be secured in the circumstances, that the Covenant was a necessary piece of machinery for effective future readjustments, that it would be a place where the public opinion of the world might focus, and that we would sacrifice no American interest by entering it and assuming a position of leadership. The main debatable points he explained again and again.

The place of the Covenant in the Treaty, he explained as follows:

"I want to remind you how the permanency of peace is at the heart of this treaty. This is not merely a treaty of

[20]

peace with Germany. It is a world settlement; not affecting those parts of the world, of course, which were not involved in the war, because the Conference had no jurisdiction over them, but the war did extend to most parts of the world, and the scattered, dismembered assets of the Central Empires and of Turkey gave us plenty to do and covered the greater part of the distressed populations of the world. It is nothing less than a world settlement, and at the centre of that stands this covenant for the future which we call the Covenant of the League of Nations. Without it the Treaty cannot be worked, and without it it is a mere temporary arrangement with Germany. The Covenant of the League of Nations is the instrumentality for the maintenance of peace."

The following will sufficiently indicate his statements to the people on the chief points in dispute:

1. The six votes of Great Britain in the Assembly.

"But, you say, 'We have heard that we might be at a disadvantage in the League of Nations.' Well, whoever told you that either was deliberately falsifying or he had not read the Covenant of the League of Nations. I leave him the choice. I want to give you a very simple account of the organization of the League of Nations and let you judge for yourselves. It is a very simple organization. The power of the League, or rather the activities of the League, lie in two bodies. There is the Council, which consists of one representative from each of the principal Allied and Associated Powers—that is to say, the United States, Great Britain, France, Italy, and Japan, along with four other representatives of smaller powers chosen out of the general body of the membership of the League. The Council is the source of every active policy of the

[21]

League, and no active policy of the League can be adopted without a unanimous vote of the Council. That is explicitly stated in the Covenant itself. Does it not evidently follow that the League of Nations can adopt no policy whatever without the consent of the United States? The affirmative vote of the representative of the United States is necessary in every case. Now, you have heard of six votes belonging to the British Empire. Those six votes are not in the Council. They are in the Assembly, and the interesting thing is that the Assembly does not vote. I must qualify that statement a little, but essentially it is absolutely true. In every matter in which the Assembly is given a voice, and there are only four or five, its vote does not count unless concurred in by the representatives of all the nations represented in the Council, so that there is no validity to any vote of the Assembly unless in that vote also the representative of the United States concurs. That one vote of the United States is as big as the six votes of the British Empire. I am not jealous for advantage, my fellow citizens, but I think that is a perfectly safe situation. There is no validity in a vote, either by the Council or the Assembly, in which we do not concur. So much for the statements about the six votes of the British Empire.

"Look at it in another aspect. The Assembly is the talking body. The Assembly was created in order that anybody that purposed anything wrong should be subjected to the awkward circumstance that everybody could talk about it. This is the great assembly in which all the things that are likely to disturb the peace of the world or the good understanding between nations are to be exposed to the general view, and I want to ask you if you think it

[22]

was unjust, unjust to the United States, that speaking parts should be assigned to the several portions of the British Empire? Do you think it unjust that there should be some spokesman in debate for that fine little stout republic down in the Pacific, New Zealand? Do you think it was unjust that Australia should be allowed to stand up and take part in the debate—Australia, from which we have learned some of the most useful progressive policies of modern time, a little nation of only five million in a great continent, but counting for several times five in its activities and in its interest in liberal reform? Do you think it unjust that that little republic down in South Africa, whose gallant resistance to being subjected to any outside authority at all we admired for so many months and whose fortunes we followed with such interest, should have a speaking part? Great Britain obliged South Africa to submit to her sovereignty, but she immediately after that felt that it was convenient and right to hand the whole self-government of that colony over to the very men whom she had beaten. The representatives of South Africa in Paris were two of the most distinguished generals of the Boer army, two of the realest men I ever met, two men that could talk sober counsel and wise advice along with the best statesmen in Europe. To exclude General Botha and General Smuts from the right to stand up in the parliament of the world and say something concerning the affairs of mankind would be absurd. And what about Canada? Is not Canada a good neighbour? I ask you, Is not Canada more likely to agree with the United States than with Great Britain? Canada has a speaking part. And then, for the first time in the history of the world, that great voiceless multitude, that throng

[23]

hundreds of millions strong in India, has a voice. . . .
I, for my part, have no jealousy whatever of those five
speaking parts in the assembly. Those speaking parts
cannot translate themselves into five votes that can in
any matter override the voice and purpose of the United
States."

2. *Article X.*

"Go to other matters with which I have less patience,
other objections to the League. I have spoken of Article
X. Those who object to Article X object to entering the
League with any responsibilities whatever. They want
to make it a matter of opinion merely, and not a matter
of action. They know just as well as I know that there is
nothing in Article X that can oblige the Congress of the
United States to declare war if it does not deem it wise to
declare war. We engage with the other nations of the
world to preserve as against external aggression—not as
against internal revolution—the territorial integrity and
existing political independence of the other members of
the League; and then, in the next sentence, it is said that
the Council of the League of Nations shall advise with
regard to the measures which may be necessary to carry
out this promise on the part of the members. . . .
These gentlemen would have you believe that our armies
can be ordered abroad by some other power or by a com-
bination of powers. They are thinking in an airtight com-
partment. America is not the only proud nation in the
world. I can testify from my share in the counsels on
the other side of the sea that the other nations are just as
jealous of their sovereignty as we are of ours. They would
no more have dreamed of giving us the right of ordering
out their armies than we would have dreamed of giving

[24]

them the right to order out our armies. The advice can come from the United States only after the United States representative votes in the affirmative."

He stated his position again as to this article in slightly different form, asserting that it was absurd to talk about the League being a supergovernment, saying:

"That affords emphasis to the point I wish you to keep distinctly in mind with regard to reservations and all the qualifications of ratification which are being discussed. No active policy can be undertaken by the League without the assenting vote of the United States. I cannot understand the anxiety of some gentlemen for fear something is going to be put over on them. I cannot understand why, having read the Covenant of the League and examined its constitution, they are not satisfied with the fact that every active policy of the League must be concurred in by a unanimous vote of the Council, which means that the affirmative vote of the United States is in every instance necessary. That being the case, it becomes sheer nonsense, my fellow citizens, to talk about a supergovernment being set up over the United States; it becomes sheer nonsense to say that any authority is constituted which can order our armies to other parts of the world, which can interfere with our domestic questions, which can direct our international policy even in any matter in which we do not consent to be directed. We would be under our own direction just as much under the Covenant of the League of Nations as we are now. . . .

"What is the Covenant for? To hear most of the debate, you would think that it was an ingenious contrivance for a subtle interference with the affairs of the United States. On the contrary, it is one of the most solemn

[25]

covenants ever entered into by all the great fighting powers of the world that they never will resort to war again without first having either submitted the question at issue to arbitration and undertaken to abide by the verdict of the arbitrators or submitted it to discussion by the Council of the League of Nations, laying all the documents, all the facts, before that council, consenting that that council should lay all those documents and all those facts before the world; they agree to allow six months for that discussion, and, even if they are not satisfied with the opinion, for it is only an opinion in that case, rendered by the Council, they agree not to go to war for three months after the opinion has been rendered. There you have nine months' submission to the moral judgment of the world. In my judgment, that is an almost complete assurance against war."

3. Monroe Doctrine.

As to the Monroe Doctrine, he had this to say:

"'But the Monroe Doctrine,' I must admit to you, my fellow citizens, I do not know how the Monroe Doctrine could be any more explicitly accepted than it is in the Covenant of the League of Nations. It says that nothing in the Covenant shall be interpreted as impairing the validity of the Monroe Doctrine. What more could you say? . . . I tell you, my fellow citizens, that is the most extraordinary sentence in that treaty, for this reason: Up to that time, there was not a nation in the world that was willing to admit the validity of the Monroe Doctrine. I have made a great many speeches in my life, perhaps too many, but I do not think that I ever put so much of what I hope was the best in me as I put in the speech in the Conference on the League of Nations in

[26]

favour of the Monroe Doctrine, and it was upon that occasion that it was embodied. And we have this extraordinary spectacle, of the world recognizing the validity of the Monroe Doctrine. Yet these gentlemen seem to want something more. What more could you get? Shall we get them to express their belief in the deity of the Monroe Doctrine? They accept it for the first time in the history of the world, and they say that they will do nothing that will interfere with it. I must submit that it is absolutely irrational to ask for anything more."

4. Domestic affairs.

That domestic affairs were not within the province of the League, he emphasized in the following language:

"But there is the question of somebody interfering with the domestic policies of the United States—immigration, naturalization, tariffs; matters of that sort. There, again, I cannot understand or feel the weight of the difficulty, because the Covenant says that if any international difficulty is brought under discussion and one of the parties claims and the Council finds that it is a matter of domestic jurisdiction, the Council shall cease to discuss it and shall make no report about it. The only way you could make the document more clear would be by enumerating the domestic questions you had in mind. Very well. I ask any lawyer here if that would be safe? Might you not be in danger of leaving out something? Might you not be in danger of not mentioning something that would afterward become important? The danger of making a list is that the mention of the things you do mention constitutes the exclusion of the things you do not mention. Inasmuch as there is no dispute of any authoritative students of international law that these matters that we are

[27]

most concerned about—immigration, naturalization, tariff, and the rest—are domestic questions, it is inconceivable that the Council should ever seek to interfere with or to discuss such questions, unless we had ourselves deliberately made them matters of international agreement, and even the opponents of the League admit they would be suitable and proper subjects for discussion."

5. Shantung.

He took great pains to explain the provision of the Treaty with reference to Shantung. He pointed out that Germany had acquired Shantung by force and that America at the time had not protested, that Japan had been allowed by a treaty signed on our own territory to take from Russia the concession of Port Arthur which had belonged to China, and that the negotiations leading to this treaty had taken place under the direct intervention of President Roosevelt, at Portsmouth. And he continued:

"The Treaty was written here; it was written under the auspices, so to say, of our own public opinion, but the government of the United States was not at liberty to protest and did not protest; it acquiesced in the very thing which is being done in this treaty. What is being done in this treaty is not that Shantung is being taken from China. China did not have it. It is being taken from Germany, just as Port Arthur was not taken from China but taken from Russia and transferred to Japan. Before we got into the war, Great Britain and France had entered into solemn covenant by treaty with Japan that, if she would take what Germany had in Shantung by force of arms, and also the islands lying north of the Equator which had been under German dominion in the Pacific, she could

[28]

keep them when the peace came and its settlements were made. They were bound by a treaty of which we knew nothing, but which, notwithstanding our ignorance of it, bound them as much as any treaty binds. This war was fought to maintain the sacredness of treaties. Great Britain and France, therefore, cannot consent to a change of the Treaty in respect of the cession of Shantung, and we have no precedent in our history which permits us even to protest against it until we become members of the League of Nations. . . . But that is not all. America, as I have said, was not bound by the agreements of Great Britain and France on the one hand, and Japan on the other. We were free to insist upon a prospect of a different settlement, and at the instance of the United States Japan has already promised that she will relinquish to China immediately after the ratification of this treaty all the sovereign rights that Germany had in Shantung Province—the only promise of that kind ever made, the only relinquishment of that sort ever achieved—and that she will retain only what foreign corporations have all over China—unfortunately, but as a matter of fact—the right to run the railroad and the right to work the mines under the usual conditions of Chinese sovereignty and as economic concessionaires, with no political rights or military power of any kind. . . .

"And the alternative? If you insist upon cutting out the Shantung arrangement, that merely severs us from the Treaty. It does not give Shantung back to China. The only way you can give Shantung back to China is by arms in your hands, armed ships and armed men, sent against Japan and France and Great Britain. A fratricidal strife, in view of what we have gone through!

[29]

We have just redeemed France. We cannot, with arms in our hands, insist that France break a covenant, however ill judged, however unjust; we cannot as her brothers in arms commit any such atrocious act against the fraternity of free people. So much for Shantung. Nobody can get that provision out of that treaty and do China any service whatever, and all such professions of friendship for China are empty noise, for the gentlemen who make those professions must know that what they propose will be not of the slightest service to her."

6. *Reservations.*

And again and again he pointed out that while he was opposed to amendments to the Treaty and to reservations which were made a part of the act of ratification because the whole thing would have to be done over again, he was not opposed to interpretative reservations. His explanations were along the following lines:

"You will say, 'Well, why not go in with reservations?' I wonder if you know what that means. . . .

"The Treaty is not susceptible of misunderstanding. I do not object to painting the rose or refining fine gold; there is not any phrase in the Covenant of the League of Nations that can legitimately be said to be of doubtful meaning, but if the Congress of the United States wants to state the meaning over again in other words and say to the other nations of the world, 'We understand the Treaty to mean what it says,' I think that is a work of supererogation, but I do not see any moral objection to it. But anything that qualifies the Treaty, anything that is a condition to our ratification of it, must be submitted to all the others, and we must go over this process again; this process which took six months of intensive labour, which took six months of very difficult adjustment and arrangement, which quieted jealousies, which allayed suspicions, which set aside controversies, which brought about the most extraordinary union of minds that was ever brought about in so miscellaneous an assembly, divided by so many interests. All that must be gone over again, and in the meantime the world must wait and its unrest grow deeper, and all the pulses of life go slower, waiting to see what is going to happen, all because the United States asks the other governments of the world to accept what they have already accepted in different language. That is all that it amounts to; I mean, all that the reasonable reservations amount to. Some of them amount to staying out altogether, some of them amount to a radical change of the spirit of the instrument, but I am speaking now of those which some men of high conscience and of high public purpose are seriously pressing in order that there may be no misunderstanding. You can avoid a misunderstanding without changing the document. You can avoid a misunderstanding without qualifying the terms of the document, because, as I have said and shall say again and again, America is at liberty as one of the voting members of the partnership to state how she understands the articles of copartnership."

In passing, he adverted to the possibility of a separate peace with the Central Empires and said:

"A separate peace with the Central Empires could accomplish nothing but our eternal disgrace, and I would like, if my voice could reach him, to let this German counsellor know that the red he sees upon the horizon is not the red of a new dawn, but the red of a consuming fire which will consume everything like the recent purposes of the

Central Empires. It is not without significance, my fellow citizens, that coincidentally with this debate with regard to the ratification of this treaty the whole pro-German propaganda has shown its head all over the United States. I would not have you understand me to mean that the men who are opposing the ratification of the Treaty are consciously encouraging the pro-German propaganda. I have no right to say that or to think it, but I do say that what they are doing is encouraging the pro-German propaganda, and that it is bringing about a hope in the minds of those whom we have just spent our precious blood to defeat that they may separate us from the rest of the world and produce this interesting spectacle, only two nations standing aside from the great concert and guaranty of peace—beaten Germany and triumphant America.

"See what can be accomplished by that. By that the attitude of the rest of the world toward America will be exactly what its recent attitude was toward Germany, and we will be in the position absolutely alien to every American conception of playing a lone hand in the world for our selfish advantage and aggrandizement. The thing is inconceivable. The thing is intolerable. The thing can and will never happen."

And finally he reminded his audiences of the purposes for which we had entered the war, its cost in wealth and in human lives, and the duty that the nation and he, himself, owed to the men who had made the great sacrifice. Concerning the nation's duty and its pledge, he said:

"We went into this war to do a thing that was fundamental for the world, and what I have come out upon this journey for is to ascertain whether the country has forgotten it or not. I have found out already. The country

[32]

has not forgotten, and it never will permit any man who stands in the way of the fulfilment of these great pledges ever to forget, the sorrowful day when he made the attempt."

"What of our pledges to the men that lie dead in France? We said that they went over there, not to prove the prowess of America or her readiness for another war, but to see to it that there never was such a war again. It always seems to make it difficult for me to say anything, my fellow citizens, when I think of my clients in this case. My clients are the children; my clients are the next generation. They do not know what promises and bonds I undertook when I ordered the armies of the United States to the soil of France, but I know, and I intend to redeem my pledges to the children; they shall not be sent upon a similar errand.

"Again and again, my fellow citizens, mothers who lost their sons in France have come to me and, taking my hand, have shed tears upon it not only, but they have added, 'God bless you, Mr. President!' Why, my fellow citizens, should they pray God to bless me? I advised the Congress of the United States to create the situation that led to the death of their sons. I ordered their sons overseas. I consented to their sons being put in the most difficult parts of the battle line, where death was certain, as in the impenetrable difficulties of the forest of Argonne. Why should they weep upon my hand and call down the blessings of God upon me? Because they believe that their boys died for something that vastly transcends any of the immediate and palpable objects of the war. They believe, and they rightly believe, that their sons saved the liberty of the world. They believe that wrapped up with

[33]

the liberty of the world is the continuous protection of that liberty by the concerted powers of all civilized people. They believe that this sacrifice was made in order that other sons should not be called upon for a similar gift—the gift of life, the gift of all that died—and if we did not see this thing through, if we fulfilled the dearest present wish of Germany and now dissociated ourselves from those alongside whom we fought in the war, would not something of the halo go away from the gun over the mantelpiece, or the sword? Would not the old uniform lose something of its significance? These men were crusaders. They were not going forth to prove the might of the United States. They were going forth to prove the might of justice and right, and all the world accepted them as crusaders, and their transcendent achievement has made all the world believe in America as it believes in no other nation organized in the modern world. There seems to me to stand between us and the rejection or qualification of this treaty the serried ranks of those boys in khaki, not only these boys who came home, but those dear ghosts that still deploy upon the fields of France.

"My friends, on last Decoration Day I went to a beautiful hillside near Paris, where was located the cemetery of Suresnes, a cemetery given over to the burial of the American dead. Behind me on the slopes was rank upon rank of living American soldiers, and lying before me upon the levels of the plain was rank upon rank of departed American soldiers. Right by the side of the stand where I spoke there was a little group of Frenchwomen who had adopted those graves, had made themselves mothers of those dear ghosts by putting flowers every day upon those graves, taking them as their own sons, their own beloved,

[34]

because they had died in the same cause—France was free and the world was free because America had come! I wish some men in public life who are now opposing the settlement for which these men died could visit such a spot as that. I wish that the thought that comes out of those graves could penetrate their consciousness. I wish that they could feel the moral obligation that rests upon us not to go back on those boys, but to see the thing through, to see it through to the end and make good their redemption of the world. For nothing less depends upon this decision, nothing less than the liberation and salvation of the world."

His final words to the people of the nation on this adventure were as follows:

"The arrangements of justice do not stand of themselves, my fellow citizens. The arrangements of this treaty are just, but they need the support of the combined power of the great nations of the world. And they will have that support. Now that the mists of this great question have cleared away, I believe that men will see the truth, eye to eye and face to face. There is one thing that the American people always rise to and extend their hand to, and that is the truth of justice and of liberty and of peace. We have accepted that truth and we are going to be led by it, and it is going to lead us, and through us the world, out into pastures of quietness and peace such as the world never dreamed of before."

CHAPTER XXIII

THE PRESIDENT'S COLLAPSE

Ignorance of His Condition Amongst Cabinet—President Advises Against the Incorporation of Lodge Reservations in Treaty —Agrees to Hitchcock Reservations—The Treaty Beaten

ON THE morning of September 26th, word reached me that the President had given up his trip and was hurrying to Washington. It was reported that he was due in Washington on Sunday the twenty-eighth. I realized that only a very serious situation would cause him to abandon the trip. I heard that he had suffered some sort of collapse. I was exceedingly apprehensive. On Monday I sent a note of sympathy and some flowers to the White House. The rumour was that the President was very nervous and could not sleep. I had nothing to go upon except rumours. There was no direct or authoritative word of any sort even to members of the Cabinet from the White House or from the physician. I regarded it as a serious mistake for those in touch with the situation not to give the public, and especially the Cabinet, the fullest and frankest information about the President's condition. We canvassed the matter among ourselves but none of us could furnish any light.

On Friday, October 3d, I saw Secretary Baker at the Shoreham. When he saw me, he said: "I am scared literally to death." He looked it. Saturday, I saw Tumulty at the Shoreham. He gave me the first direct word

[36]

I had had concerning the President. He said that the President was paralyzed in one leg and one arm. He expressed grave alarm over the situation. We agreed that it would be one of the tragedies of the ages if the President was incapacitated or were to become incapacitated.

Sunday I happened to lunch at the Shoreham. I saw the Vice President and Mrs. Marshall sitting at one of the tables. I went up to them and paid my respects. The Vice President was evidently much disturbed and expressed regret that he was being kept in the dark about the President's condition. He asked me if I could give him the real facts, which I was unable to do. I could not even repeat what had been told to me, because it had been said in confidence. The Vice President expressed the view that he ought immediately to be informed; that it would be a tragedy for him to assume the duties of President, at best; and that it would be equally a tragedy for the people; that he knew many men who knew more about the affairs of the government than he did; and that it would be especially trying for him if he had to assume the duties without warning. He showed resentment that the doctors were keeping the situation a mystery so far as he especially was concerned, and asserted that they ought to be frank with the public. I told him that I hoped to be in a position to know more the next day.

On Friday, October 3d, I had received word from Secretary Lansing that there would be a meeting of the Cabinet in the Cabinet room, Monday at eleven o'clock, to consider the situation. He had sent this word when the news was spread that the President's condition was worse. I was surprised when I received the call for a meeting on an unusual day, as I was apprehensive that our meeting

[37]

at an odd time would arouse undue apprehension. But I said that I would attend the meeting. When we met Lansing said that it was necessary to decide whether or not we should continue to carry on the government—that there was nothing to guide us as to who would decide the question of the ability of the President to discharge the duties of his office.

After the Secretary of State had outlined the situation, someone suggested that, if it was necessary to take the matter up at all, we should do so only after we had se-- cured direct information as to the President's condition and that we should first consult the President's physician. It was decided to ask Doctor Grayson to meet us and to tell us everything he could. While we were waiting we talked informally about the legal situation. There were no pressing matters requiring the President's decision and signature, and, therefore, there was no need for haste. Garfield was incapacitated from July 2d to September 19th, and no action was taken.

Doctor Grayson and Mr. Tumulty soon came into the Cabinet room. Doctor Grayson stated that the President's condition had improved over Sunday, but that he could not say when he would be out of danger—that the scales might tip either way. He added that they might tip the wrong way especially if he was harassed by business matters, and that he should be bothered as little as possible. He told us that the President's mind was very clear, but that he was suffering from a nervous breakdown, from indigestion and a depleted system. Doctor Grayson was asked if he could tell us more exactly what was the trouble. He replied that he could add nothing to what he had already said. He added with a sort of twinkle in his eye:

"The President asked me what the Cabinet wanted with me and by what authority it was meeting while he was in Washington without a call from him." He said that the President showed no little irritation when he heard that we were holding a Cabinet meeting.

After some further discussion of the matter, the Secretary of State asked Doctor Grayson to tell the President that we met primarily to express our interest in his condition, to get information about him, to extend our sympathy, and to consider such departmental matters as needed attention, as there had been no Cabinet meeting for a month.

This seemed to me to be an inadequate statement. It looked as if the Secretary for some reason had changed his mind as to the purpose of the meeting since the members had begun to gather. If he had called the meeting for the regular day, it might have been sufficient and reasonable for him to say that we had held Cabinet meetings at the request of the President during his absence, that we had had no meeting for a month and that, since he was ill, it seemed not inappropriate or in any way at variance with his views that we should meet. Our meeting at the regular time, as I have stated, would have been reassuring to the public, properly creating the picture in their mind that the government was going ahead. But the message the Secretary sent was hardly a satisfactory explanation for our meeting at an unusual time.

The problem presented by the illness of the President is one for the handling of which machinery ought to be created. The Cabinet is in good position to pass upon the government's exigencies, perhaps in better position than any other body, but, for various reasons, it is not the body that should be charged with the final determination of the inability of a president to discharge his duties. The Congress also is not the proper body. It might be of different political complexion from the President and there might be situations in which partisanship would enter. It would seem that either a Commission should be set up composed possibly of Supreme Court justices, members of the Cabinet, and members of Congress, to sit as a jury and to determine the matter, or the determination might be left to the Supreme Court. But whatever may be the best machinery, it is clear that some machinery should be set up.

In the meantime, the fight over the League continued, the lines of opposition being more tightly drawn. As the battle developed, apparently the disposition of the opposition changed. An able Republican Senator said that, in his opinion, Lodge had not started the fight on the League with the thought that he could kill it, but rather with the hope that he might give it a Republican veneer, partly for political purposes and partly to impair the prestige of Mr. Wilson, but that as time passed and such Senators as Borah, Johnson, and Reed, became more and more outspoken and hostile, he discovered, much to his surprise, that the League could be killed and that he then set out to kill it. Lodge's way of putting it was that he proposed to Americanize the Treaty and the Covenant. In other words, he would show the people that the Republicans had sufficiently rewritten the Treaty to save the situation. Amendments and reservations were proposed, debated, adopted, or rejected, until in November, 1919, the Lodge resolution of ratification, containing fourteen amendments or reservations, was voted upon and rejected by the vote of 41 "ayes" to 51 "noes," 3 not voting, most of the Democrats voting against the Lodge ratification resolution. Just before the vote was taken, Senator Lodge had inserted in the record a letter from President Wilson, dated November 18, 1919, and addressed to Senator Hitchcock.

The White House,
Washington, 18 November, 1919.

MY DEAR SENATOR:

You were good enough to bring me word that the Democratic Senators supporting the Treaty expected to hold a conference before the final vote on the Lodge resolution of ratification and that they would be glad to receive a word of counsel from me.

I should hesitate to offer it in any detail, but I assume that the Senators only desire my judgment upon the all-important question of the final vote on the resolution containing the many reservations by Senator Lodge. On that I cannot hesitate, for, in my opinion, the resolution in that form does not provide for ratification but, rather, for the nullification of the Treaty. I sincerely hope that the friends and supporters of the Treaty will vote against the Lodge resolution of ratification.

I understand that the door will probably then be open for a genuine resolution of ratification.

I trust that all true friends of the Treaty will refuse to support the Lodge resolution.

Cordially, and sincerely, yours,
(Signed) WOODROW WILSON.

Hon. G. M. Hitchcock,
  United States Senate.

[41]

The resolution of ratification containing fourteen amendments or reservations was as follows:

"RESOLVED (two thirds of the Senators present concurring therein), That the Senate advise and consent to the ratification of the Treaty of Peace with Germany concluded at Versailles on the 28th day of June, 1919, subject to the following reservations and understandings, which are hereby made a part and condition of this resolution of ratification, which ratification is not to take effect or bind the United States until the said reservations and understandings adopted by the Senate have been accepted by an exchange of notes as a part and a condition of this resolution of ratification by at least three of the four principal Allied and Associated Powers, to wit, Great Britain, France, Italy, and Japan:

"1. The United States so understands and construes Article I that in case of notice of withdrawal from the League of Nations, as provided in said Article, the United States shall be the sole judge as to whether all its international obligations and all its obligations under the said Covenant have been fulfilled, and notice of withdrawal by the United States may be given by a concurrent resolution of the Congress of the United States.

"2. The United States assumes no obligation to preserve the territorial integrity or political independence of any other country or to interfere in controversies between nations—whether members of the League or not—under the provisions of Article X, or to employ the military or naval forces of the United States under any article of the Treaty for any purpose, unless in any particular case the Congress, which, under the Constitution, has the sole power to declare war or authorize the employment of the military or naval forces of the United States, shall by act or joint resolution so provide.

"3. No mandate shall be accepted by the United States under Article XXII, Part I, or any other provision of the Treaty of Peace with Germany, except by action of the Congress of the United States.

"4. The United States reserves to itself exclusively the right to decide what questions are within its domestic jurisdiction, and declares that all domestic and political questions relating wholly or in part to its internal affairs, including immigration, labour, coastwise traffic, the tariff, commerce, the suppression of traffic in women and children, and in opium and other dangerous drugs, and all other domestic questions, are solely within the jurisdiction of the United States and are not under this treaty to be submitted in any way either to arbitration or to the consideration of the Council or of the Assembly of the League of Nations, or any agency thereof, or to the decision or recommendation of any other power.

"5. The United States will not submit to arbitration or to inquiry by the Assembly or by the Council of the League of Nations, provided for in said Treaty of Peace, any questions which in the judgment of the United States depend upon or relate to its long-established policy, commonly known as the Monroe Doctrine; said Doctrine is to be interpreted by the United States alone and is hereby declared to be wholly outside the jurisdiction of said League of Nations and entirely unaffected by any provision contained in the said Treaty of Peace with Germany.

"6. The United States withholds its assent to Articles CLVI, CLVII, and CLVIII, and reserves full liberty of action with respect to any controversy which may arise under said Articles between the Republic of China and the Empire of Japan.

"7. The Congress of the United States will provide by law for the appointment of the representatives of the United States in the Assembly and the Council of the League of Nations, and may in its discretion provide for the participation of the United States in any commission, committee, tribunal, court, council, or conference, or in the selection of any members thereof and for the appointment of members of said commissions, committees, tribunals, courts, councils, or conferences, or any other representatives under the Treaty of Peace, or in carrying out its provisions, and until such participation and appointment have been so provided for and the powers and duties of such representatives have been defined by law, no persons shall represent the United States under either said League of Nations or the Treaty of Peace with Germany or be authorized to perform any act for or on behalf of the United States thereunder, and no citizen of the United States shall be selected or appointed as a member of said commissions, committees, tribunals, courts, councils, or conferences except with the approval of the Senate of the United States.

"8. The United States understands that the Reparations Commission will regulate or interfere with exports from the United States to Germany, or from Germany to the United States, only when the United States by act or joint resolution of Congress approves such regulation or interference.

"9. The United States shall not be obligated to contribute to any expenses of the League of Nations, or of the secretariat, or of any commission, or committee, or conference, or other agency, organized under the League of Nations or under the Treaty or for the purpose of carrying out the Treaty provisions, unless and until an appropriation of funds available for such expenses shall have been made by the Congress of the United States.

"10. If the United States shall at any time adopt any plan for the limitation of armaments proposed by the Council of the League of Nations under the provisions of Article VIII, it reserves the right to increase such armaments without the consent of the Council whenever the United States is threatened with invasion or engaged in war.

"11. The United States reserves the right to permit, in its discretion, the nationals of a covenant-breaking state, as defined in Article XVI of the Covenant of the League of Nations, residing within the United States or in countries other than that violating said Article XVI, to continue their commercial, financial, and personal relations with the nationals of the United States.

"12. Nothing in Articles CCXCVI, CCXCVII, or in any of the annexes thereto or in any other article, section, or annex of the Treaty of Peace with Germany shall, as against citizens of the United States, be taken to mean any confirmation, ratification, or approval of any act otherwise illegal or in contravention of the rights of citizens of the United States.

"13. The United States withholds its assent to Part XIII (Articles CCCXXCVII to CCCCXXVII, inclusive) unless Congress by act or joint resolution shall hereafter make provision for representation in the organization established by said Part XIII, and in such event the participation of the United States will be governed and conditioned by the provisions of such act or joint resolution.

"14. The United States assumes no obligation to be bound by any election, decision, report, or finding of the Council or Assembly in which any member of the League and its self-governing dominions, colonies, or parts of empire, in the aggregate have cast more than one vote, and assumes no obligation to be bound by any decision, report or finding of the Council or Assembly arising out of any dispute between the United States and any member of the League if such member, or any self-governing dominion, colony, empire, or part of empire united with it politically has voted."

A little later in the day, Senator Underwood of Alabama offered the following straight resolution of ratification:

"RESOLVED (two thirds of the Senators present concurring therein), That the Senate do advise and consent to the ratification of the Treaty of Peace with Germany concluded at Versailles on the 28th day of June, 1919."

This resolution was rejected by almost a straight party vote, 38 "ayes" to 53 "noes," 4 not voting. Therefore, the Senate was unable to ratify the Treaty, with reservations as proposed either by Lodge or by Hitchcock, or without reservations; and the Senate adjourned the same day.

This leaves the country and the world in confusion. Our action will impair our prestige and prevent us from assuming leadership at a time when it would be most gladly accepted and would count for most. It will retard the processes of recovery. It leaves us in a state of war with Germany and will make it difficult for trade to reopen. It leaves the executive departments in suspense in reference to many measures which are purely war measures.

As time passed, no progress was made in the matter of the ratification of the Treaty. Shortly before Jackson Day (January 8th), I was informed that the President would prepare and send to those present at the Jackson Day banquet in Washington, a letter dealing mainly with the Treaty situation. Tumulty spoke to me about it after Cabinet meeting Tuesday, January 6th, and stated that he wished to bring the Attorney General and the Under-secretary of State to my office to go over the letter with me. He did so at 4:30. He read the letter at the conference. It was unsatisfactory. The President said in it that he could not accept the Senate's action, that its action and the delay left the stage set for the old plots, that the world was left without a treaty, that Germany was free to become a menace once more, and that she need not give up armaments, or Alsace-Lorraine, or make reparation. I did not say so, but I doubted if the President had had anything to do with the preparation of this letter. I could not understand how he could make such statements. I suggested that the letter be changed. It contained erroneous statements. There was a Treaty. All the other powers had agreed to the Versailles Treaty. The fact was that we only had not accepted it. Germany was not free to become a menace. She would have to give up armaments and surrender Alsace-Lorraine and properly make reparation. Germany's armament was already largely gone; her fleet was gone, and France already had Alsace-Lorraine. The letter, as it stood, I said, would arouse great adverse comment and would irritate the Allies.

[47]

The statement that the only course left was for the nation to have a referendum on the Treaty at the next election was, I thought, unwise. It was a flat declaration, in effect, against further attempts to agree on reservations and would, if assented to, make the Treaty a partisan issue in an election, while the people were in bad humour and might be interested in many other things besides the Treaty. The conference asked me to revise the address.

In the circumstances, I agreed to do what I could to alter the letter. I realized that it would be difficult to do more than reshape the statements which contained errors of fact or interpretation. I knew that it would be impossible to avoid saying that our acceptance of the Treaty should be left to a referendum. I revised the letter to indicate plainly that the President was not opposed to reservations of an interpretative character but that if the Senate did not accept the Treaty outright or with such reservations, the only course left would be to submit the matter to the people.

I sent the revised letter to Tumulty at twelve o'clock Wednesday. On the afternoon of the eighth, I called him up and asked if there was any news. He replied that everything was fine and that the letter as revised would be substantially accepted.

At the banquet the letter was read. Apparently, the audience approved the President's statement that he would accept reservations as indicated but that, if the Senate persisted in its course, the Treaty should be submitted to a referendum.

About this time Mr. Bryan managed to give the people the benefit of his views on the Treaty. Among other things, he informed the people that minorities were supposed to conform, and that, since the Republicans had organized the Senate, the President ought to have let them assume responsibility and have their way. He overlooked the little facts that the Constitution does not provide for majority ratification of treaties but for a two thirds majority, and that the Senate did not act because it could not get a two thirds vote on any proposition.

On January 31st, a few weeks later, Lord Grey published a letter in a London paper in which he indicated that the Allies would show a sympathetic attitude toward the ratification of the Treaty with the Lodge reservations and that the British Empire would not resent the amendments except the one providing a modification of the provision dealing with its six votes in the assembly. People in Washington were more surprised at this action of Lord Grey's than I was, because, at a dinner in Washington, I happened to be standing within a foot of him and Lodge and could not avoid overhearing him sympathetically commenting on Lodge's handling of the Treaty and on his reservations. In spite of the fact that the President had said in August, 1919, to the Senate Committee on Foreign Relations, that he would accept interpretative reservations, in spite of the fact that he reiterated this in his speeches on his Western trip, in spite of the fact that he restated it in his Jackson Day letter, apparently his position did not get over to the people; and many very intelligent men were insisting that the President was committed to the ratification of the Treaty without the "change of a dot of an *i* or the cross of a *t*." This, of course, I knew to be untrue and wondered why it was that it was so difficult to get his attitude before the public. I knew, not only from his speeches but from other sources, what the President's attitude was. On February 9, 1920, when the Treaty again came before the Senate for consideration, Senator Hitchcock read the following letter:

The White House,
January 26, 1920.

MY DEAR SENATOR HITCHCOCK:

I have greatly appreciated your thoughtful kindness in keeping me informed concerning the conferences you and some of your colleagues have had with spokesmen of the Republican party concerning the possibility of ratification of the Treaty of Peace, and send this line in special appreciative acknowledgment of your letter of the twenty-second. I return the clipping you were kind enough to inclose.

To the substance of it I, of course, adhere. I am bound to. Like yourself, I am solemnly sworn to obey and maintain the Constitution of the United States. But I think the form of it very unfortunate. Any reservation or resolution stating that "the United States assumes no obligation under such and such an article unless or except" would, I am sure, chill our relationship with the nations with which we expect to be associated in the great enterprise of maintaining the world's peace.

That association must in any case, my dear Senator, involve very serious and far-reaching implications of honour and duty which I am sure we shall never in fact be desirous of ignoring. It is the more important not to create the impression that we are trying to escape obligations.

But I realize that negative criticism is not all that is called for in so serious a matter. I am happy to be able to add, therefore, that I have once more gone over the

[50]

reservations proposed by yourself, the copy of which I return herewith, and am glad to say that I can accept them as they stand.

I have never seen the slightest reason to doubt the good faith of our associates in the war, nor ever had the slightest reason to fear that any nation would seek to enlarge our obligations under the Covenant of the League of Nations, or seek to commit us to lines of action which, under our Constitution, only the Congress of the United States can in the last analysis decide.

May I suggest that with regard to the possible withdrawal of the United States it would be wise to give to the President the right to act upon a resolution of Congress in the matter of withdrawal? In other words, it would seem to be permissible and advisable that any resolution giving notice of withdrawal should be a joint rather than a concurrent resolution.

I doubt whether the President can be deprived of his veto power under the Constitution, even with his own consent. The use of a joint resolution would permit the President, who is, of course, charged by the Constitution with the conduct of foreign policy, to merely exercise a voice in saying whether so important a step as withdrawal from the League of Nations should be accomplished by a majority or by a two thirds vote.

The Constitution itself providing that the legislative body was to be consulted in treaty making, and having prescribed a two thirds vote in such cases, it seems to me that there should be no unnecessary departure from the method there indicated.

I see no objection to a frank statement that the United States can accept a mandate with regard to any territory

[51]

under Article XIII, Part I, or any other provision of the Treaty of Peace, only by the direct authority and action of the Congress of the United States.

I hope, my dear Senator, that you will never hesitate to call upon me for any assistance that I can render in this or any other public matter.

Cordially and sincerely, yours,
WOODROW WILSON.

It will be noted that in this letter the President stated that he was glad to say that he accepted Senator Hitchcock's reservations as they stood. These reservations were as follows:

"2. The United States assumes no obligation to employ its military or naval forces of the economic boycott to preserve the territorial integrity or political independence of any other country under the provisions of Article X, or to employ the military or naval forces of the United States under any other article of the Treaty for any purpose, unless in any particular case the Congress, which, under the Constitution, has the sole power to declare war, shall, by act or joint resolution so provide. Nothing herein shall be deemed to impair the obligation in Article XVI concerning the economic boycott."

Proposed substitute reservations by Mr. Hitchcock to take the place of those proposed by Senator Lodge:

"That any member nation proposing to withdraw from the League on two years' notice is the sole judge as to whether its obligations referred to in Article I of the League of Nations have been performed as required in said article.

"That no member nation is required to submit to the

League, its council, or its assembly, for decision, report, or recommendation, any matter which it considers to be in international law a domestic question such as immigration, labour, tariff, or other matter relating to its internal or coastwise affairs.

"That the national policy of the United States known as the Monroe Doctrine, as announced and interpreted by the United States, is not in any way impaired or affected by the Covenant of the League of Nations and is not subject to any decision, report, or inquiry by the Council or Assembly.

"That the advice mentioned in Article X of the Covenant of the League which the Council may give to the member nations as to the employment of their naval and military forces is merely advice which each member nation is free to accept or reject according to the conscience and judgment of its then existing government, and in the United States this advice can only be accepted by action of the Congress at the time in being, Congress alone under the Constitution of the United States having the power to declare war.

"That in case of a dispute between members of the League, if one of them have self-governing colonies, dominions, or parts which have representation in the Assembly, each and all are to be considered parties to the dispute, and the same shall be the rule if one of the parties to the dispute is a self-governing colony, dominion, or part, in which case, all other self-governing colonies, dominions, or parts, as well as the nation as a whole, shall be considered parties to the dispute, and each and all shall be disqualified from having their votes counted in case of any inquiry on said dispute made by the Assembly."

[53]

On February 11th, amendments were offered by bi-partisan conferees but were rejected by Senator Hitch-cock, the Administration leader.

On March 19th, the Treaty again came before the Senate for final vote. The resolution of ratification and the reservations or amendments were substantially similar to those rejected on November 19, 1919, and need not be repeated. The Treaty was rejected at this time by a vote of 49 "ayes" to 39 "noes." On May 15th, the Knox resolution, introduced in the Senate some time before, proposing a separate treaty with Germany and amended to eliminate the request that the President should negotiate a separate treaty with Germany, passed the Senate by a vote of 43 to 38. Among the affirmative votes were three Democratic Senators: Reed of Missouri, Shields of Tennessee, and Walsh of Massachusetts. On May 21st, it passed the House by a vote of 228 to 139. And on May 27th, it was vetoed by the President in a message in which he said that he was unwilling to become a party to an action which would stain the honour of the United States. The next day, an effort was made to pass the resolution over the President's veto, but it failed by a vote of 219 to 152. And thus the deadlock continued.

Certain Republican agencies are assiduously disseminating the representation that the Treaty failed because of the obstinacy of the President. They are leading the public to believe that he insisted on the Treaty without the "change of a dot of an *i* or the cross of a *t*." It is difficult for me to see how a fair-minded man can accept the view that the President, because of his stubbornness, is mainly responsible for the failure of the Senate to ratify the Treaty, for the following reasons:

[54]

(1) In the first place, it would have entailed no risk or danger to the United States, if it had promptly accepted the Treaty as it was presented. On the contrary, it would have promoted peaceful adjustments in the world and have advanced the welfare of this country. It is pure nonsense to say that the League creates a superstate, or that it would in any way impair the independence of action of any department of our government, or that it jeopardize any of our fundamental interests. The League can take no effective action without the unanimous vote of the Council. We would have been represented on the Council. The assent of our representative would have been necessary for any effective action. His assent would not have been given without instructions from our government. No President would have given instructions in any essential matter, especially in any matter involving war, without full consultation with Congress and the necessary action by Congress. Furthermore, if the Council acted, its action would have been only advisory and the judgment of Congress would have had to be exercised as to all the facts in the case and the final course of this government.

(2) The President repeatedly asserted that he was not opposed to interpretative reservations which would make the position of this country clear and which would clarify the meaning of the Covenant. All that he asked was that these reservations accompany the act of ratification instead of being made a part of it. Unquestionably this would have put the world on notice as to our position and would have been accepted. They would have served every useful purpose. He objected to reservations which would change the structure of the League or to amend-

ments, because these would have to go back to the various ratifying parties to the Treaty, including Germany. And such a course was unnecessary. The President's view on this point seems to me to have been reasonable.

(3) He specifically and publicly assented to the Hitchcock reservations which covered all matters of real vital import.

(4) On the other hand, Lodge and the majority of the Senate Committee on Foreign Relations strenuously resisted every effort to ratify the Treaty except on the basis of the Lodge reservations, incorporated in the act of ratification.

Certainly, the stubbornness was not all on one side. Unquestionably, the President was stubborn; and I believe that his stubbornness was, in the main, justified. But can it be fairly said that he alone was stubborn? I have not been aware of the fact that Lodge, Borah, Brandegee, Johnson, and Reed were soft and pliable. Which side was the more unyielding is certainly debatable, at least. Even if the President had indicated that he was willing to have the Treaty ratified with the Lodge reservations and the Senate had acted accordingly it is by no means certain that any good would have resulted. The members of the League, and especially Great Britain and the Dominions, might have refused to accept the amendments and admit us to the League. I doubt, too, whether Lodge would, at this stage, have let the Treaty go through even with his own reservations, if he had had warning that the Democrats in the Senate would accept them. This view is based partly upon general impressions and partly upon the following incident.

At Cabinet meeting, one day, when the Treaty was under consideration, the President was called to the telephone. It was stated that a Senator wished to speak to him. He came back and said that a conference was being held and that a form of statement on Article X had been worked out, which, it was understood, Lodge would accept. The President asked what we thought about the matter. We instantly replied that he should authorize the Senator to proceed. He said that he would do so and returned to the telephone to give his assent. Before we adjourned, the President answered the telephone again. When he returned, he remarked that there was nothing doing—that Lodge would not adhere to his understanding. Later, on the floor of the Senate, Lodge was charged with his failure to stand by his agreement. It is probable that the matter could not have been carried through unless, at the time of the final vote on the reservations, the Democrats, on word from the President, had suddenly joined in an affirmative vote.

It seems clear, as I have stated, that Lodge, for various reasons, passed through an interesting mental transition in respect to the League. He, himself, had advocated an association stronger than the League. When the Treaty was brought back to this country, it would appear that Lodge's first thought was that it would be popular to permit the Treaty's ratification, but, as I have said, with just sufficient changes to enable him to ascribe credit to the Republicans. Later, because of attacks made on the Treaty and the Covenant, by "irreconcilable" Senators, and particularly by a large section of the press, he began to change his mind and to feel that it would be possible and popular to defeat the Treaty.

The situation then was that the matter was to be left for determination of the American people in a solemn referendum. The Democratic party in its platform flatly declared for the League of Nations and applauded the President's courage. It rejected the Republican view. The Republican party announced its approval of an agreement among nations to preserve the peace of the world. It advocated an international association based upon international justice. Its plank seemed to call for an instant and general international conference, whenever peace was threatened by political action. It approved the stand of the Senators who insisted upon reservations. The suggestion of occasional general international conferences, whenever peace was threatened, was, of course, not new. It was a suggestion that the world return to pre-war practices which had failed. It evidenced no awareness of changed conditions, or of a need for a permanent body, which should study situations, seek to remove the causes of friction, and prevent disturbances of peace.

The campaign itself was hectic. It was obvious that the League would be only one of numerous factors on which the people would base their judgments. It was clear that all the forces of unrest would operate. No clear stand was taken by the Republican party and it was impossible to get a frank declaration from the Republican candidate as to the course he would pursue. Senator Harding revealed the same inability or unwillingness to understand the meaning of the Covenant which he had revealed when the President received the Foreign Affairs Committee in August, 1919. He indulged in reckless assertions, such as that the League was utterly impotent, that it could not be a preventive of wars, and that Europe was abandoning the League. He went further, apparently, than his platform by declaring as follows:

"The other type is a society of free nations, or an association of free nations, or a league of free nations, animated by considerations of right and justice, instead of might and self-interest, and not merely proclaimed an agency in pursuit of peace, but so organized and so participated in as to make the actual attainment of peace a reasonable possibility. Such an association I favour with all my heart, and I would make no fine distinction as to whom credit is due. One need not care what it is called. Let it be an association, a society, or a league, or what not, our concern is solely with the substance, not the form thereof."

Later, a body of thirty-one eminent Republican leaders assured the people of the nation that the quickest way for them to get the nation into the League was to vote for the Republican candidate. It is incredible that this could have been done without the knowledge of the Republican National Committee and also of Senator Harding.

CHAPTER XXIV

APPOINTED SECRETARY OF THE TREASURY

Financial Conditions in 1920—The President Asks Lansing to Resign—Appointment of Bainbridge Colby

I AWOKE Sunday morning, January 25, 1920, at five o'clock, with the grippe. I was aching and chilly and had a temperature of 101. At 11:30 I was called up by the White House and was told that Mrs. Wilson wished me to call at 4:30 that afternoon. I hesitated for a moment, on account of my slight illness, but finally said that I would be glad to call as requested. There were three things, any one of which I imagined the President possibly wished to canvass with me—the Treasury vacancy, the Treaty situation which I had been discussing with Tumulty, or a successor to Lane, whose resignation had been announced in the press. Later, I called up the White House, spoke to Mrs. Wilson, and told her I had a cold and fever. I added that perhaps she would be afraid to have me come on her account. She replied that she had a cold herself and would take a chance if I would. She said: "I am not afraid of you, if you are not afraid of me." I called at the appointed time. Mrs. Wilson was in the downstairs sitting room. She greeted me very graciously and discussed various matters until the servants had finished serving tea. Then she said: "You are wondering why I wanted to see you and why I sent for you this afternoon. Of course, you know that I did not ask you to take the trouble to come merely to drink tea. The President asked me to tell you that he is very anxious for you to accept the Secretaryship of the Treasury. He is reluctant to have you give up Agriculture, but still he thinks he now needs you more in the Treasury. He thought of putting you there twice before—first, when McAdoo thought of resigning, and second, when he did resign—but could not make up his mind to have you leave the Department of Agriculture."

When she finished, I said: "Please give my greetings to the President and tell him that I am very grateful to him for this further evidence of his confidence. I am in the harness until March 4, 1921, if he wishes it, and as long as I am with him I will dig stumps, or act as Secretary of the Treasury, or assume any other task he assigns me." Mrs. Wilson smiled and replied: "That is very interesting. That is just what the President said you would say."

Mrs. Wilson said that the President would like to know whether I had anybody in mind to suggest for Secretary of Agriculture. I asked if he was thinking about anybody. She answered: "Yes, Meredith." I replied that Meredith came from the right section, that he was in touch with agricultural problems through his newspaper, and that it seemed to me that he ought to fill the position acceptably. I told her that I had at one time sounded him out as to whether he would take the Assistant Secretaryship, that I had suggested him for membership on the War Agricultural Council, and that I had mentioned his name for membership on the Industrial Conference, but that I knew very little about his intellectual ability and whether he was Cabinet size or not. I added: "If I had to select a Secretary of Agriculture, I would draft President W. O.

[61]

Thompson of the University of Ohio. He is a man of very independent judgment. He is an independent in politics, but I understand that he voted for Mr. Wilson both in 1912 and in 1916. He is a man of unusual ability, of great wisdom, and of sound views. He has been the Dean of the Presidents of the Land-Grant colleges. I know of no one who stands higher in the agricultural field among leaders and sensible thinkers."

She then asked whether I had anybody in mind whom I could suggest for the position of Secretary of the Interior. She added: "The President is somewhat embarrassed. Secretary Lane has resigned—in the press. The President has not yet been officially informed of his going. He would like your judgment." I told her that I had nobody in mind at the moment, but that I would think it over. She said that the President would really prefer somebody not from the Far West, since the Interior Department problems lie mainly in the West, and that it was difficult to find a Western man who would take a sufficiently detached or national view.

When I went to the Treasury, much nonsense was being talked concerning the economic situation in the United States and in the foreign field. It was clear to me that there was no short cut to recovery either at home or abroad. There is no short road to a stabilization of exchange. It can be rectified only when the underlying economic forces are satisfactorily operating and production and trade improve. The exchange will be stabilized when a reasonable recovery from the effects of the war is made. This will be hastened if Europe will stop fighting, disarm as largely as possible, cut down expenditures, stop the printing presses, and abate foolish trade restrictions. Incidentally, the Allies must be reasonable in their exactions against the Central Powers. They must give them a chance. They, too, have been hard hit. The indemnity amount will have to be reduced and fixed; and it must be recognized that no substantial payments can be made in the near future. The world cannot recover as long as the central part of Europe is in chaos; and unless assistance is rendered, Germany and Austria will sink deeper into the mire and draw others in with them. If the Allies want actually to get something, they must ask less. They could not take what they ask even if Germany could produce it and give it. French producers would bitterly fight the importation of large quantities of competitive German commodities.

In the meantime, Europe will have to cut down her consumption and to import less. Exports from the United States will decline. Prices will fall, especially prices of agricultural products. Europe will first try to produce her own foodstuffs, and she will turn in part to other countries where she can get them at lower rates. At any rate, if we export, we must take lower prices. That this would occur, I warned the farmers in the fall of 1918 and throughout 1919. I predicted before and just after the Armistice that, on the return of peace, there would probably be a period of optimism and of feverish trading, that there would then begin a decline, especially of agricultural prices, that this would start an agrarian movement, and that the farmers, in ignorance of underlying causes, would see a conspiracy on the part of the bankers to ruin them. I felt that the farmers would not be able to control their production quickly and that, because of the lessened demand from Europe, for the reasons I have indicated, and

[63]

for the further reason that we had stopped lending Europe money, prices might go very low. And yet, business men were urging that farmers produce and produce. I protested against this in the Industrial Conference in Washington in the late fall of 1918, saying that farmers should not be urged to produce as much as they had or more, unless business men were prepared to protect them against a drop in price. This, I knew, could not be done. I warned the Conference that a drop in general prices would come and that, if they were prudent, they would arrange to weather the storm. I advised farmers to return to a balanced agriculture and to pursue practices best suited to their own needs and to those of their community. I urged this in official statements and in addresses in the latter part of 1918, and, especially, in 1919 and 1920.

On February 10, 1920, I received a letter from the Secretary of State, telling me that, on the seventh, he had received a letter from the President indicating that he would not consider it proper for the Cabinet to meet except at his personal summons. The Secretary stated that in view of this letter, he had requested the Executive Office to notify the members of the Cabinet that there would be no meeting on the tenth and no further meetings unless they were summoned by the President, himself. This is the letter:

The Secretary of State,
Washington,
February 10, 1920.

MY DEAR MR. SECRETARY:

I received on the seventh a letter from the President indicating that he did not consider it proper for the Cabinet

[64]

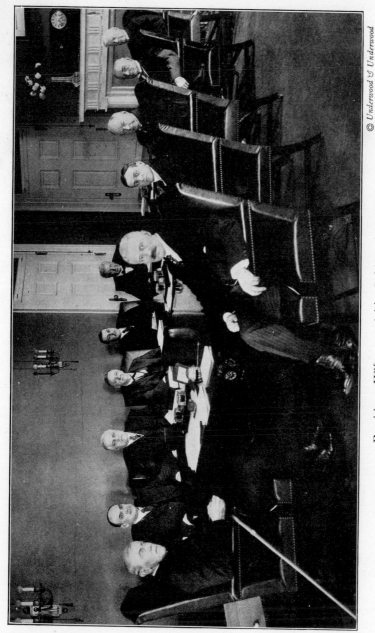

President Wilson and his Cabinet in 1920

to meet except at his personal summons.   In view of this letter, I requested the Executive Office to notify the members of the Cabinet that there would be no meeting to-day, and in compliance with the intimation contained in the letter there will be no meetings in the future unless summoned by the President himself.

I am notifying the other Cabinet Officers to this effect.

Very sincerely yours,

ROBERT LANSING.

Honourable David F. Houston,
    Secretary of the Treasury.

I was puzzled over this letter.   I wondered what was back of it.   We had been having Cabinet meetings during the President's absences.   When he first went to Paris, he requested us to hold Cabinet meetings, which we did. When he went West for a long absence, we continued to hold Cabinet meetings.   When he returned, evidently very ill, although he was in Washington, it seemed not only natural but desirable that we should hold Cabinet meetings for its effect on the public mind.   The public was excited.   It seemed that it would be a good thing to hold up the picture before the public that the government was going forward with its ordinary activities in about the usual way.   The only question I had when the Cabinet meeting was held, after the President's return from the West, was as to the time fixed by the Secretary of State for the first meeting.   It was called for an unusual day. It was called, so far as I knew, by Mr. Lansing without consultation.   It would have been better to call it for the usual day.   It seemed obvious that calling it for an unusual day would raise questions.   Several members of

[65]

the Cabinet doubted the wisdom of holding meetings at all.

We could, of course, take no action as a Cabinet. We could, however, in this way more conveniently discuss matters of general interest and particularly of departmental interest. And we could, if necessary, after canvassing problems, advise the President of our conclusions. We did so specifically in respect to the coal and railroad situations. In the coal matter, I, myself, went over to the White House at the request of the Cabinet to explain our views to Mrs. Wilson for transmission to the President. The President replied in writing and raised no question about our meeting. Obviously, it would have been possible and better if the matter of continuing to hold Cabinet meetings had been taken up with the President and we had ascertained his wishes in respect to them.

On Saturday, February 14th, I dined at a friend's house. Doctor Grayson was there. I talked to him about a number of matters. I stressed especially the desirability of the President's filling vacancies on the Tariff Commission. The Chairman of the Commission had been disturbed about these vacancies for a long time. I asked Doctor Grayson to tell the President that I thought the vacancies should be filled and that it would be desirable for him to appoint a man who would be recognized as a regular Republican. I said that the Commission should be obviously bi-partisan. It had been said that it was essential to get someone not too much identified with the protected industries. I remarked that this seemed to me not to be the main question; that it would be difficult to get a good business man and a Republican who had not been tied to something, that the chief consideration was to get an able

[66]

and honest man and then to trust him and his colleagues, and that this was essential to keep the Commission out of politics. It would not do to assume that a man could not take a broad or fair view because of his particular business relations.

Apparently, it was difficult for the President, except during the war, to get his consent to appoint a straight-out Republican even to a bi-partisan board. As a rule, he selected men who belonged to the Progressive wing, some of whom had gone off with Mr. Roosevelt, deserting the Republican party. He seemed to feel that it would be difficult for such a regular Republican to take a fair and unbiassed view. I regarded this as unfortunate from many points of view. I knew that the regular Republicans would not consider it fair play, and that when they came to power they might retaliate. Such a course would necessarily mean the breakdown of any bi-partisan regulatory board, or board of inquiry. And it would necessarily lead to Republican resentment and opposition.

Doctor Grayson told me that the President had asked for Lansing's resignation. I was surprised, not that Lansing was asked to resign, but that he should have been asked to resign at that time. From what I had heard, the question was raised in my mind why he had not been asked to go sooner. I recalled that the President had said to me originally that he would not appoint Lansing, because he had no imagination and would not oppose him to his face in any serious matter. It was apparent, after Lansing came back from Paris, that he was not in sympathy with the President on vital points in the Treaty. He did not succeed in disguising his differences. It came to me in various ways that he was against the Shantung settlement and against Article X, and that he thought it would have been better merely to provide that the members of the League should respect one another's territorial integrity and neutrality. It was believed that Lodge and also certain diplomats knew his views. It had come out in the hearing before the Committee of the Senate, when the President was in the West, that Lansing had not been in sympathy with the President.

I asked Doctor Grayson if he knew who would succeed Lansing. He said that the President was very much worried; in fact, that he was worrying himself sick over the matter. I asked him why. He replied that the President was no longer in position to write his notes and papers as he formally was, and that he wanted somebody who had great facility in this direction. I said that it would be very easy to get a fine man very near at hand. Grayson asked whom I had in mind. I replied: "Frank Polk, of course." "Just what I told him," Grayson said. I added: "Polk is every inch a gentleman. He has ability. He knows the domestic and foreign situations. He has good judgment. He has a fine spirit and good sense. He knows Europe and is well liked. The Treasury has many points of contact with the State Department and, with Polk at the head of the State Department, I could cooperate with him easily in common matters." I remarked further that Polk had great loyalty and courage and that, if I had a dozen villains attacking me at the same moment, I did not know anybody I should prefer to have at my side. Doctor Grayson again observed that the President wanted somebody who had special facility in writing. I replied then that I would make another suggestion. "Let him make Polk Secretary of State. Have him send word to President Alderman, of the University of Virginia, to come to see him. Let him tell Alderman that, as he is sick, he would like to draft him into the State Department as First Assistant Secretary, with nothing to do but write." I asserted that Alderman could say "No" to foreign diplomats in words which would make them weep in gratitude for his considerate refusal. I added that I felt sure that Alderman, although his health was not good, would not refuse, in the circumstances. Grayson said: "I am going to see the chief before he goes to sleep, and I shall tell him exactly what you have said."

The following morning, Bainbridge Colby's appointment appeared in the papers. That afternoon I saw Doctor Grayson near the Treasury. I asked him what had happened. He replied that he saw the President and gave him my message, and that the President smiled a grim smile and said: "You and Houston are freight wagons. Why did you not think of this yesterday afternoon? I have already acted."

The Lansing correspondence appeared Saturday. In the circumstances, I was somewhat surprised that the President placed emphasis on Lansing's action in calling the Cabinet meetings. It was apparent that there was more back of the correspondence than appeared. I recalled Doctor Grayson's statement, at our first Cabinet meeting after the President's illness, that the President was irritated over the report that we were meeting, and wanted to know by whose authority we had met, adding that, if he had wanted us to meet, he would have let us know.

A Cabinet meeting was held in the President's study in the old Cabinet room in the White House proper on April

13th. This was the first meeting with the President since August, 1919, the first meeting since he went on his Western trip. I arrived several minutes late. The President was already seated behind a desk at the far end of the room. I noted that I was ushered into his presence by the White House aide, and was announced by him to the President. This struck me as singular, and I wondered why it was done. The President looked old, worn, and haggard. It was enough to make one weep to look at him. One of his arms was useless. In repose, his face looked very much as usual, but, when he tried to speak, there were marked evidences of his trouble. His jaw tended to drop on one side, or seemed to do so. His voice was very weak and strained. I shook hands with him and sat down. He greeted me as of old. He put up a brave front and spent several minutes cracking jokes. Then there was a brief silence. It appeared that he would not take the initiative. Someone brought up the railroad situation for discussion. The President seemed at first to have some difficulty in fixing his mind on what we were discussing. Doctor Grayson looked in the door several times, as if to warn us not to prolong the discussion unduly for fear of wearying the President. The discussion dragged on for more than an hour. Finally, Mrs. Wilson came in, looking rather disturbed, and suggested that we had better go.

At the next meeting, on Tuesday, April 27th, the President seemed rather better and took a much more lively part in the discussions.

CHAPTER XXV

CONGRESS ENCROACHES ON THE EXECUTIVE

The President Requests Draft of a Veto of Legislative, Executive, and Judicial Appropriation—Vetoing the Budget Measure Because of Its Encroachments—Opinions on the Budget

FOR some time, it had been apparent that members of Congress were bent, not only on obstructing the President in his policies, but also upon having Congress usurp certain executive functions. They had planned, when we entered the war, to have a Congressional Committee on the conduct of the war, such as existed during the Civil War. It would be a fatal thing to have such a body now, just as it was almost fatal then. If the Congress had succeeded in its plans to interfere in the conduct of the war, it would have made as great a mess of things as it did, not only in the Civil War, but also in the Mexican War. In both these wars, Congress hideously failed as a military agency. It would have been irritating, if it had not been amusing, to hear charges of Presidential usurpation, of which there was none, when, as a matter of fact, there were glaring instances of Congressional invasion of the executive field. This fact had come to my attention months before, when I was in the Department of Agriculture. In May, 1920, it came out sharply in connection with the Legislative, Executive, and Judicial Appropriation Bill for the fiscal year ending June 30, 1921.

[71]

On April 15, 1920, I wrote the President a personal letter, calling his attention to the increasing disposition on the part of the Congress to encroach upon fields clearly in the province of the executive. I pointed out a number of proposals and provisions of law evidencing this disposition, including the transfer of the Bureau of Efficiency from the executive to the legislative, the Commission on Public Buildings, and the provision relating to printing. I suggested that, in view of the seriousness of the matter, he obtain the opinion of the Attorney General. Nothing was done until the passage of the Appropriation Bill referred to. On May 3d, I wrote the President the following letter:

The Secretary of the Treasury,
Washington,
May 3, 1920.

DEAR MR. PRESIDENT:

I return herewith Bill H. R. 12610, "making appropriations for the legislative, executive, and judicial expenses of the government for the fiscal year ending June 30, 1921, and for other purposes," and recommend that you veto this bill. Section 8 of the bill amends Section 11 of the Act approved March 1, 1919, by adding a proviso prohibiting mimeographing, multigraphing, and other processes used for the duplication of typewritten and printed matter, except under such regulations as may be adopted by the Congressional Joint Committee on Printing. Previously the jurisdiction of the Joint Committee on Printing has been limited to public printing and binding and distribution of publications. Whatever may be said for the existing administrative powers of this Joint Committee of Congress, the provision contained in this bill is such an encroachment upon the province of the executive that I feel it should be brought to your attention. For the Committee to undertake to establish regulations governing every process for duplicating typewritten matter means that it proposes to enter into every department of the government and determine what information shall be made public. For instance, the Treasury habitually makes public current information concerning the financial operations of the government which will be of general interest. I think that the Treasury of the United States should not be subjected to the meddling of a Joint Committee of Congress in a matter of this sort. I believe the same principle ought to govern in every other department. No question of coördination is involved; each department has its own typewriters, stenographers, and supplies of paper and duplicating machinery. Under the terms of the bill, the Joint Committee on Printing would have the power to prohibit even the making of carbon copies of anything other than official correspondence and office records. I believe that the time has come when you should make an issue of this legislative usurpation of executive functions, particularly when it arises on such a matter as the attempt of the Joint Committee on Printing to exercise a censorship over the executive departments. I consider it one of the first duties of the Treasury in particular to make public information concerning its financial operations, and I should feel very much concerned indeed to see such a provision as this become a law. It seems to me it involves a very important principle.

Quite obviously the question is one which must affect other departments as well as mine, and I have no doubt you will wish to consult other members of the Cabinet and ascertain their views.

In this connection, I call your attention to my personal letter of April 15, 1920. The Senate amendment transferring the Bureau of Efficiency from the jurisdiction of the President to that of the Congress, mentioned in that letter, was eliminated in conference, but the provision enlarging the powers of the Joint Committee on Printing, as outlined above, was retained.

The Treasury has two other objections to the bill which I feel obliged to call to your attention in view of my recommendation that the bill be vetoed, although I should not regard them as sufficiently serious in themselves to warrant a veto.

Cordially yours,
D. F. HOUSTON.
Secretary.

The President,
The White House.

The President replied in his own handwriting that he would be very grateful if the Secretary of the Treasury would draft a veto message for him.

On receiving this direction, I decided that it would be desirable for me to confer with the Attorney General as I had advised the President. I did so and was referred to the Solicitor General, who gave me an informal statement to the effect that he was unable to advise that the Act was unconstitutional. I was not satisfied with his opinion, but I felt obliged, in the circumstances, not only to inform the President of it, but also, partly to relieve him from embarrassment, formally to withdraw my ten-

[74]

tative recommendation that he veto the bill, which I did under date of May 7th as follows:

The Secretary of the Treasury,
Washington,
May 7, 1920.

DEAR MR. PRESIDENT:

I received your note asking me to prepare for your consideration a message vetoing the Legislative, Executive, and Judicial Appropriation Bill for the reasons suggested in my letter to you of the 3d instant. I shall of course be glad to prepare the message if after reading this letter you still desire me to do so.

It was my own view that the proviso in Section 8 of the bill, that no journal, magazine, periodical, or similar government publication shall be printed, issued, or discontinued by any branch or office of the government service unless authorized under regulations prescribed by the Joint Committee on Printing, and that nothing should be mimeographed or multigraphed other than official correspondence, would not only interfere with administrative work, but that it constituted an invasion of the executive power and was unconstitutional. It was upon the assumption that this proviso did constitute an invasion of the executive power and was unconstitutional that I tentatively suggested that you should veto the measure. I felt, however, that you would desire that I consult the Department of Justice as to the legal phase of the matter, particularly in view of the fact that in my personal letter to you of April 15th I had suggested that the Attorney General be requested to inquire into the constitutionality of several pending legislative proposals, including the one

[75]

now under consideration. I therefore asked the advice of the Attorney General. He referred me to the Solicitor General, who informally advises me that the proviso does not constitute an invasion of the Executive power and is constitutional. He bases his opinion on the wide control of Congress over the public funds and its right to impose conditions with respect to their expenditure.

While I still think that such legislation is administratively objectionable, I am of the opinion that, since the constitutional objection cannot be raised, it would be inadvisable for you to veto the bill because it contains this proviso. I think that at some time in the future the propriety of such legislation may be raised on its merits and a reconsideration be secured, and that the defects as to the two items of appropriation can also be cured in time to prevent any great inconvenience. In these circumstances, I feel obliged to withdraw my tentative recommendation that you veto the bill, and to suggest that you sign it.

Faithfully yours,
D. F. Houston.

The President,
    The White House.

The President noted in his own handwriting on the letter which he returned:

"I still hold your original view and would be greatly obliged for a draft of a veto.

"W. W."

Immediately upon receipt of this direction, I prepared a veto message which the President transmitted to Congress under date of May 13, 1920. It is, in part, as follows:

TO THE HOUSE OF REPRESENTATIVES:

I am returning, without my signature, H. R. 12610, "An Act Making Appropriations for the Legislative, Executive, and Judicial Expenses of the Government for the Fiscal Year Ending June 30, 1921, and for other purposes."

I object to, and cannot approve, Section 8 of the bill, which amends Section 11 of the Act approved March 1, 1919, as follows:

"Sec. 8. That Section 11 of the Act entitled 'An Act Making Appropriations for the Legislative, Executive and Judicial Expenses of the Government for the fiscal year ending June 30, 1920, and for other purposes' is hereby amended by striking out the first proviso and inserting the following in lieu thereof:

"Provided, That hereafter no journal, magazine, periodical, or similar government publication, shall be printed, issued, or discontinued by any branch or officer of the government service unless the same shall have been authorized under such regulations as shall be prescribed by the Joint Committee on Printing, and such publications shall not contain any commercial advertisements: Provided, further, That the foregoing provisions of this section shall also apply to mimeographing, multigraphing, and other processes used for the duplication of typewritten and printed matter, other than official correspondence and office records."

Without raising any constitutional question, I think that this section, which would give the Congressional

[77]

Joint Committee on Printing power to exercise censorship over the executive departments, is an encroachment on the functions of the Executive and incompatible with good government. I am in entire sympathy with the efforts of the Congress and the departments to effect economies in printing and in the use of paper and supplies, but I do not believe that such a provision as this should become law. I should also call attention to the fact that by its terms the section in question absolutely forbids mimeographing, multigraphing, and other duplicating processes in the executive departments (except as permitted by regulations established by the Congressional Joint Committee on Printing) and thus imposes a flat prohibition against the exercise of executive functions.

If we are to have efficient and economical business administration of government affairs, the Congress, I believe, should direct its efforts to the control of public moneys along broader lines, fixing the amounts to be expended and then holding the executive departments strictly responsible for their use. This can be accomplished by the enactment of legislation, establishing an effective budget system which I have heretofore urged. The Congress and the Executive must function within their respective spheres. Otherwise, efficient and responsible management will be impossible and progress impeded by the wasteful forces of disorganization and obstruction. The Congress has the power and the right to grant or deny an appropriation, or to enact or refuse to enact a law; but once an appropriation is made or a law is passed, the appropriation should be administered or the law executed by the executive branch of the government. In no other way can the government be efficiently managed and responsibility fixed. The Congress has the right to confer upon its committees full authority for purposes of investigation and the accumulation of information for its guidance, but I do not concede the right, and certainly not the wisdom, of the Congress endowing a committee of either House or a joint committee of both Houses with power to prescribe "regulations" under which executive departments may operate. Under Section 8 of the bill, responsibility cannot be definitely placed upon either the executive departments or the Joint Committee on Printing. It falls between them.

I regard the provision in question as an invasion of the province of the Executive and calculated to result in unwarranted interferences in the processes of good government, producing only confusion, irritation, and distrust. The proposal assumes significance as an outstanding illustration of a growing tendency which I am sure is not fully realized by the Congress itself and certainly not by the people of the country. For that reason, I am taking the liberty of pointing out a few examples of an increasing disposition, as expressed in existing laws and in pending legislative proposals, to restrict the executive departments in the exercise of purely administrative functions.

I do not care to discuss here the powers which previously have been conferred upon the Congressional Joint Committee on Printing, as they have passed into law, but I do feel that it is proper to point to a few specific examples of the administrative authority exercised by the Committee under existing law in order to indicate the incongruity and inconsistency that already exist and which would be accentuated and aggravated if Section 8 of the bill under consideration were enacted into law. In this

[79]

connection, I invite the attention of the Congress to a letter from the Chairman of the Joint Committee on Printing to the Public Printer, under date of March 19, 1920, replying to a request from the latter for a ruling by the Committee as to the application to certain printing of Section 89 of the Printing Act of 1895, restricting the printing of reports, publications, and documents to 1,000 copies each. In the communication mentioned, the Public Printer is "directed" to apply that section of the law in accordance with the "opinion" rendered by the Chairman of the Joint Committee on Printing. To my mind, the opinion mentioned is nothing more or less than a direction to an executive officer in the performance of his executive duties. The printing laws may give the Congressional Joint Committee on Printing authority to make interpretations of the law, but if they do, I think it is a most unwise procedure and the statute should be revised.

Another example of the exercise of administrative authority by the Joint Committee on Printing is to be found in a resolution adopted by that Committee on April 2, 1920, prohibiting any person connected with any department of the government from furnishing any publication for free distribution to any private individual, corporation, or agency, in lots to exceed fifty copies "without first making application to the Joint Committee on Printing."

I also invite attention to the creation by law of what is known as the Public Buildings Commission, consisting of two Senators, two Representatives, the Superintendent of the Capitol Buildings and Grounds, the officer in charge of public buildings and grounds, and the Supervising

Architect or acting Supervising Architect of the Treasury.

That Commission, by law, is given "absolute control of and the allotment of all space in the several public buildings named, or buildings leased by the United States in the District of Columbia, with the exception of the Executive mansion and office of the President, Capitol Building, the Senate and House office buildings, the Capitol power plant, the buildings under the jurisdiction of the regents of the Smithsonian Institution, and the Congressional Library Building."

The Commission possesses the absolute power to order the several executive departments and independent establishments out of any of the buildings which they occupy, and, as a matter of fact, has directed various branches of the public service to vacate or to occupy specific space. It is organized and operates as a Congressional Commission and appears in the Congressional Directory under the heading "Congressional Commissions and Joint Committees." The Senators serving upon it are appointed by the President of the Senate, the Representatives serving upon it are appointed by the Speaker of the House, while the other officials composing the Commission are specifically named in the law. Its work, nevertheless, so far as it involves the allotting of space for administrative services and of ordering executive departments to move units into or out of government owned or leased buildings, is distinctly executive in character.

In considering bills containing the provisions mentioned above, I was willing to overlook the objectionable features for the time being with the thought that they were designed as exceptional and temporary measures to meet

[81]

unusual conditions. To permit such expedients to serve as precedents or accepted rules for legislation, would, in my judgment, be most unfortunate and destructive of proper principles for the orderly and efficient management of the government's business. I feel very strongly that the authority carried in Section 8 of the bill herewith returned should not be conferred upon a legislative committee and that the entire section should be stricken from the measure.

WOODROW WILSON.

The White House,
May 13, 1920.

The House in which the bill originated sustained the President's veto and the bill was passed by both Houses with the objectionable section omitted, and I thereupon advised the President to sign the bill, which he did. This is one of the few instances in this difficult period in which Congress sustained the President's veto. This action should put a stop to these particular efforts of Congress to usurp and to hamper the Executive.

A more interesting but less nagging and irritating invasion of the Executive function occurred in the bill passed toward the close of the session of Congress in June, 1920, to provide a national budget system. This was embodied in the section covering the removal of the Comptroller General and the Assistant Comptroller General, the provision being, in effect, that these officers, although appointed by the President with the advice and consent of the Senate, might be removed at any time by a concurrent resolution of Congress after notice and hearing, when in their judgment these officers, or either of them, were deemed incapacitated or inefficient or guilty of neglect or malfeasance in office.

The bill was sent to me by the President with the usual request that I advise him as to whether I saw any objection to its approval. After reading the measure, I became convinced that the provision for the removal of the officers mentioned was in violation of the Constitution, taking away from the President a power which he had under the Constitution. It is the duty of the President to uphold the Constitution, and he could not approve the bill with an unconstitutional provision in it. I consulted with the officers of the Department and with the Solicitor General of the United States and advised the President that he should not approve the measure with the provision mentioned. He then requested that I prepare a veto message. I did so, and he transmitted it to the Congress June 4, 1920. It was as follows:

To the House of Representatives:

I am returning, without my signature, H. R. 9783, "An Act to provide a national budget system, an independent audit of government accounts, and for other purposes." I do this with the greatest regret. I am in entire sympathy with the objects of this bill and would gladly approve it but for the fact that I regard one of the provisions contained in Section 303 as unconstitutional. This is the provision to the effect that the Comptroller General and the Assistant Comptroller General, who are to be appointed by the President with the advice and consent of the Senate, may be removed at any time by a concurrent resolution of Congress after notice and hearing, when, in their judgment, the Comptroller General or Assistant

[83]

Comptroller General is incapacitated or inefficient, or has been guilty of neglect of duty, or of malfeasance in office, or of any felony or conduct involving moral turpitude, and for no other cause and in no other manner except by impeachment. The effect of this is to prevent the removal of these officers for any cause except either by impeachment or a concurrent resolution of Congress. It has, I think, always been the accepted construction of the Constitution that the power to appoint officers of this kind carries with it, as an incident, the power to remove. I am convinced that the Congress is without constitutional power to limit the appointing power and its incident, the power of removal derived from the Constitution.

The section referred to not only forbids the Executive to remove these officers, but undertakes to empower the Congress by a concurrent resolution to remove an officer appointed by the President with the advice and consent of the Senate. I can find in the Constitution no warrant for the exercise of this power by the Congress. There is certainly no express authority conferred, and I am unable to see that authority for the exercise of this power is implied in any express grant of power. On the contrary, I think its exercise is clearly negatived by Section 2 of Article II. That section, after providing that certain enumerated officers and all officers whose appointments are not otherwise provided for shall be appointed by the President with the advice and consent of the Senate, provides that the Congress may by law vest the appointment of such inferior officers as they think proper in the President alone, in the courts of law, or in the heads of departments. It would have been within the constitutional power of the Congress, in creating these offices,

[84]

to have vested the power of appointment in the President alone, in the President with the advice and consent of the Senate, or even in the head of a department.   Regarding as I do the power of removal from office as an essential incident to the appointing power, I cannot escape the conclusion that the vesting of this power of removal in the Congress is unconstitutional, and therefore I am unable to approve the bill.

I am returning the bill at the earliest possible moment with the hope that the Congress may find time before adjournment to remedy this defect.

WOODROW WILSON.

The constitutional point raised was promptly debated in the House.   On the question, whether the House would pass the bill over the objections of the President, the vote was in the negative and the President's veto was sustained. Later, the matter was taken up and the House passed the measure with the objectionable provision eliminated, providing simply that the Comptroller should hold office for good behaviour.   When the revised measure came to the Senate, it was discussed briefly, but the Senate adjourned without taking action.

I particularly regretted this outcome.   Budgetary procedure and practice were matters in which I had had a very deep interest for more than twenty-five years.   At Harvard, under Dunbar, I had studied the history of budgets in the leading constitutional countries of Europe, their practices, and their administration, and had canvassed thoroughly the situation in this country.   Subsequently, I had frequently considered the matter of a proper budget system for the Federal Government as

[85]

well as for the states. It had been specifically brought to my attention by a civic body in 1913, and I had discussed with it the history of our Federal practices, the reasons for them, and the urgent need of change. We had inherited from England the principle of popular control of the government purse. We had provided that all financial measures must originate in the lower House. We did not, at the time, perceive that the legislative body in England was really coming to dominate the executive, and to direct the government through a responsible committee. It is reasonably clear that those who framed the government had in mind a Congressional rather than an Executive budget. They could not anticipate the development of our Congressional system and that there would be in time more than a dozen committees dealing directly with appropriations and revenues. It is true that the Secretary of the Treasury had come to be required by Congress to submit an annual Book of Estimates, but this was really a clerical task. He accepted the estimates of the heads of departments, the only check being that the President, himself, must approve the estimates of the heads of departments. This was done by President Wilson. The Secretary of the Treasury, himself, however, had no official responsibility and could not bring any actual pressure to bear. In 1912, the President ordered the various heads of departments to prepare two sets of estimates, one in accordance with the existing practice, and one in accordance with forms recommended by the President's Commission on Efficiency. This, the Congress promptly attempted to block, providing in an appropriation bill that, until otherwise directed, the estimates should be submitted only as required by law.

On September 19, 1912, in a letter to the Secretary of the Treasury, the President maintained that Congress had no right to interfere with his plan and directed the Secretary of the Treasury and the heads of departments to prepare the statements according to his order of July 10th. Here the matter rested until the formulation of the measure which the President vetoed. Because, as I have said, of my long interest in the matter, I was peculiarly distressed by the failure of the Senate to pass the revised bill which did not contain the objectionable feature. It would have been a great satisfaction to me to have participated in the organization of a budget system, even though it was very partial and incomplete. It was also a matter of general regret to the President, as he indicated in his message. It would have been easily possible for the Senate to act.

I have stated that the measure provided for an incomplete budget system. As a matter of fact, the most important feature of a budget system, from many points of view, was not incorporated, namely, limitations on the Congress, itself, as to what it should do with the estimates when they reached it. Broadly speaking, the act provided for unified estimates and for an effective audit. The evils most commonly complained of, however, in our budget practices grow out of the Congressional handling of the estimates. There has always been much logrolling in Congress. There was no unified view of appropriations and no coördination of appropriations and receipts. It is apparent that we shall not have a budget system until Congress adopts rules affecting its consideration of the estimates. In Great Britain, where the budget practice has reached its highest and best development, the Parliament in reality makes a contract with the Executive to run the government for so much a year. It never thinks of giving the Executive more than it asks for, and it does not usually diminish the items or seriously alter the proposals for revenue changes. The Congress could provide by rule that it would make no increases in the estimates recommended by its own committees, and it might perhaps make a rule that its committees should not recommend an increase in the estimates except by an unusual majority, say two thirds. In my Annual Report for 1920, submitted to the Congress, I touched upon the budget, indicating the merits and defects of the proposed measure. As to the matter just referred to, I said:

"In the second place, the budget should receive initial consideration by the Congress through a single great budget committee for each House. These committees should consider both the appropriations and the ways of raising the revenue to meet them. There should be a rule that, after the committees have made their reports, no addition can be made to any item in the budget except by an unusual vote, such, for instance, as two thirds. It would be an important achievement if the Congress would go further and, as far as the budget presented by the President is concerned, impose a limitation on the right to increase any item either in committee or on the floor, unless recommended by the Secretary of the Treasury or approved by two thirds of the membership of the Congress. The Congress should, of course, retain the right to reduce items in the budget, but if the President is to be held responsible for a financial programme it should exercise restraint in increasing the budget as submitted by him. In order that there may be no interference with the

[88]

constitutional right of the Congress to appropriate money apart from the budget, it appears to me that such appropriations should be made in separate bills. These should also provide for the necessary revenue to meet the proposed expenditures in case the estimated revenues of the government are not sufficient. A plan of this character would definitely place the responsibility for expenditures before the people of the country."

I also expressed the opinion that, while the responsibility for the preparation of the budget should be placed upon the President, he should meet this responsibility through the Secretary of the Treasury as the chief fiscal officer of the government, saying:

"I believe that the budget bureau should be established in the office of the Secretary of the Treasury. He is the officer charged by law to provide funds for expenditures. It would appear that the preparation of the budget should be the principal function of the chief government finance officer. It is indefensible that he should be charged with the duty of keeping an adequate balance in the general fund to meet any and all demands and denied any word with respect to the determination of the expenditures of the government outside his own department. To place the budget bureau in the office of the President, as is sometimes urged, would mean the creation of an establishment likely to overshadow, or to be overshadowed by, the great departments of the government and, what is more important, would mean a division of responsibility with respect to receipts and expenditures which should be centralized under one control. The Secretary of the Treasury, acting for the President, should have power to reduce and revise the estimates. Under his direction the bureau of the budget should make a continuous study of the various government agencies, with a view to the elimination of duplicated work and wasted effort. If this responsibility is placed upon the Treasury, the Bureau of War Risk Insurance, the Public Health Service, the Office of the Supervising Architect, the General Supply Committee, and the prohibition unit of the Bureau of Internal Revenue simultaneously should be transferred to the jurisdiction of some other department, as recommended later in this report."

The objection had been offered that other heads of departments would resent the power accorded to one of their colleagues. My own judgment is that they would not resent that as much as they would the power accorded to a subordinate officer created by the act. They would have frequent opportunities to confer with the Secretary of the Treasury and they would recognize that after all he was acting, as all of them were, under the President. I believe that making someone else than the Secretary of the Treasury responsible under the President for the budget will in time be found to give rise to complications and seriously to interfere with the effectiveness of the Secretary of the Treasury in the discharge of his duties as the chief fiscal officer of the government.

CHAPTER XXVI

POLITICS AND FINANCE

The President's Belief in Cox's Election and Vindication of League—President's Attitude toward Harding—Financial Programme in 1921 to Abolish Excess Profits Tax, Reduce Super Tax to 25 per cent., and Repeal Nuisance Taxes

DURING the summer of 1920, the public mind was fixed mainly on the course of the campaign. Cabinet meetings were relatively few. On Tuesday, October 19th, the regular Cabinet meetings were resumed and were held in the President's study in the main part of the White House. The President had not changed much in appearance in the interval. He still looked weak and strained. As before, he was seated at his desk when we entered, and each of us was announced to him. It was evident that his eyesight had been impaired. He evidently had difficulty in distinguishing us at a distance. I recall someone saying at this time that he had practically lost the sight of one eye and had not had the use of it for some time, and that the other was impaired.

Again I was impressed with the fact that the President would not take the initiative in bringing matters to the attention of the Cabinet or in discussions. For several minutes things dragged somewhat embarrassingly. The President's mind seemed inactive until a discussion was started, and then he would become alert and take part in the discussion, expressing himself admirably. He thought better and spoke better than most of his associates, and displayed all his old-time courage.

The matter of the approaching election was mentioned by a member of the Cabinet. The President expressed a very strong conviction of its favourable outcome. He said that he was confident that Cox would be elected and that the League would be the issue with which the people would mainly concern themselves, and that on it they would go with Cox. He said that the people were a good jury, that they were especially fitted to pass judgment on matters of a moral character, that the causes upheld by the Democrats were moral causes and were sound, and that the people would see this and act accordingly.

I did not share the President's confidence. I agreed with him that the people judge rightly as a rule in the long run. I said this, but stated that the run had not been long enough and that the people could play the mischief in the short run. I added that the issues were very complex, that people had been hit in many directions by the war and its aftermath, that there was much soreness and some hysteria, that there had been no effective presentation of the Democratic views, and that there had been very effective misrepresentation by many agencies. I felt, too, that Mr. Cox had not at first made a very satisfactory campaign. At the outset he held aloof from Mr. Wilson and avoided the League. Apparently, the faction which had urged him as the nominee was not particularly favourable to the League, and at first he seemed to take his cue from them. He wasted much time on charges of corruption which he had difficulty in proving. Finding that he was not making headway, he turned about when

[92]

it was too late and made a zealous campaign for the League.

What a drop there will be to either Cox or Harding. If Mr. Harding is elected, the contrast will be painful. It will be somewhat tragic to have a man of Mr. Wilson's intellect and high standards succeeded by a man of Mr. Harding's mediocre mind and ordinary standards of thinking and action. At this time, particularly, the nation needs a leader, and Mr. Harding will not be a leader. He cannot be. He has never stood for any great cause. He knows very little, has no vision, very little sense of direction, and no independence. He was not nominated to lead. He was selected because he was colourless and pliable. If he is elected, he will be the tool of such tried leaders as Lodge, Penrose, and others. He will play the game of the Senate. The Senate will be supreme. The old policies will be revived. Protection will raise its head again and raise it higher than ever. The revolt of the people against the Paine-Aldrich Tariff Bill will be forgotten. This element of the Republican party which will be in the ascendant knows exactly where it is going. It will go back to where it was before 1915. What a trial it will be to have to witness Mr. Harding's efforts to think and his efforts to say what he thinks.

At the Cabinet meeting, Tuesday, November 2d, someone referred to the approaching election and said to the President that he was apprehensive as to Cox's chances. The President interrupted him and said in substance: "You need not worry. The American people will not turn Cox down and elect Harding. A great moral issue is involved. The people can and will see it. In the long run, they do the right thing. They are on to the Republicans. I am receiving letters from people throughout the country which indicate that they are not going to be deceived."

Believing myself that Cox would be defeated, and fearing the possible effects on the President of the shock, I spoke up and again said that I, too, was inclined to think that Cox would not succeed. I gave my reasons briefly. I added, however, that I did not believe that Harding's success would mean the final loss of the fight for the League, that sooner or later the country would decide that it would have to go in, and that it would some day do so. I added: "Whatever the verdict be in this election, you may be certain that history will justify your course. It will give your Administration a high place for its foreign as well as for its domestic achievements, and above all, for giving the country a pure and sincere government free from the dictation of any groups, and for heroic efforts to secure a just peace."

The President thanked me but said: "You need not worry. The people will not elect Harding."

I somewhat dreaded to go to Cabinet meeting Tuesday, November 9th, after the election. I could not help feeling that the President, particularly in his state of broken health, might show bad effects from the defeat of Cox and from his disappointment. I had forgotten for the moment that he was a sturdy Scotch Presbyterian. He looked worried but somewhat better physically. He showed no concern whatever for himself, but he expressed grave concern for the country and for the world. He felt that progress toward peace and restoration would be greatly retarded.

A member of the Cabinet said: "Mr. President, you can

put Mr. Harding and the Republican party in a hole. All you have to do is to put the Treaty on the Vice President's desk."

The President quickly interrupted him, saying: "But I do not wish to put Mr. Harding in a hole. The situation of the nation and of the world is too serious to make it thinkable that I or any good citizen should desire to hamper the next President. I should like to help Mr. Harding, and I hope that every good citizen will try to help him."

The calendar year 1921 was an exceptionally difficult, and, therefore, exceptionally interesting year in the Treasury. It was interesting because of the size and character of the financial operations, of the chance presented for advancing a programme for handling the floating debt and the Victory Loan, and of the opportunity for suggesting a plan of taxation; and it was certain to be trying because of the necessity of dealing with those whose interests had been seriously hit in the aftermath of the war.

The very scale of operations, in itself, was striking. The nation had been called upon in a few years to spend about $16,000,000,000 more than it had spent in the entire time from the adoption of the Constitution to the beginning of the war, that is, about $42,000,000,000. Much of the expenditure had been met from taxation, as was the case in Great Britain. And it was because of this that this nation was able to carry on in orderly fashion, just as drastic taxation had kept Britain's finances on a vastly more solid footing than those of any other European country. These two countries had resorted to heavy taxation from the outset. In one year, England raised by taxes more by a billion dollars than France raised in the five years following the outbreak of the Great War. Other Continental nations pursued a less sound policy even than France; and, if nothing else had happened, they would have become practically fiscally bankrupt. Continental nations had never shown a willingness or an ability to fight wars by taxing the people. Only democracies have shown the wisdom, ability, and courage to do this. The year 1920 stands out in our history to date as the year in which the largest collections were made from the people through taxation, the total ordinary receipts being in excess of $6,700,000,000.

But in spite of the enormous sacrifices which the people made, there had been accumulated a huge public debt, which, in August, 1919, amounted to more than $26,596,000,000. Of this, there was outstanding in the form of loan and tax certificates approximately $3,268,000,000. And there was the Victory Loan of about $4,250,000,000, which would in whole or in part become a floating debt after May, 1923.

The most pressing task was the handling of the Treasury certificates to meet in part the current requirements of the government. The chief financial operations of the Treasury during the year centred around these certificates. There had to be frequent offerings. In fact, during the period from February, 1920, to February 15, 1921, there were thirteen such offerings, ranging in amount from $100,000,000 to $500,000,000 at a time. And the amount subscribed ranged from about $130,000,000 to approximately $590,000,000, the subscriptions to the thirteen offerings exceeding $4,000,000,000.

When I went to the Treasury, the offerings had been in

rates out of line with the market rates. The Treasury was, therefore, exercising a predominating influence in the financial market and vitally affecting the entire business of the country, somewhat adversely. The certificates were being taken, but too many of them were lodging in the hands of the subscribers and were not being distributed satisfactorily to investors. This was an undesirable and a menacing situation. The first issue after I went to the Treasury was on March 15th, at a 4¾ per cent. rate, and although the books were open for almost two weeks, the total amount subscribed was only $201,000,000. In April, an issue at a higher rate was made. This process continued until the rate was in line with the market rate and the certificates were put on an investment basis. Subscriptions became heavy, and the distribution of the certificates among investors proceeded satisfactorily.

In thinking of the Treasury's enormous transactions during and following the war, one would have been staggered had he not had a full appreciation of the virility and financial strength of the nation. I had made it a special point to try to keep up with the growth of the nation, and I was aware of its enormous development. I knew something of the nation's productive power, of the ability of the people to meet financial burdens, and of the margin which would permit even greater saving if they had the desire and the will power to make them. Having this in mind, on one occasion I asked the Actuary of the Treasury to give me an estimate of what the people were spending in twelve months on what the law classed as luxuries. He reported this amount to be $22,000,000,000, nearly enough to extinguish the entire national debt. The items greatly interested me. They were as follows:

Chewing gum	$ 50,000,000
Candy	1,000,000,000
Soft drinks	350,000,000
Ice cream...........................	250,000,000
Confections.........................	350,000,000
Cereal beverages	230,000,000
Cigarettes	800,000,000
Cigars	510,000,000
Cigar and cigarette holders	1,000,000
Tobacco and snuff	800,000,000
Toilet soaps, etc.	400,000,000
Jewellery, watches, etc................	500,000,000
Perfumery and cosmetics	750,000,000
Admissions to places of amusement and dues	800,000,000
Pianos, organs, victrolas, etc...........	250,000,000
Fur articles	300,000,000
Carpets, rugs, luxurious wearing apparel, etc.................................	1,500,000,000
Hunting garments, liveries, firearms and shells	60,000,000
Art works	25,000,000
Yachts	1,000,000
Portable electric fans	8,000,000
Sporting goods	25,000,000
Luxurious service....................	3,000,000,000
Luxuries in hotels and restaurants	75,000,000
Luxurious articles of food, etc..........	5,000,000,000
Other luxuries, including joy riding, pleasure resorts, races, etc................	3,000,000,000
Automobiles and parts................	2,000,000,000

Think of one item—an expenditure of $50,000,000 a year
for chewing gum! It occurred to me that people who
could chew $50,000,000 worth of chewing gum in one
year could accomplish anything.

I was also interested in discovering what part of our
entire national expenditure up to 1920 had gone into
constructive undertakings and what part had been
used for war or destructive purposes. I asked the
Actuary to give me this figure, and he reported that of the
$67,000,000,000 which the nation had expended to June
30, 1920, about $58,000,000,000 of it had been expended
for war, including the interest on the public debt (which
was mainly a war debt), pensions, and other things, while
$9,000,000,000 had been spent for ordinary civil activ-
ities.

A third thing occurred to me in this connection as I
happened to look at the portrait of the first and greatest
Secretary of the Treasury, which was hanging on the wall
on my left. I was thinking of the enormous receipts
which were coming into the Treasury and the correspond-
ing expenditures. I was just in the act of approving a
railroad voucher for $40,000,000. It occurred to me to
ask how much the Treasury had received and how much
Secretary Alexander Hamilton had handled in the six and
a quarter years of his direction of the Treasury. I discovered that the amount was approximately $28,000,000
for the entire period, and that one warrant which I was
then approving, and which was a minor transaction, exceeded this amount by $12,000,000. But I reflected that
it was more difficult for him and the nation to raise and
handle the small amounts in that day than it was for us
to handle the large amounts in our day, and that it was

not any more difficult to think straight in billions than it was in hundreds of thousands or millions of dollars.

There was a further task in connection with the debt and that was to suggest a programme which would involve the orderly working of a sinking fund and other operations for the retirement of the debt. This was worked out under the direction of the brilliant Assistant Secretary, Mr. Leffingwell, and his successor, Mr. Parker Gilbert.

The second task which confronted the President and the Treasury related to taxation. It was necessary, in the first place, that everything possible be done to secure the maximum of economy. And this, the President insisted upon; and with his approval I laid special emphasis upon it in my report to the Congress. We particularly warned the Congress and the people against any new raids on the Treasury. More especially, we took a sharp and effective stand against the soldiers' bonus. With the President's full approval, I not only wrote on May 18, 1920, to Mr. Fordney a letter opposing a bonus in any form no matter how financed, but I went before the Committee of Ways and Means and emphasized my reasons against such a proposal.

We realized, however, that, in spite of the utmost economy, it would be necessary for the time being, in order to meet the requirements of the government and to proceed with the public debt programme in sensible fashion, to keep receipts from taxation for several years, that is, until about the end of 1923, to approximately $4,000,000,000. It was not possible, therefore, at the time, to make recommendations for tax reduction as a whole such as we would have liked to make. It was desirable, however, to make suggestions for tax reform or revision; and this I did in some detail, notwithstanding the fact that I knew that Congress would be sensitive in the matter. The following are the chief items of the recommendations:

(1) The abolition of the excess profits tax, primarily because of its complexity and of its lack of equity as among different classes of business.

(2) The reduction of surtaxes to approximately 25 per cent. making the total maximum income tax, including the normal tax, 31 per cent.

(3) The abolition of the nuisance taxes.

(4) The necessity of having a final determination of a taxpayer's liability and the settlement of tax claims.

Also, in this connection, I urged that, in the matter of providing a budget system, the Congress go much further than it had gone in the bill which the President vetoed, namely, as I have heretofore stated, that it should place limitations on itself in handling the estimates.

I also outlined the situation with reference to the loans to the Allies, opposed the cancellation of this indebtedness, and suggested that the course to pursue was to proceed under the terms of the existing law and to have the demand notes of the Allies funded into long-term bonds.

Finally, I suggested that certain non-fiscal activities, such as public health, public buildings, and prohibition, be transferred from the Treasury to some other department, and urged the creation of the position of Undersecretary of the Treasury, and that more attractive financial conditions be created so that the Treasury could secure and retain in key positions men of the requisite ability and experience.

The foregoing problems and activities were interesting and important, but they were not nagging. The things which plagued those who had the official responsibility in respect to them grew out of the general economic situation. After the Armistice, a wave of optimism swept over the nation; business men had a feeling that, since the war had closed, business would quickly set up, and enterprises were entered upon to an extent not justified by the underlying conditions. About the time of the Armistice, I had predicted that this would happen. I had stated that there would be a period of rather feverish activities because of the close of the war, that prices would mount even higher, and that there would then come a collapse. I urged that caution should be observed by business men and that farmers should redirect their activities along lines suited to their own community needs. Very soon there was a nation-wide outcry against the mounting prices and the high cost of living. In fact, the pressure was so great that there were many conferences, including official conferences, to see what steps, if any, could be taken to afford relief. It was recognized that little or nothing could be done as long as the people were extravagant, as long as there was reckless speculation, and until production set up on a larger scale both here and abroad. Some indications of a change appeared toward the close of 1919. Industries showed signs of hesitation. This tendency became more marked the latter part of February, 1920. The prices of manufacturing commodities in some cases fell and then, very suddenly, toward the beginning of summer, it became evident that there would be a great decline in the prices of foodstuffs.

CHAPTER XXVII

THE FARMERS BEGIN TO DEMAND RELIEF

A Delegation Demanding Federal Aid for German Cotton Purchases—The Hysteria for Revival of the War Finance Corporation

WE WERE no sooner out of the difficulties presented by the high cost of living than we were confronted by a more difficult situation, that caused by the sharp decline of prices of agricultural commodities, about midsummer and thereafter. The first impulse of many who were hit by the declining prices was to turn to the government, and especially to the Treasury, as the sole recourse for their salvation. This disposition had developed before the war. It was reinforced during hostilities. I was flooded by letters demanding that the Treasury do something. Many delegations appeared, insistently urging that the Treasury see that the high prices that had prevailed were maintained, and even demanding that in some way they be enabled to secure even higher prices.

This tendency can be illustrated by reference to the visit of one of the many groups which was most insistent. I was asked to meet a large delegation from the South. I agreed to do so. About forty appeared. Before the meeting, several Senators came in another door and told me in substance that they knew I could not do what the delegation was going to urge, but that they had to appear to be sympathetic, and that they hoped that I understood their situation. I felt like telling them that I did, and that I clearly recognized that they were taking an unfair position, that, if they agreed with me, it was their duty to tell their constituents the truth. I listened for an hour or more to reports by various members of the conference of conditions with which I was entirely familiar. I knew that the price of cotton had suddenly dropped nearly 50 per cent. I inquired what I could do. The leader announced that I could lend money to the farmers of the South. I pointed out that this would not secure a market for their cotton and that the government was not buying cotton and could not assist them in that way. The leader then announced that the trouble would be remedied if Germany were enabled to buy Southern cotton. I said that would be true if Germany wanted the cotton and had the money or the credit to secure it. One of the Senators jumped up and said that we had to assist Germany. I asked him how. He replied that we could lend her money. I reminded him that we were still in the state of war with Germany as the Senate had not ratified the Treaty of Peace. I also asked him on what security the Treasury could lend money to Germany, even if it had the power, as the Allies had a claim on what little resources Germany had. He shouted that I could lend on German bonds. I asked him if he would lend money to Germany on German bonds, or if he, a cotton planter, would sell his cotton to Germany and take German bonds. He said that of course he would. I asked him to consider the matter carefully, because that very morning a representative from Germany had called on me to see if by any means she could secure cotton. I told the Senator that I felt sure that I could arrange for him to secure all the

[104]

German bonds he would take if he would give his cotton in exchange. I asked if he would make the exchange. He replied that he declined to be quizzed in any such fashion. The conference ended without result.

It was not true, of course, that exports were not going forward to Europe. As a matter of fact, they continued to go in stupendous volume. In 1918, the last year of the war, their value was $6,149,000,000. In 1919, it approximated $8,000,000,000. In the first quarter of 1920, the exports exceeded those for the first quarter of 1919. The business agencies of the country were finding means to facilitate exports to Europe in amazing quantities, and a large percentage, in fact, approximately 50 per cent., consisted of agricultural products. But the prices for these were not so high as the farmers had been receiving or desired to receive. The trouble arose from the fact that the war had closed, that the first thing Europe undertook to do was to produce her food supplies and return to such countries as Australia and Argentina, from which they had been shut off during the war by the submarine. This was coupled with the fact that the farmers could not quickly control their supply as manufacturers could, and had an immense outpouring of commodities. The war had caused prices to rise greatly. The close of the war caused prices to fall, particularly the prices of commodities the supply of which was great, as in the case of agricultural products.

The ignorant part of the community, including many demagogues, in and out of public life, unable or unwilling to see the facts, resorted to the easy and usual practice of attributing the financial ills to the banking machinery of the country, even going so far as to charge that there was a deliberate conspiracy on the part of the Reserve Board and of many bankers to crush the farmers. Their usual way of putting it was that the Federal Reserve Board was deflating the farmers. It was obvious that they did not know what they really meant. They did not really understand what is meant by deflation. They knew that there was a fall in the prices of certain commodities, and they called that deflation. They were unaware that by deflation is meant a lessening of the money or credit of the nation, and that a decrease of the volume of credit in itself would affect all prices equally. If there was real deflation and it alone was operating, there would not be at the same time, because of it, a tremendous drop in farm prices, a smaller decline in prices of many industrial products, and an increase in the prices of others. Their easy explanation also did not account for the great fall of prices of farm products in the other countries of the world. The truth is that, while some prices, particularly those of farm products, greatly declined, there was no real deflation. There was no decline in the volume of credit during 1920, when prices of agricultural products dropped so sharply. There was, as a matter of fact, an enormous increase. Between the date of the Armistice and October 1, 1920, the loans and investments of all banks increased more than $7,000,000,000, and the Federal Reserve notes more than $740,000,000. In the period from January 23, 1920, to the end of September, by which time the drop in agricultural products had occurred, the loans and investments of all the banks expanded a billion dollars or more, and the Federal Reserve note circulation $460,000,000. What is more important is the fact that accommodations extended to agriculture, industry, and commerce, increased in the same period between $3,000,000,000 and $4,000,000,000. From the beginning of the crop-moving season in July, to October 16th, the bills discounted and purchased by the Federal Reserve banks gained at an average rate of $22,000,000 a week, and the Federal Reserve note circulation at the rate of $20,000,000. The peak of the credit expansion was not reached until the close of the year. When the declining loans appeared, in 1921, it was not primarily because of any action of the Federal Reserve System but because business had fallen off and the demand for loans had decreased.

What the Federal Reserve System did, and it was a very important thing, was to save the nation from a financial collapse and from going in the direction that Poland, Austria, Russia, and other continental countries had gone, of stupendous inflation. The Federal Reserve banks, recognizing the danger and the vast amount of unwarranted speculative activities, did take steps to attempt to control further enormous expansion. The main criticism at the time was that they acted too late and too weakly. They first made some change in rediscount rates in the latter part of 1919. They made further changes in 1920. It was necessary to do this, not only to prevent undue expansion for speculative purposes, but to protect the banking reserves. They had reached or were reaching the legal limit and in some cases were below the limit. Loans for speculative purposes were discouraged and reduced so that loans for legitimate purposes might remain high and might even be increased. The desire of the Board was to facilitate essential businesses. And special consideration was given to demands for loans on agricultural paper. There was not only no contraction but, as I have said, a considerable expansion. And there was not a great deal which could be done, except of a temporary character, to aid the people in distress. Time alone, and the readjustment of the industry of this nation and of the world, could bring the necessary relief. It was clear that steps could be taken directly to organize financial relief mainly through the banks of the Northwest, for the aid of the farmers. This had been done during the war through the $5,000,000 which I got the President to set aside. And I had approved in principle a measure which could not come up for final action before I left Washington, a proposal that Congress appropriate a large sum of money for the aid of farmers particularly in the West and South, to be extended through banks.

In the circumstances, a clamour set up for a revival of the War Finance Corporation. It was contended that, under the power which it then had of lending money to exporters to facilitate exports to Europe, it might do something to restore and maintain higher prices for farm products. At my request, in May, 1920, the activities of the War Finance Corporation had been suspended. It was a war agency. At the time there was a great cry that all war agencies should be abolished. It was desirable that they should cease to function. Up to May, the Corporation had rendered very little assistance through the only power it had which bore on the situation. To November, 1920, the advances to aid exports had not exceeded $47,000,000, while the total exports in the year ran at the rate of $8,000,000,000. Before taking the action of suspending the activities of the Corporation, I advised with the President, received his cordial assent, but told him that I thought I had better consult certain leaders in the Senate. I did so. After two long conferences, they agreed with me that I should suspend the activities of the Corporation, and they went even further. They told me that if I would frame a bill to place it in liquidation they would pass it.

The agitation for relief became hysterical. The demand that the War Finance Corporation should resume operations was insistent. I was confident that it would be unwise and futile to revive the Corporation. I was convinced that there would be few legitimate applications from exporters of agricultural commodities for loans and that its activities would have no appreciable effect on prices. I had to continue to meet delegations of Congressmen and of interested groups and I had to write many letters explaining the situation and the reason for my course.

In this period I received support in Washington only from the President and from my colleagues in the Treasury, including my associates on the Federal Reserve Board, with one exception. I received support from many intelligent people throughout the nation and was encouraged by letters from various parts of the country.

I made it a point to keep the President informed about this difficult and nagging state of affairs. I did this in Cabinet meeting, particularly in October, because I had become aware that two of my associates in the Cabinet did not understand the situation and did not agree with me, and that it was being said that they thought I was taking the wrong stand. Several representatives and visitors informed me that one of my colleagues had told them that he took a different view from mine. At the Cabinet meeting I summarized the situation for the President. I told him about the pressure and about the numerous conferences I was having. I outlined the character of the discussion and my conclusions. Two of my colleagues in the Cabinet made it clear during the discussion that they had a different view from mine. The President listened patiently for a little while, then expressed his absolute concurrence with me and approval of the position which I had taken. He added: "I admire your optimism and your patience in attempting to argue this matter with the people who are interested, and particularly with members of Congress, many of whom know better." One of my colleagues interrupted, indicating that he was sympathetic with those who were insisting that the Treasury do something. The President showed some impatience and said: "Let's talk about something more interesting. It is no use trying to reason with people into whose minds reason has never entered."

The Congress persisted and passed a resolution directing, in effect, the revival of the activities of the War Finance Corporation. Following the usual custom, the President sent the resolution to me, requesting me to inform him whether I had any objection to its approval. I replied that I had and that in my judgment it should be vetoed. He then directed me to prepare a veto message, which I did, and which he sent to the Senate. I insert the message, in part, because it gives a further picture of the conditions and additional reasons for the Administration's belief that artificial efforts would be abortive and would only mislead the farmers. The letter from the President's private secretary, my reply, and the message, in part, follow:

The White House,
Washington,
December 23, 1920.

MY DEAR MR. SECRETARY:

The President directs me to send you the accompanying Joint Resolution, S. J. Res. 212, Joint Resolution directing the War Finance Corporation to take certain action for the relief of the present depression in the agricultural sections of the country, and for other purposes, with the request that you inform him, at your earliest convenience, whether there are any objections to its approval.

Sincerely yours,
J. P. TUMULTY.
Secretary to the President.

Hon. D. F. Houston,
    Secretary of the Treasury.

December 30, 1920.

DEAR MR. PRESIDENT:

I am sending herewith for your consideration the draft of a message vetoing S. J. Res. 212. It is long, but I believe that a somewhat full survey will serve a useful purpose.

Faithfully yours,
D. F. HOUSTON.

The President,
    The White House.

[111]

To THE SENATE OF THE UNITED STATES:

I am returning, without my signature, S. J. Res. 212, "Joint Resolution directing the War Finance Corporation to take certain action for the relief of the present depression in the agricultural sections of the country, and for other purposes."

This Resolution was passed by the Congress apparently in view of the recent sudden and considerable fall in prices, especially of agricultural commodities, with the thought that some European countries to which certain products were customarily shipped before the war might again be enabled to resume their importation, and that larger masses of domestic exports to European countries generally might be stimulated, with the resulting enhancement of domestic prices. I am in full sympathy with every sound proposal to promote foreign trade along sound business lines. I am not convinced that the method proposed is wise, that the benefits, if any, would offset the evils which would result, or that the same or larger advantages cannot be secured without resort to government intervention. On the contrary, I apprehend that the resumption of the Corporation's activities at this time would exert no beneficial influence in the situation in which improvement is sought, would raise false hopes among the very people who would expect most, and would be hurtful to the natural and orderly processes of business and finance.

Large government credits were extended during the war to certain European governments associated with us in the struggle. These ceased several months after the Armistice, except for commitments already made. They should not now be resumed, either directly or indirectly.

The recent Brussels Conference, composed of experts from many European countries and from other nations, itself expressed the opinion that further credits should not be accorded directly by governments. I do not believe that they should be accorded indirectly.

Exports of domestic products have not declined since the Armistice. On the contrary, they have greatly increased. From an aggregate value before the war of less than $2\frac{1}{2}$ billions of dollars, and of about 6 billions the last year of hostilities, they rose in the calendar year 1919 to more than $7,900,000,000, and this figure will probably be exceeded this calendar year. For the first eleven months of this calendar year we exported more than $7\frac{1}{2}$ billion dollars' worth of domestic merchandise. These have been largely privately financed. The difficulty in the way of still larger exports does not seem to lie so much in the lack of financial ability here as in Europe's lack of means to make payment. Her productive energies and the services which she renders have not yet reached a point where they balance the value of commodities taken from this nation, and her ability to furnish for additional exports securities which business men would feel justified in taking is restricted. The experts of the Brussels Conference reported that "one of the chief obstacles to the granting of credits is the absence in borrowing countries of sufficient securities for ultimate repayment."

Under the law, if the activities of the Corporation were resumed, no direct advances could be made to producers and, if they could be, they would not accomplish the objects in view. They would not create demand for our products. They could be made only to exporters or to banks engaged in financing exports and if they did in some measure stimulate exports they would probably not have the effect apparently most desired, of substantially increasing those of agricultural commodities. Already, with the larger volume of exports which Europe is taking from us, she is exercising her option of taking a smaller volume of some of our principal agricultural products, such as meats, presumably because she herself has become more largely self-sufficient, or is again providing herself with supplies from distant countries which, with the opening up of shipping since the Armistice, have once more found their place in the markets of the world.

It is highly probable that the most immediate and conspicuous effect of the resumption of the Corporation's activities would be an effort on the part of exporters to shift the financing of their operations from ordinary commercial channels to the government. There is no question that the borrowing of the government should be limited to the minimum requirements, and that the government should not be called upon further to finance private business at public expense. To the extent that Europe is able to furnish additional securities, private financial institutions here will doubtless find means of giving the necessary accommodation. Through reliance on such enterprises, rather than through government intervention, may we expect to secure a return to stable business relations. For many months there has been a demand that war agencies should be abolished and that there should be less government interference with business. I have sympathized with this view, and believe that it is applicable to foreign trade as well as to domestic business. I am of the opinion that now, more than two years after the Armistice, the nation should resume its usual business methods and return to its reliance on the initiative, intelligence, and ability of its business leaders and financial institutions.

We shall not witness an immediate satisfactory adjustment of domestic and international trade relations. The burdens of war are not lifted when the fighting ceases. One sad thing about war is that it leaves behind it a legacy of economic ills and of suffering from which there is no escape. Conditions, however, are improving both here and abroad. The difficulties with which we are now confronted are of small consequence in comparison with those which we have met and overcome. Fuller restoration awaits the adoption of constructive measures of large consequence: the secure establishment of a just peace in the world; the cessation of fighting everywhere; the more complete resumption in Europe of the normal courses of industry, the return of her people to sounder fiscal and banking policies, and the breaking down within her borders of harmful restrictions

WOODROW WILSON.

The White House,
3 Jan., 1921.

In the absence of support of any consequence among the general run of public officials in Washington, I derived what consolation I could from the conviction that the right course was being pursued. My main comfort, however, came from the fact that the President fully understood the situation and was, I knew, strongly behind what was being done. As usual, I knew that if I could decide on the right course and pursue it, he would give

[115]

me the strongest sort of backing. If I had not known this, I would scarcely have been willing to struggle with the forces with which I had to contend. Under any other chief, under a chief who was hesitant or lacking in courage, the task would not have been worth while.

CHAPTER XXVIII

ATTEMPTS TO SETTLE THE WAR DEBTS

The Wording of the Debt Contract—Rathbone's Mission to Great Britain—Chamberlain Suggests United States Offer Cancellation —Message Refusing —Correspondence with Lloyd George—American Policy Outlined

DURING 1920, the problem presented by the loans to foreign governments had given the Treasury a great deal of concern. But the worry was internal until the early part of 1921. Then, extracts appearing in the papers and an agitation precipitated by one of the papers and furthered by a Senator caused official recognition to be taken of the matter by the Senate. A Senate resolution was passed requesting the Secretary of the Treasury to furnish certain information. For various reasons, I preferred to present the whole matter to the Committee on Foreign Affairs, and on February 12, 1921, I did so.

When we entered the war it was generally believed, as I have elsewhere stated, that the largest assistance we could render the Allies would be through economic and financial measures. Within a few days after our entry into the struggle, the Congress passed an act, that of April 24, 1917, authorizing the Secretary of the Treasury to establish credits in favour of foreign governments engaged in war with enemies of the United States, and to the extent of these credits to make advances to such governments through purchase of their respective obligations at par. Three other acts were passed before the Armistice, and the total credits authorized as fixed by the appropriations were $10,000,000,000. The net credits actually established up to November 15, 1920, aggregated approximately $9,710,000,000, of which the principal amounts in round numbers were:

To Great Britain	$4,277,000,000
France	3,048,000,000
Italy	1,666,000,000
Belgium	349,000,000
Russia	188,000,000

The amounts received by the foreign governments under these credits were to meet their commitments in the United States for food and military supplies. The dealings in every case were single and direct with each of the several governments, and not indirect and unified. The suggestion had been made by one government that it would stand in a way as sponsor for other governments and be the vent through which these loans should flow. This suggestion was flatly rejected by the Secretary of the Treasury. The acts of Congress authorizing the loans, which acts must have been known to the foreign governments, make it clear that the governments were to be dealt with separately and on their own responsibility. Certainly, every act after the first one does so. The Second Liberty Bond Act authorized the Secretary of the Treasury to establish credits for "any foreign government" waging war with enemies of the United States, and to purchase "from such foreign governments respectively the several obligations." It was directed by the acts that the obligations of foreign governments should bear the same rate of interest and contain in essence the same terms and conditions as those of the United States. It was contemplated that they should be long-term obligations. In the course of the financial operations, short-term obligations were accepted and the Secretary of the Treasury was authorized to convert any such short-term obligations into long-time bonds, maturing not later than the bonds of the United States.

The certificates indicating the indebtedness of foreign governments were signed in the name of the respective governments by their representatives designated to the Treasury by the Department of State as being authorized to sign them in the name and on behalf of the respective governments. The following is a skeleton copy of an obligation received under one of the acts.

CERTIFICATE OF INDEBTEDNESS

$ [Amount in Figures]

The government of [name of foreign government], for value received, promises to pay to the United States of America, or assigns, the sum of [number of dollars in words] on demand, with interest from date hereof at the rate of [rate per cent.] per cent. per annum. Such principal sum and the interest thereon will be paid without deduction for any [name of foreign government] taxes, present or future, in gold coin of the United States of America of the present standard of weight and fineness at the Subtreasury of the United States in New York, or, at the option of the holder, at the Treasury of the United States in Washington.

[119]

This certificate will be converted by the government of [name of foreign government] if requested by the Secretary of the Treasury of the United States of America, at par with an adjustment of accrued interest into an equal par amount of [rate per cent.] per cent. convertible gold bonds of the government of [name of foreign government], conforming to the provisions of acts of Congress of the United States known, respectively, as Second Liberty Bond Act, Third Liberty Bond Act, and Fourth Liberty Bond Act. If bonds of the United States issued under authority of said acts shall be converted into other bonds of the United States bearing a higher rate of interest than $4\frac{1}{2}$ per cent. per annum, a proportionate part of the obligations of the government of [name of foreign government] of this series acquired by the United States under authority of said acts shall, at the request of said Secretary of the Treasury, be converted into obligations of said government of [name of foreign government], bearing interest at a rate exceeding that previously borne by this obligation by the same amount as the interest rate of the bonds of the United States issued upon such conversion exceeds the interest rate of [rate of this obligation] per cent. but not less than the highest rate of interest borne by such bonds of the United States.

[Signature of representative of foreign government]
For the government of [name of foreign government]
Dated the —— day of ——

It will be particularly observed that the foreign government signing such a certificate pledged itself, if requested by the Secretary of the Treasury, to convert the certificate at par into gold bonds conforming to the provision of the acts of Congress.

It became the duty of the Secretary of the Treasury to secure the compliance by foreign governments with their obligations and to see that the governments proceed with the funding. In spite of approaches by the Secretary of the Treasury to certain foreign governments to get them to comply with the law, little or no headway was made. The only country which seemed even to face the matter seriously and to show signs of compliance was Great Britain. It seemed impossible to induce France, Italy, and other governments, to direct their thoughts toward the matter of funding. And this in spite of the fact that they had signed a certificate pledging themselves to fund at the request of the Secretary of the Treasury.

The first discussion over the funding of the demand obligations was in 1917. It soon died down. The real discussions began in the autumn of 1919, when Mr. Rathbone, Assistant Secretary of the Treasury, then in charge of foreign loans, went to Paris. He made little headway there. In April, 1920, he went to London and, for a month or more, was in active discussion with the British Treasury as to the funding of the British Government's obligations. He carried the negotiations to the point where I believed that a full agreement would be reached and that I would soon receive the agreement for final action. I had been in communication with Mr. Rathbone, and all the difficulties seemed to have been ironed out.

But just at this juncture, on May 25th, Mr. Rathbone received a communication from the Chancellor of the Exchequer stating that he had reported to the Cabinet the tenor of the discussions. He suggested that Mr. Rathbone, who had temporarily gone to the Continent, see him again before he sailed for America. Before Mr. Rathbone had time to reply, he received a telephone message quoting a telegram from the Chancellor to the effect that it would be unnecessary for him to return to London. The Cabinet had given the matter consideration. The Prime Ministers of Great Britain and France had had a conference at Hythe, and on the initiative of the French, an agreement had been reached that the settlement of the debts between them and other European Allies should proceed on parallel lines with the reparation debts. The matter of the European indebtedness to America had not been discussed, it was stated. But it was concluded to be necessary that the treatment of the British debt to the United States which was intended to form a basis for settlements with other nations should be canvassed in its relation to the general situation. It was added that the Prime Minister, who had discussed the matter with President Wilson in Paris, proposed to resume the discussions directly with the President.

This put an end to the negotiations by Mr. Rathbone in Europe. He soon returned home.

Prior to this, following a conversation between Mr. Leffingwell, the Assistant Secretary of the Treasury, and the Counsellor of the British Embassy in Washington, there was transmitted to me informally by the British Counsellor under date of February 9th, a telegram from Mr. Chamberlain, the Chancellor of the Exchequer. It discussed briefly the financial difficulties in Europe and closed by saying that they would welcome a proposal for a general cancellation of any governmental war debts. It is to be noted that Mr. Chamberlain did not propose a cancellation, but indicated his disposition to welcome a proposal. The situation seemed to me to justify a prompt answer. I prepared such an answer and transmitted it to the President for his consideration and approval. He promptly returned the message with his approval noted upon it in pencil in his own writing, and I transmitted it to the Chancellor through Mr. Lindsay, the Counsellor. It was as follows:

March 1, 1920.

DEAR MR. LINDSAY:

Mr. Leffingwell has handed me your note of February 9th, enclosing a message from the Chancellor of the Exchequer. I have read the Chancellor's message with considerable interest, and shall be pleased to have you transmit to the Chancellor the enclosed reply from me.

I am, my dear Mr. Lindsay,

Very sincerely yours,

(Signed) D. F. HOUSTON.

Honourable Ronald C. Lindsay,
  Counsellor, British Embassy,
    2339 Massachusetts Avenue,
      Washington, D. C.

MESSAGE FROM THE SECRETARY OF THE TREASURY TO THE CHANCELLOR OF THE EXCHEQUER

Your recent message through the British Embassy, in which among other things you suggest a general cancellation of inter-governmental war debts, has been received,

[123]

and Rathbone has transmitted a copy of the communication sent him by Blackett dealing with the funding of the demand obligations of the Allied governments held by the United States and England respectively, in which the same subject is raised.

I concur with your view that the financial and economic problems of all the world are closely connected and that Great Britain and the United States naturally look with concern upon the difficulties which confront Continental Europe. The United States Treasury has been greatly interested in information reaching it concerning the situation of Great Britain, and has viewed with pleasure and satisfaction the progress which your government has been making toward a return to a peace basis. While we are at present confronted with difficult problems, our financial situation is not at all critical. On the contrary, it is such that I have reason to think that credits from private sources may be made available to Continental Europe on sound and adequate security and on terms which recognize the world-wide shortage of capital resulting from five years of warfare.

Funding of the short-term obligations into long-term obligations is a matter as to which no question has been raised by our Congress, and there should be no difficulty in dealing with this phase of the proposed arrangements in the manner outlined by Mr. Rathbone. As you have no doubt heard from Mr. Rathbone, it may be impossible to reach, without Congressional approval, a final settlement in respect to the interest accruing during the next two or three years.

I regret that conditions are such as to cause you concern in respect to the Anglo-French loan maturing this fall, and sincerely hope you will have no difficulty in making satisfactory arrangements to take care of it.

As to the engagement of the British Government in respect to advances for the purchase of silver under the Pittman Act, this matter is being dealt with by Mr. Rathbone, who undoubtedly will give full consideration to any proposal that you have to make in that connection. It is unfortunate that the Indian Government has not seen fit to take steps to limit the importation of gold into India. Failure to do this is making heavy demands on our gold reserves. If continued, this is likely materially to impair the ability of our financial markets to assist Europe.

As to the general cancellation of inter-governmental war debts suggested by you, you will, I am sure, desire that I present my views no less frankly than you have presented yours. Any proposal or movement of such character would, I am confident, serve no useful purpose. On the contrary, it would, I fear, mislead the people of the debtor countries as to the justice and efficacy of such a plan, and arouse hopes the disappointment of which could only have a harmful effect. I feel certain that neither the American people nor our Congress, whose action on such a question would be required, is prepared to look with favour upon such a proposal.

Apparently, there are those who have been labouring for some time under the delusion that the inevitable consequences of war can be avoided. As far back as January, a year ago, before it could possibly be foreseen whether any measures were necessary other than the adoption of sound economic policies, various schemes, including that of a cancellation of inter-governmental war

[125]

debts, were launched. Of course, I recognize that a general cancellation of such debts would be of advantage to Great Britain, and that it probably would not involve any losses on her part. As there are no obligations of the United States Government which would be cancelled under such a plan, the effect would be that in consideration of a cancellation by the United States Government of the obligations which it holds for advances made to the British Government and the other Allied governments the British Government would cancel its debt against France, Italy, Russia, and her other allies. Such a proposal does not involve mutual sacrifices on the part of the nations concerned. It simply involves a contribution mainly by the United States. The United States has shown its desire to assist Europe. Negotiations for funding the principal of the foreign obligations held by the United States Treasury and for postponing or funding the interest accruing during the reconstruction period are in progress. Since the Armistice, this government has extended to foreign governments financial assistance to the extent of approximately four billions of dollars. What this government could do for the immediate relief of the debtor countries has been done. Their need now is for private credits. The indebtedness of the Allied governments to each other and to the United States is not a present burden upon the debtor governments, since they are not paying interest or even, as far as I am aware, providing in their budgets or taxes for the payment of either principal or interest. At the present time, the foreign obligations held by the government of the United States do not constitute a practical obstacle to obtaining credits here, and I do not think that the European countries would obtain a dollar additional credit as a result of the cancellation of those obligations. The proposal does not touch matters out of which the present financial and economic difficulties of Europe chiefly grow. The relief from present ills, in so far as it can be obtained, is primarily within the control of the debtor governments and peoples themselves. Most of the debtor governments have not levied taxes sufficient to enable them to balance their budgets, nor have they taken any energetic and adequate measures to reduce their expenditures to meet their income. Too little progress has been made in disarmament. No appreciable progress has been made in deflating excessive issues of currency or in stabilizing the currencies at new levels, but in Continental Europe there has been a constant increase in note issues. Private initiative has not been restored. Unnecessary and unwise economic barriers still exist. Instead of setting trade and commerce free by appropriate steps there appear to be concerted efforts to obtain from the most needy discriminatory advantages and exclusive concessions. There is not yet apparent any disposition on the part of Europe to make a prompt and reasonable definite settlement of the reparation claims against Germany or to adopt policies which will set Germany and Austria free to make their necessary contribution to the economic rehabilitation of Europe.

After taking all the measures within their power, one or more of the debtor governments may ultimately consider it necessary or advantageous to make some general settlement of their indebtedness. In such a case, they would, I presume, propose to all creditors, domestic and foreign, a general composition which would take into account advantages obtained by such debtor country under the Treaty of Peace. How the American people or the American Congress would view participation in such a composition, I cannot say. It is very clear to me, however, that a general cancellation of inter-governmental war debts, irrespective of the positions of the separate debtor governments, is of no present advantage or necessity. A general cancellation as suggested would, while retaining the domestic obligations intact, throw upon the people of this country the exclusive burden of meeting the interest and of ultimately extinguishing the principal of our loans to the Allied governments. This nation has neither sought nor received substantial benefits from the war. On the other hand, the Allies, although having suffered greatly in loss of lives and property, have, under the terms of the Treaty of Peace and otherwise, acquired very considerable accessions of territories, populations, economic and other advantages. It would therefore seem that, if a full account were taken of these and of the whole situation, there would be no desire or reason to call upon the government of this country for further contributions.

* * *

When Mr. Rathbone's cable came announcing the breaking off of the negotiations and conveying the information that the Prime Minister desired to communicate directly with the President, I thought it necessary that the matter be not permitted to drop and that I should prepare a communication to be sent to the Chancellor of the Exchequer. This I did and, after receiving approval from the President, I transmitted the following:

"I have consulted with the President concerning a

cable which we have received from Mr. Rathbone, Assistant Secretary of the Treasury, transmitting a letter from the Chancellor of the Exchequer to him, in which he states that the Cabinet, before proceeding further with the consideration of detailed proposals for the treatment of the British debt to the United States Government, feel that their applicability to the general situation must be further explored, and that there are raised questions of great importance unsuited for departmental treatment between the two treasuries; and that the Prime Minister will communicate on this subject with the President. A copy of the letter from the Chancellor of the Exchequer and a copy of Mr. Rathbone's reply to the Chancellor, of which I approve, are attached hereto. The President has approved my expressing the position of this government, which is as follows:

"The letter above referred to from the Chancellor to Mr. Rathbone and Mr. Rathbone's reply are the outcome of negotiations which have been conducted for many months between the British and the American treasuries and which in effect began at the inception of our loans to the British Treasury. The communication from the Chancellor to Mr. Rathbone is the more surprising in that Mr. Rathbone had been in Europe in this connection for six months, the last of which he spent in London for the sole purpose of conducting with the British Treasury discussions which had resulted in agreement on nearly all points, including the exchange of the demand obligations of the British Government held by this government into time obligations, and there was fair promise that agreement would be reached speedily on the few matters that remained to be settled. We are especially surprised that

[129]

the negotiations should thus have been terminated on the ground that the applicability of detailed proposals for the treatment of the debt of the British Government to the American Government in the general situation must be further explored, and that this raises questions of importance too great for departmental treatment between our two treasuries. On several occasions during the Peace Conference, suggestions were made with a view to injecting the subject of the debts among the Associated and Allied governments into the question of the settlement to be made with the enemy. This government then took the position that its loans to the respective Allied governments have no relation to the other indebtedness of those governments or to the German Government to them, and that matters relating to the indebtedness of any government to this government were properly to be dealt with by the treasuries of the two countries and not at the Peace Conference. All proposals contradictory to this principle were rejected. The position of this government has not changed.

"With reference to so much of the Chancellor's letter as states that discussions on this subject took place at an earlier period between the President and the Prime Minister, and that the Prime Minister proposes now to resume these discussions and will send a communication for the President's consideration, the President recalls that he stated his views at length in a letter dated the 5th of May, 1919, to the Prime Minister. The views so expressed have been maintained constantly since that time, and this government now adheres to them, and holds the opinion that no useful purpose can be served by now reopening such questions. Although this government

[130]

fully realizes that a wise and constructive policy regarding the reparations due from Germany will greatly accelerate the rehabilitation of Europe and consequently the power of the debtor governments to pay what they owe, only future developments can show whether or not the ability of any allied government to discharge its indebtedness is dependent upon what it collects from Germany.

"Should the British Government conclude that matters concerning British obligations held by the United States are not a departmental matter, to be dealt with by the Chancellor of the Exchequer, the fact would remain that as to such obligations and all other obligations received by the Secretary of the Treasury of the United States on account of advances made by him under the Liberty Bond acts, Congress has delegated only to the Secretary of the Treasury the power within certain limitations to deal with them. Since questions concerning the British indebtedness to the United States arise only out of the existence of such obligations or under the laws under which they were received and necessarily concern the disposition of them, it is proper and necessary that such questions be dealt with by the American Treasury. The Secretary of the Treasury must adhere to the position which he has always maintained and which, as he understood, had been accepted by the British Government, that matters concerning the disposition and payment of the obligations of the British Government held by this government must be dealt with independently of the debt due from other governments to the British Government or of the financial position of such other governments. We had, however, hoped that the British and American treasuries might agree that the obligations to be received by them from

[131]

governments debtor to both in exchange for the obligations now held might be similar as to maturity, rate of interest, and certain other matters."

The matter drifted for some months. I assumed that there would be a prompt communication from Mr. Lloyd George to the President, but nothing came from him until August 5, 1920. In the course of his letter, he touched upon the reparation question and said that it was the view of the French Government, which had been made known to the British Government, that France could not remit any part of the reparations due under the Treaty except as a part of an all-round settlement of Inter-allied indebtedness. He added that the British Government would agree to any equitable arrangement for a reduction, provided such a reduction applied all round.

There was nothing new in this. Mr. Lloyd George had taken the matter up with the President early in the course of the negotiations in Paris. He transmitted to the President a document dated April, 1919. It revealed that the thought in the minds of the Allies was that the loans of the United States should be tied up with reparations, that there should be a joint consideration of debts, and that if the reparations were reduced our loans should be scaled accordingly. It proposed, among other things, that German bonds to the face value of £1,200,000,000 at 4 per cent. and 1 per cent. for sinking fund, should be issued, that certain bonds should be issued by the other enemy countries, and that these should be guaranteed jointly and severally by the enemy states. It further provided that, if any of the enemy guarantees fell down, they should be guaranteed by the Allied and Associated governments, by the Scandinavian governments and Holland and

[132]

Switzerland. In the event of any of the guaranteeing governments failing to meet their guarantees, the remaining states should make good their failure. The proceeds of most of the bonds were to be paid over on account of sums due for reparations. The bonds were to be accepted at their par value with interest in payment of all indebtedness between any of the Allied and Associated governments. They were to be acceptable as collateral for loans at the central banks of all the issuing or guaranteeing states. The United States, Great Britain, and France were to guarantee 20 per cent. each, Italy and Japan 10 per cent. and the other states the remainder. The effect of this would have been to make anything that we might receive dependent upon German reparations and to make the United States the principal effective guarantor of the transaction.

The President replied under date of May 5th, emphatically turning down the proposition, pointing out the impossibility of our acceptance and the lack of equity in the proposal. Incidentally, he pointed out the injury which the reparation claims, as they stood, would do to Germany and the harm which uncertainty would cause the Allies.

Mr. Lloyd George's letter of August 5, 1920, was presented to me and, after full consideration, I drafted a reply for the President's approval and for his transmission to the Prime Minister. In the early part of October, the President transmitted a reply to Mr. Lloyd George, the pertinent parts of which are as follows:

"I turn now to the problem of inter-allied indebtedness, which you raise. I must deal with this matter with great frankness, as I am sure you wish me to do. It is desirable that our position be clearly understood in order to avoid

[133]

any further delay in a constructive settlement of reparations which may arise from the hope that the debts of this government can form a part of such settlement. It will be helpful if first of all I indicate our legal situation.

"The Secretary of the Treasury is authorized by United States law to arrange for the conversion of the demand obligations of the British Government into its obligations having a fixed date of maturity, in accordance with the agreement of the British Government to make such exchange on demand contained in its existing obligations. In connection with such exchange, the Secretary of the Treasury has authority to arrange for the postponement of interest payments. No power has been given by the Congress to any one to exchange, remit, or cancel any part of the indebtedness of the Allied governments to the United States represented by their respective demand obligations. It would require Congressional authority to authorize any such dealing with the demand obligations and, as stated in the letter of November 18, 1919, from Mr. Rathbone to Mr. Blackett of the British Treasury, the Congress has the same authority to authorize any disposition of obligations of the British Government held by the United States, whether represented by demand obligations or by obligations having a fixed date of maturity. It is highly improbable that either the Congress or popular opinion in this country will ever permit a cancellation of any part of the debt of the British Government to the United States in order to induce the British Government to remit, in whole or in part, the debt to Great Britain of France or any other of the Allied governments, or that it would consent to a cancellation or reduction in the debts of any of the Allied governments as an inducement toward a practical settlement of the reparation claims. As a matter of fact, such a settlement in our judgment would not in itself increase the ultimate financial strength of the Allies.

"You will recall that suggestions looking to the cancellation or exchange of the indebtedness of Great Britain to the United States were made to me when I was in Paris. Like suggestions were again made by the Chancellor of the Exchequer in the early part of the present year. The United States Government, by its duly authorized representatives, has promptly and clearly stated its unwillingness to accept such suggestions each time they have been made and has pointed out in detail the considerations which caused its decision. The views of the United States Government have not changed, and it is not prepared to consent to the remission of any part of the debt of Great Britain to the United States. Any arrangements the British Government may make with regard to the debt owed to it by France or by the other Allied governments should be made in the light of the position now and heretofore taken by the United States, and the United States, in making any arrangements with other Allied governments regarding their indebtedness to the United States (and none are now contemplated beyond the funding of indebtedness and the postponement of payment of interest) will do so with the confident expectation of the payment in due course of the debt owed the United States by Great Britain. It is felt that the funding of these demand obligations of the British Government will do more to strengthen the friendly relations between America and Great Britain than would any other course of dealing with the same.

[135]

"The United States Government entirely agrees with the British Government that the fixing of Germany's reparation obligation is a cardinal necessity for the renewal of the economic life of Europe and would prove to be most helpful in the interests of peace throughout the world; however, it fails to perceive the logic in a suggestion in effect either that the United States shall pay part of Germany's reparation obligation or that it shall make a gratuity to the Allied governments to induce them to fix such obligation at an amount within Germany's capacity to pay. This government has endeavoured heretofore in a most friendly spirit to make it clear that it cannot consent to connect the reparation question with that of inter-governmental indebtedness.

"The long delay which has occurred in the funding of the demand obligations is already embarrassing the Treasury, which will find itself compelled to begin to collect back and current interest if speedy progress is not made with the funding. Unless arrangements are completed for funding such loans and in that connection for the deferring of interest, in the present state of opinion here, there is likely to develop a dangerous misunderstanding. I believe it to be highly important that a British representative with proper authority proceed to Washington without delay to arrange to carry out the obligation of the British Government to convert its demand obligations held by our Treasury into long-time obligations.

"The United States Government recognizes the importance, in the interests of peace and prosperity, of securing the restoration of financial and industrial stability throughout Europe. The war debts of the Allied governments, the treaty obligations of Germany under the reparation clauses of the Treaty of Versailles and the annexes thereto, and of other enemy and ex-enemy countries under the treaties negotiated with them, the administration of countries under the mandates provided for by such treaties, and the existing arrangements between the governments of various countries, have or may have an important bearing in making plans to accomplish such restoration. It is the view of the United States Government that in accrediting a representative to Washington for the purpose mentioned, it might prove expedient that the British Government should authorize him to enter into discussions of all of these matters with the proper representatives of the United States Government."

When I ascertained that this letter had been sent, I inquired if the Treasury might again take up the matter. I received an affirmative answer. I approached the British Ambassador and suggested the desirability of concluding negotiations. I was informed that Britain would soon send a representative here to continue the discussion. And here the matter rested.

It seemed to me unfortunate that there should have been any delay. I was convinced that delay would simply give interested persons an opportunity to make trouble, and that suspicion and ill-feeling might result. I regarded it as particularly unfortunate that certain positions should be taken by one of the leading governments in reference to this matter. I knew that it would not help matters to place the debts due the United States in the same category with reparations claimed from Germany. When we made the loans, those eagerly seeking them did not suggest that their funding or their repayment be made dependent on what they might subsequently receive from any direction,

[137]

especially from reparations from Germany. They did not then know, of course, that they would receive reparations from Germany. They did not then know that they would be victorious over Germany. Any reparations were made possible by the participation of the United States in the war, and by her financial aid. The United States from the outset had vigorously protested against the excessive amount of reparations which was fixed. It would not sit well to have any nation assert that her repayment of loans would depend upon her receipt of reparations and be a part and parcel of them, that if there was any reduction in the reparations amount, which, of course, was an impossible amount, the United States must help make up the difference by cancelling her loans in part or whole. I was confident that the people of the United States, while they might be prepared to recognize all the economic facts and be generous, would not be put in the position of paying part of an indemnity amount which in the nature of things could not be paid by Germany. The further argument that we should cancel our debts because we did not enter the war soon enough was likewise irritating. Whether we were to enter the war or not and when was a decision for us alone to make. Likewise, the suggestion that we had not, in fact, pooled our resources with the Allies, and especially the suggestion that Great Britain had acted as an intermediary for her Allies and as a guarantor for their debts to us, was as irritating as it was untrue.

In my report for 1920, I reviewed the matter of credits and indicated my strong opposition to a cancellation of the foreign loans and pointed out that the American people would scarcely entertain with favour the proposition to cancel them without consideration, realizing that, if the debts were cancelled, they must pay the taxes to meet the interest and to redeem the principal. I then believed and still believe that generous terms would be made, and especially if this country were convinced that the Allies would settle down to readjustment along sound lines and would abate many of the evils that tend to cause friction and war. I emphasized the fact that the reasonable and proper course to take at the time was to proceed under the terms of the law, and for those indebted to fund their demand notes into obligations with a distant maturity, with rates of interest, low at first and later gradually increasing, coupled with authority for the time being to defer interest payments. I recognized that the period of maturity should be a very long one and that it would do this country no good, looking at the matter broadly, to receive any payments of either interest or principal in the existing state of international finance and international trade.

CHAPTER XXIX

THE LAST DAYS OF THE ADMINISTRATION

Luncheon at the White House—Requested to Draft Veto of Tariff on Agricultural Products—Farewell Letter

ON THURSDAY, February 24th, Mrs. Houston and I, at the invitation of the President and Mrs. Wilson, went to the White House for luncheon. This was the first time that we had taken any meal with the President and Mrs. Wilson when no other guests were present. It was a somewhat pathetic experience. The President looked fairly well and made a brave show of good spirits. He repeated a great many of his favourite stories and was exceptionally kindly and friendly.

I asked him what he thought of the new Cabinet. He replied that he did not have mind enough to encompass the entire body, and asked which I had particularly in mind. I was more especially concerned with the Secretary of the Interior, Senator Fall. I had known of his attitude toward conservation. He was one of a crowd that we had been fighting for a number of years. I knew that he had about the same interest in the conservation of the natural resources of the nation that a tiger has in a lamb, and I was astounded when I noticed his appointment.

When I mentioned his name, the President said he had never wanted to hit a man in his life as badly as he did Senator Fall on a certain occasion. He reminded us of the fact that, after his serious illness, Senator Fall had called at the White House, as the President expressed it, "as a member of a smelling committee," to find out whether he was all there or not, and added: "I was lying in bed flat on my back. After the committee had discussed certain matters with me and had, I think, discovered that I was very much all here, the committee turned to leave. Senator Fall paused a moment and said: 'Mr. President, I want you to know that I am praying for you.'" The President remarked: "If I could have got out of bed, I would have hit the man. Why did he want to put me in bad with the Almighty? He must have known that God would take the opposite view from him on any subject."

As we were leaving, he walked on his crutches with me as far as the elevator, making headway with great difficulty. As we parted, he laid his hand on my arm and with some emotion simply said: "Houston, old man, God bless you." This was the first evidence of personal affection or emotion I ever saw him exhibit.

The last important matter affecting the Treasury I had to take up with the President was the bill imposing temporary duties upon agricultural products and for other purposes. The President had the bill sent to me with the usual request that I advise him whether I had any objections to his approval. I replied that I had objection and prepared and sent to him for his consideration a veto message which he transmitted to the Congress. It was as follows:

THE HOUSE OF REPRESENTATIVES:
I return herewith, without my approval, H. R. 15275, an act imposing temporary duties upon certain agricul-

tural products to meet present emergencies, to provide revenue, and for other purposes.

The title of this measure indicates that it has several purposes. The report of the Committee on Ways and Means reveals that its principal object is to furnish relief to certain producers in the nation who have been unable to discover satisfactory markets in foreign countries for their products and whose prices have fallen. Very little reflection would lead any one to conclude that the measure would not furnish in any substantial degree the relief sought by the producers of most of the staple commodities which it covers. This nation has been for very many years a large exporter of agricultural products. For nearly a generation before it entered the European war, its exports exceeded its imports of agricultural commodities by from approximately $200,000,000 to more than $500,000,000. In recent years this excess has greatly increased, and in 1919 reached the huge total of $1,904,292,000. The excess of exports of staple products is especially marked. In 1913, the nation imported 783,481 bushels of wheat valued at $670,931, and in 1920, 35,848,648 bushels worth $75,398,834; while it exported in 1913, 99,508,968 bushels worth $95,098,838, and in 1920, 218,280,231 bushels valued at $596,957,796. In the year 1913, it imported 85,183 barrels of wheat flour valued at $347,877, and in 1920, 800,788 barrels valued at $8,669,300; while it exported in the first year, 12,278,206 barrels valued at $56,865,444, and in 1920, 19,853,952 barrels valued at $224,472,448. In 1913, it imported $3,888,604 worth of corn, and in 1920, $9,257,377 worth, while its exports in the first year were valued at $26,515,146, and in 1920, at $26,453,681. Of unmanufactured cotton in 1920 it imported approximately 300,000,000 pounds valued at $38,743,000, while it exported more than 3,179,000,000 pounds, worth over $1,136,000,000.

Of preserved milk in the same year it imported $3,331,812 worth and exported $65,239,020 worth. Its imports in the same year of sugar and wool of course greatly exceeded its exports. It is obvious that for the commodities, except sugar and wool, mentioned in the measure, which make up the greater part of our agricultural international trade, the imports can have little or no effect on the prices of the domestic products. This is strikingly true of such commodities as wheat and corn. The imports of wheat have come mainly from Canada and Argentina and have not competed with the domestic crop. Rather they have supplemented it. The domestic demand has been for specific classes and qualities of foreign wheat to meet particular milling and planting needs. They are a small fraction of our total production and of our wheat exports. The price of wheat is a world price; and it is a matter of little moment whether the Canadian wheat goes directly into the markets of the other countries of the world or indirectly through this country. The relatively small quantity of corn imported into this country has a specialized use and does not come into competition with the domestic commodity.

The situation in which many of the farmers of the country find themselves cannot be remedied by a measure of this sort. This is doubtless generally understood. There is no short way out of existing conditions, and measures of this sort can only have the effect of deceiving the farmers and of raising false hopes among them. Actual relief can come only from the adoption of constructive measures of a broader scope, from the restoration of peace everywhere in the world, the resumption of normal industrial pursuits, the recovery particularly of Europe, and the discovery there of additional credit foundations on the basis of which her people may arrange to take from farmers and other producers of this nation a greater part of their surplus production.

One does not pay a compliment to the American farmer who attempts to alarm him by dangers from foreign competition. The American farmers are the most effective agricultural producers in the world. Their production is several times as great for each worker as that of their principal foreign rivals. This grows out of the intelligence of the American farmer, the nature of his agricultural practices and economy, and the fact that he has the assistance of scientific and practical agencies which in respect to variety of activity, of personnel, and of financial support exceed those of any other two or three nations in the world combined. There is little doubt that the farmers of this nation will not only continue mainly to supply the home demand but will be increasingly called upon to supply a large part of the needs of the rest of the world.

What the farmer now needs is not only a better system of domestic marketing and credit, but especially larger foreign markets for his surplus products. Clearly, measures of this sort will not conduce to an expansion of the foreign market. It is not a little singular that a measure which strikes a blow at our foreign trade should follow so closely upon the action of Congress directing the resumption of certain activities of the War Finance Corporation, especially at the urgent insistence of representatives of the

[144]

farming interests, who believed that its resumption would improve foreign marketing. Indeed, when one surveys recent activities in the foreign field and measures enacted affecting the foreign trade, one cannot fail to be impressed with the fact that there is consistency only in their con- tradictions and inconsistencies. We have been vigorously building up a great merchant marine and providing for improvement of marketing in foreign countries by the passage of an export-trade law and of measures for the promotion of banking agencies in foreign countries. Now it appears that we propose to render these measures abor- tive in whole or in part.

I imagine there is little doubt that, while this measure is temporary, it is intended as a foundation for action of a similar nature of a very general and permanent character. It would seem to be designed to pave the way for such action. If there ever was a time when America had any- thing to fear from foreign competition, that time has passed. I cannot believe that American producers, who in most respects are the most effective in the world, can have any dread of competition when they view the fact that their country has come through the great struggle of the last few years, relatively speaking, untouched, while their principal competitors are in varying degrees sadly stricken and labouring under adverse conditions from which they will not recover for many years. Changes of a very radi- cal character have taken place. The United States has become a great creditor nation. She has lent certain governments of Europe more than $9,000,000,000, and as a result of the enormous excess of our exports, there is an additional commercial indebtedness of foreign nations to our own of perhaps not less than $4,000,000,000. There

[145]

are only three ways in which Europe can meet her part of her indebtedness, namely, by the establishment of private credits, by the shipment of gold, or of commodities. It is difficult for Europe to discover the requisite securities as a basis for the necessary credits. Europe is not in a position at the present time to send us the amount of gold which would be needed, and we could not view further large imports of gold into this country without concern. The result, to say the least, would be a larger disarrangement of international exchange and disturbance of international trade. If we wish to have Europe settle her debts, governmental or commercial, we must be prepared to buy from her, and if we wish to assist Europe and ourselves by the export either of food, of raw materials, or of finished products, we must be prepared to welcome commodities which we need and which Europe will be prepared, with no little pain, to send us.

Clearly, this is no time for the erection here of high trade barriers. It would strike a blow at the large and successful efforts which have been made by many of our great industries to place themselves on an export basis. It would stand in the way of the normal readjustment of business conditions throughout the world, which is as vital to the welfare of this country as to that of all the other nations. The United States has a duty to itself as well as to the world, and it can discharge this duty by widening, not by contracting, its world markets.

This measure has only slight interest so far as its prospective revenue yields are concerned. It is estimated that the aggregate addition to the nation's income from its operation for ten months would be less than $72,000,000, and of this more than half would arise from the proposed duty on sugar. Obviously, this and much more can be secured in ways known to the Congress, which would be vastly less burdensome to the American consumer and American industry.

The rates, however, have a peculiar interest. In practically every case, they either equal or exceed those established under the Payne-Aldrich Act, in which the principle of protection reached its high-water mark, and the enactment of which was followed by an effective exhibition of protests on the part of the majority of the American people. I do not believe that the sober judgment of the masses of the people of the nation, or even of the special class whose interests are immediately affected by this measure, will sanction a return, especially in view of conditions which lend even less justification for such action, to a policy of legislation for selfish interests which will foster monopoly and increase the disposition to look upon the government as an instrument for private gain instead of an instrument for the promotion of the general well being. Such a policy is antagonistic to the fundamental principle of equal and exact justice to all, and can only serve to revive the feeling of irritation on the part of the great masses of the people and of lack of confidence in the motives of rulers and the results of government.

WOODROW WILSON.

The White House,
3 March, 1921.

Tuesday, March 1, 1921, we held our last Cabinet meeting. It had been decided to hold it in the regular Cabinet room in the executive offices. I arrived a few minutes early and saw the President coming through the White

House grounds toward the room. He was walking with great difficulty. It was a brave but tragic spectacle. I turned away and walked into an adjoining room so that he might get seated, and then I entered and took my place at his left. We discussed a few measures which were still before the Congress, and something was said about the part the President would take in the exercises during the inauguration. He had not then had presented to him the full plans. He made it clear that he expected and intended to carry out his full part in the exercises.

A brief pause ensued. Then one of the members of the Cabinet asked the President how he was going to pass his time and if it was likely that he would write a history of the Administration. The President replied that he would not write a history of his Administration, saying that he was too near the events and too closely personally associated with them to make it desirable or possible for him to do so. He said, in substance: "I cannot write a history of these eight years. It is unnecessary for me to attempt to write anything new. The people know everything that I have thought. There has been nothing which it was necessary or desirable for me to keep secret." The same member of the Cabinet said: "But you must do something! What will you do?" The President reflected a moment and said: "I am going to try to teach ex-presidents how to behave." Then he added: "There will be one very difficult thing for me, however, to stand, and that is Mr. Harding's English."

After the business was disposed of, our minds naturally turned to the experiences of our eight strenuous years together and particularly to the President's personal struggles and heroic endeavours. A short pause ensued.

[148]

Then the Secretary of State, properly speaking first, said in effect:

"Mr. President, if I may presume to voice the sentiments of my colleagues, I have the honour of saying that it has been a great distinction to serve you and with you in the most interesting and fateful times of modern history. It has been a most satisfactory and inspiring service. We shall keep watch of your progress toward better health with affectionate interest and shall pray that your recovery may be rapid."

It was then my part to say something. I turned toward the President and started to speak but noticed that he was struggling under a powerful emotion and was trying to control himself. His lips were trembling. He began to speak but hesitated a moment as tears rolled down his cheeks. Then he said, brokenly: "Gentlemen, it is one of the handicaps of my physical condition that I cannot control myself as I have been accustomed to do. God bless you all." This was a very touching statement. No greater trial could come to a Scotch Presbyterian whose whole philosophy of life was self-control, to be unable to master himself.

We got up quietly, shook hands with him, bade him farewell, and left the room. That afternoon I returned to my office and dictated this letter which I sent him on Thursday:

March 3, 1921.

Dear Mr. President:

I feel impelled to say just a word to you before I vacate my office and our official relations are severed. I need not tell you that I have felt greatly honoured by my association with you in one of the greatest periods of American history. You conferred on me great distinction in making me first the head of the Department of Agriculture and later the head of the Treasury Department. These happen to be the departments of government dealing with activities in which my interests for many years have mainly centred. I have therefore derived immense interest, pleasure, and satisfaction from supervising their activities, including not only the problems of rural life and of finance, also those of commercial and farm-loan banking, not to speak of many others. At all times my problems have been numerous and difficult, but my tasks have been rendered tolerable by your unfailing support. I have had no doubt at any time of the principle by which I should be guided. I knew that the principle was the one by which you yourself are guided. I have known you too long and been associated with you too intimately not to know that there is only one question in which you are interested, and that is whether a given course is right or wrong. May I say that I have had knowledge of the fact that no other man has occupied your position who was so well prepared by training and experience to pass judgment on problems in this spirit or who had in higher degree the willingness and courage to follow the course deemed to be in the public interest? I am serenely confident that the sober judgment of the people of this nation now is that you have given the nation as effective and as clean an administration as it has ever had, and that no man in the world has laboured more valiantly and successfully than you to promote real and civilized purposes. I know that the verdict of history will be to this effect.

I have deeply appreciated your many personal courtesies. I have been distressed that your numerous tasks weighed on you and almost overwhelmed you physically, and I have followed with immense satisfaction your course of recovery. I hope that you will be rapidly restored to normal physical strength.

May I say just another personal word? I feel that I cannot close this note without an expression of indebtedness to Mrs. Wilson, and of admiration for the part she has played and the judgment she has shown in dealing with important matters.

With great affection and gratitude, I am,

Faithfully yours,

D. F. HOUSTON.

The President,
  The White House.

AN ESTIMATE OF
WOODROW WILSON

AN ESTIMATE OF WOODROW WILSON

THUS far the record speaks for itself. It gives the story of things as I saw them, for the day, or the week, or the month or, in a few instances, for a longer period, when no new developments appeared and there seemed to be no special need for recording anything. The memoranda having been made at the time, little opportunity was offered to look backward or forward, and an effort was made not to do so. The comments are those of the moment, on the happenings of the moment, and there is, therefore, little in the record in the way of broad criticism or of a controversial nature.

Perhaps it would be wiser to stop with the record, but I find it difficult to resist the temptation to take a somewhat freer range, in particular to give my estimate of the central figure of the period, and, for that matter, the central world figure in this great period of the world's history. I prefer to yield to the temptation and run the risk of being counted unwise and even rash. It is rash to attempt to give an estimate of any man—to say that he was thus and so, and that he acted from such and such motives. No man fully understands himself, or is able always, even after reflection, to state satisfactorily to himself the grounds of his decision and the reasons for his action.

It is peculiarly risky for any one to essay to analyse Woodrow Wilson and to picture what manner of man he was and why he acted as he did on many of the smaller and larger matters rapidly pressing upon him for decision in the most momentous and rapidly shifting scenes of modern history. It was easy for omniscient persons on the outside to ascertain and determine at the time why he did certain things and what he should have done. They were hampered neither by facts nor by responsibility; and many of those who were most vocal, at a time of great national peril even, were more concerned with making political capital than they were in soberly discovering the right course. Not a few of them of the prima donna type were constantly seeking the limelight and were deeply resentful of the fact that in such stirring and dramatic times others had the leading rôles and positions of power. There were a few conspicuous leaders of the opposing party, some in political positions of influence, others in private life who were peculiarly affected with this resentment and could not conceal it. They revealed it at all times, frequently in harmful ways—in outbursts of furious criticism or in petty partisan tactics. It is not necessary that I mention names. They will readily occur to the reader.

Few men see a thing or a man in the same light, and I do not for a moment assume that any one else will accept my estimate of Woodrow Wilson in full, or even in large measure. It is not even satisfactory to me, and I shall doubtless revise it as I get sidelights from his other friends, from his critics, and from new materials.

The sum of Mark Twain's later philosophy about man is that he is the creature of heredity and environment. How far this is sound is a matter for debate, but there is no question that there is a measure of truth in it. Woodrow Wilson revealed sharply the influence of his heredity and of his environment. He came from stern ancestors and for fifty-eight years of his life his environment was confined and specialized. "My ancestors," he said, "were troublesome Scotsmen, and among them were some of that famous group that were known as Covenanters." His maternal grandfather was a Scotsman. He was a Scotch Presbyterian. He was a Calvinist; a follower of John Knox. He was at one time a missionary in Canada and later became the pastor of a church in Chillicothe, Ohio. He was a graduate of the University of Glasgow. Woodrow Wilson's father was also a Presbyterian of a severe, intellectual type. He was a graduate of Jefferson College, Pennsylvania. At one time, he taught in a Presbyterian school. He was a student in a theological school at Alleghany; also in the Theological School at Princeton; Professor of Rhetoric in Jefferson College; then a Professor in Hamden-Sidney, a Presbyterian college in Virginia; a Presbyterian preacher, and a professor of Theology in Columbia, South Carolina. Woodrow Wilson's uncle, Dr. James Woodrow, of Scotch ancestry, was also a Presbyterian theologian. He was a graduate of a German university; a scientist and linguist; a highly refined, intellectual type of scholar; a versatile man of affairs; a stubborn, relentless fighter for his convictions and for intellectual freedom. I knew him well and had the good fortune to be with him much during the stress of the period when he was being tried for heresy because of his views on evolution.

Furthermore, Woodrow Wilson's first wife was the daughter of a Presbyterian clergyman and the granddaughter of one. Truly, Woodrow Wilson was the son of the manse; and his environment was that of the manse

[157]

until he changed it for that of the college. The first college he attended—Davidson in North Carolina, founded by followers of Witherspoon of Princeton—was Presbyterian, and Princeton, where he spent four years as a student, is, of course, strictly Presbyterian in descent. From 1874 to October 20, 1910, with the exception of one year, Woodrow Wilson's environment was that of the college.

Wilson was, therefore, a dyed-in-the-wool Scotch Presbyterian, a Scotch-Presbyterian Christian, with all that that implies—in philosophy, ethics, morals, standards of conduct, and practices. Those who do not recognize this waste their time in trying to understand him, and to those who do recognize and remember this those who evilly gossiped about him will sink into their proper places. There were many such evil-minded, stupid creatures gossiping during Woodrow Wilson's life, and there are still some left. They abounded in Washington, which, in a way, is the national headquarters of gossips, who, with more money than brains or morals, occupy a position of commonplace social leadership and who, having no worthy intellectual interest to commend them, busy themselves with manufacturing and disseminating unwholesome rumours about those in high political positions, particularly about the President. It has always interested me to observe that the lower classes everywhere, throughout history, have taken a peculiar pride in imputing immorality to their rulers. Few Presidents have escaped and few hereafter will escape. Washington, Jefferson, Jackson, Lincoln, Cleveland, Roosevelt, and Wilson have all been victims of their venom. The more outstanding the character, the more venomous have been their assaults.

[158]

I said that Woodrow Wilson was a Scotch-Presbyterian Christian. With him God was an immanent presence. He was with him in the White House, and if he could discover what He wanted, he gave no heed to what anybody else or everybody else wanted or thought. Reference has been made to the meeting of the Cabinet before our forces took Vera Cruz, when he startled the Cabinet by asking those who still believed in prayer to pray over the matter. That he did so constantly admits of no doubt. Mr. Wilson believed in an Over-ruling Providence. This is revealed in many of his addresses, and there is abundant evidence of his solemn reliance on Its guidance. To illustrate, in his address to the Confederate Veterans at Washington, June 5, 1917, he said:

"Many men, I know, particularly of our own generation, have wondered at some of the dealings of Providence, but the wise heart never questions the dealings of Providence, because the great, long plan as it unfolds has a majesty about it and a definiteness of purpose, an elevation of ideal, which we are incapable of conceiving as we tried to work things out with our own short sight and weak strength."

This recognition of an Over-ruling Providence was strikingly reflected in a statement Mr. Wilson made not long before his death. A friend who was visiting him expressed deep regret that the nation still had not ratified the Treaty of Versailles or entered the League of Nations. Mr. Wilson said, in substance: "I am not so sure that the delay is not for the best. The people should be unmistakably back of the government's action. After all, Providence knows more about these things than any of us. Any one is a fool who questions Its ways."

It follows that Mr. Wilson had a strong belief in the might of right. In all my contacts with him, in everything I heard him say, I was impressed by this more than by anything else, viz.: That he was interested above all things in discovering what was right: what was the right thing to say and the right course to pursue. He was nervous only about the possibility of being wrong. The only real appeal one could make to him was on the right or wrong of a matter. He had little stomach for compromises of any sort, and none for compromises which had a shade of the compromising in them. He was content when he felt that he had arrived at the heart of a matter and had the right of it. He was then prepared to go ahead regardless of consequences. In his assessment of measures, personalities, personal equations, personal ambitions, and self-seeking were ruthlessly brushed aside. He had, in his processes and actions, in very high degree, the element of objectivity. In all his thinking and actions in the field of government and economics, his mind directed itself to the merit of the question, and he assumed that others were equally unselfish and devoted. He, of course, regarded government as an agency for promoting the general welfare through the establishment of justice and rules of conduct and through the creation of conditions under which each individual or group of individuals could most satisfactorily work out its own salvation. He recognized, of course, that government was coöperation, and that certain things could better be done by joint action than by individual effort, and that without coöperative effort through government certain things could not get done at all. He resented the theory of personal, or group, or sectional favour, or special privilege. He likewise detested the idea of paternalism and patronage, and that government should be used to foster certain interests or classes on the assumption that they would pass on to the public its share of the benefit.

Mr. Wilson had something more than this objectivity in all public matters. He was strikingly selfless, or unselfish. He had no personal ends to serve and no thought of attempting to serve them. It was difficult to get him to take any interest in himself; and in my eight years of contact with him, it never occurred to me at any time to raise a question as to how a proposed course of action might affect him or his fortunes. I knew that he would resent it. On a few occasions, when someone ventured a suggestion of the kind, he met with a very prompt and stern rebuke. Mr. Wilson worked for the approval of his own conscience and for that of mankind, or as he expressed it, for the verdict of history.

He was utterly sincere when he asserted that he had never been interested in fighting for himself, but that he was always intensely interested in fighting for the things he believed in. He was speaking naturally when he said that it was a matter of personal indifference to him what the verdict of the people was in 1916.

Never at any time did he attempt to make personal capital out of his high position. He was humbled rather than exalted by it, and his keen wit penetrated quickly the atmosphere with which lesser spirits surrounded themselves when they descended upon Washington in their official dignity. He was amused at the front the average man threw when he assumed high position, and especially when one of them heard himself addressed as, for instance, "Senator" or "Mr. Secretary." "There are two sorts of men who come to Washington," he said: "those who swell and those who grow, and the former are greatly in the majority." Those little understood him who represented that his main motive in going to Europe was to capitalize his position and to win personal glory and acclaim. This representation was as cruel as it was untrue. He went to Europe through his stern sense of duty to the nation and to those whom he had sent to Europe to offer their lives for humanity.

Having this high conception of his position and of government, this selfless and objective state of mind, he had a deep suspicion of the ordinary run of professional politicians and an innate hostility to them. They appeared to him to have primarily only a selfish interest in the government and to be determined to use it mainly for personal ends and the ends of their friends and adherents. He could not easily bring himself to take interest in the solicitude of Senators and Congressmen for their political fences and their desire to keep them in order by seeking local and national positions for their party supporters. Doubtless he carried this attitude too far. Doubtless he took too little account of poor human nature, its weaknesses and foibles. Calvinists habitually do so. Doubtless he was disposed unconsciously to subject it to an unduly severe strain. Possibly he could have yielded something without sacrificing principle. If he had done so, he might have been a more successful party leader and had back of him to the end a united fighting force instead of finally a disorganized and half-hearted Congressional line-up, but if he had I should not now cherish the same admiration for him that I had from the beginning and still have.

Mr. Wilson's faith in the people was a complement and a natural resultant of his Christian philosophy and his reliance on Providence. He had a deep faith in the moral judgments of the people. "I have found that the flame of moral judgments burns just as bright in the man of humble and limited experience as in the scholar and man of affairs," he said to his audience more than once. He relied on the unselfishness of the people of the lower walks of life and, like Lincoln, believed that in the long run they would do the right thing. In his oration on Lincoln he paid eloquent tribute to men of humble station:

"No more significant memorial could have been presented to the nation than this. It expresses so much of what is singular and noteworthy in the history of the country; it suggests so many of the things that we prize most highly in our life and in our system of government. How eloquent this little house within this shrine is of the vigour of democracy! There is nowhere in the land any home so remote, so humble, that it may not contain the power of mind and heart and conscience to which nations yield and history submits its processes. Nature pays no tribute to aristocracy, subscribes to no creed of caste, renders fealty to no monarch or master of any name or kind. Genius is no snob. It does not run after titles or seek by preference the high circles of society. It affects humble company as well as great. It pays no special tribute to universities or learned societies or conventional standards of greatness, but serenely chooses its own comrades, its own haunts, its own cradle even, and its own life of adventure and of training. Here is proof of it. This little hut was the cradle of one of the great sons of men, a man of singular, delightful, vital genius, who presently emerged upon the great stage of the nation's history, gaunt, shy, ungainly, but dominant and majestic, a natural ruler of men, himself inevitably the central figure of the great plot. No man can explain this, but every man can see how it demonstrates the vigour of democracy, where every door is open, in every hamlet and countryside, in city and wilderness alike, for the ruler to emerge when he will and claim his leadership in the free life. Such are the authentic proofs of the validity and vitality of democracy.

"Here, no less, hides the mystery of democracy. Who shall guess this secret of nature and providence and a free polity? Whatever the vigour and vitality of the stock from which he sprang, its mere vigour and soundness do not explain where this man got his great heart that seemed to comprehend all mankind in its catholic and benignant sympathy, the mind that sat enthroned behind those brooding, melancholy eyes, whose vision swept many an horizon which those about him dreamed not of—that mind that comprehended what it had never seen, and understood the language of affairs with the ready ease of one to the manner born—or that nature which seemed in its varied richness to be the familiar of men of every way of life. This is the sacred mystery of democracy, that its richest fruits spring up out of soils which no man has prepared and in circumstances amidst which they are the least expected. This is a place alike of mystery and of reassurance.

"It is likely that, in a society ordered otherwise than our own, Lincoln could not have found himself or the path of fame and power upon which he walked serenely to his death. In this place, it is right that we should remind ourselves of the solid and striking facts upon which our

[164]

faith in democracy is founded.   Many another man besides Lincoln has served the nation in its highest places of
counsel and of action whose origins were as humble as his.
Though the greatest example of the universal energy,
richness, stimulation, and force of democracy, he is only
one example among many.   The permeating and all-
pervasive virtue of the freedom which challenges us in
America to make the most of every gift and power we
possess, every page of our history serves to emphasize and
illustrate.   Standing here in this place, it seems almost
the whole of the stirring story.

"Here Lincoln had his beginnings.   Here the end and
consummation of that great life seem remote and a bit
incredible.   And yet there was no break anywhere between beginning and end, no lack of natural sequence anywhere.   Nothing really incredible happened.   Lincoln
was unaffectedly as much at home in the White House as
he was here.   Do you share with me the feeling, I wonder,
that he was permanently at home nowhere?   It seems to
me that, in the case of a man—I would rather say of a
spirit—like Lincoln, the question where he was is of little
significance, that it is always what he was that really ar-
rests our thought and takes hold of our imagination.   It
is the spirit always that is sovereign.   Lincoln, like the
rest of us, was put through the discipline of the world—a
very rough and exacting discipline for him, an indispens-
able discipline for every man who would know what he
is about in the midst of the world's affairs; but his spirit
got only its schooling there.   It did not derive its character or its vision from the experiences which brought it
to its full revelation.   The test of every American must
always be, not where he is, but what he is.   That, also, is

of the essence of democracy, and is the moral of which this place is most gravely expressive.

"We would like to think of men like Lincoln and Washington as typical Americans, but no man can be typical who is so unusual as these great men were. It was typical of American life that it should produce such men with supreme indifference as to the manner in which it produced them, and as readily here in this hut as amidst the little circle of cultivated gentlemen to whom Virginia owed so much in leadership and example. And Lincoln and Washington were typical Americans in the use they made of their genius. But there will be few such men at best, and we will not look into the mystery of how and why they come. We will only keep the door open for them always, and a hearty welcome—after we have recognized them."

Again he said:

"I believe in the ordinary man. If I did not believe in the ordinary man, I would move out of a democracy and, if I found an endurable monarchy, I would live in it.

"The very conception of America is based upon the validity of the judgments of the average man. . . . I call you to witness that the average judgments of the voters of the United States have been sound judgments."

Mr. Wilson longed to have the people like him and applaud his course. He craved popularity, but only on its own basis. This was his statement of it:

"I am sometimes very much interested when I see gentlemen supposing that popularity is the way to success in America. The way to success in this great country, with its fair judgments, is to show that you are not afraid of anybody except God and His final verdict. If I did not believe that, I would not believe in democracy. If I did not believe that, I would not believe that people can govern themselves. If I did not believe that the moral judgment would be the last judgment, the final judgment, in the minds of men as well as the tribunal of God, I could not believe in popular government. But I do believe these things, and, therefore, I earnestly believe in the democracy, not only of America, but of every awakened people that wishes and intends to govern and control its own affairs."

This is a stern code, but only a natural expression of his whole philosophy of life. It was not of late fruitage; he came by it early. He was a great admirer of Burke, Bright, and Pitt. Several times I heard him say that he was so familiar with Burke's writings, and they were so much a part of him, that he could not be sure whether he was using his own phraseology or Burke's. He wrote essays on Bright and Pitt, and they also aided him to formulate his principles. Writing of Bright in 1888 he says:

"The lessons of his life are not hard to seek or hard to learn. It is that duty consists not in the cultivation and practice of the arts of intrigue, nor in the pressure of all the crooked intricacies of the paths of party management, but in the lifelong endeavour to lead first the attention and then the will of the people to the acceptance of truth in its applications to the problems of government; that not the adornments of rhetoric, but an absorbing love of justice and truth and a consuming, passionate devotion to principle, are the body and soul of eloquence; that complete identification with some worthy cause is the first and great prerequisite of abiding success."

[167]

In contemplating the life of Pitt, writing in 1887, he gives his ideal of statesmanship:

"Statesmanship, that resolute and vigorous advance towards the realization of high, definite, and consistent aims, which issue from the unreserved devotion of a strong intellect to the service of the state and to the solution of all the multiform problems of public policy."

In criticizing Pitt, he made a further revelation of his own thought. In the same article he adds this:

"And yet his errors were many and grave. They were, however, such as are incident upon a policy whose authors seek with whole-souled ardour, with keen enthusiasm, to carry out great principles in all their integrity. Such a policy is always admirable, in the abstract, but, in practice, seldom safe. In a free government, founded upon public opinion, the governmental machinery is so nicely balanced, opposite parties, opposing forces of thought, generally exercise powers so nearly equal that great principles must be worked cautiously, step by step, seldom attaining triumphant ascendency by a course of uninterrupted success—by only a few bold strokes. Public opinion must not be outstripped, but kept pace with."

It is not a little singular that one who so aptly and discriminatingly pointed out the error of Pitt in pressing relentlessly for the acceptance of a great principle, should himself not have taken the principle to heart when he was facing a great struggle over a programme in which he was equally concerned.

It is possible that he might have had larger success in his fight for the Treaty if he had worked more cautiously and had not striven "to attain triumphant success by a few bold strokes."

Mr. Wilson's thinking was, I believe, hampered by two things. In the first place, his mind was a single-track mind. He frequently acknowledged this characteristic. In writing to George Harvey he said, "Every day I am confirmed in the judgment that my mind is a one-track road and can run only one train of thought at a time." He made a similar confession publicly a number of times. He was right. He had difficulty in quickly turning his thoughts and attention from one problem to another, or in seeing many things at the same moment, or in quick succession. Doubtless, this trait caused him to fail to see all the implications of statements he made. It also helps to explain his limiting himself more exclusively to a particular field—to the field of Foreign Affairs—than he would have done if he had been differently constituted. It further helps to explain his very complete reliance on his subordinates in other fields. It is good administration for a chief to select the right sort of subordinates and then to trust them, but he must and will, if he possesses administrative ability of the highest order, be alert to know their problems; to be aware of the extent to which they handle them properly and to get rid of them if they do not do so. Because of this defect, Mr. Wilson was not an administrator of the first rank, but, as an administrator, I should say that he was superior to Lincoln.

Mr. Wilson's other defect arose, in part, from the fact that for so long a time he led a cloistered life, shut off in a measure from the busy world of affairs. This reinforced a certain intellectual tendency, inbred or acquired. It does not appear that Mr. Wilson ever had any large experience in the business world, or intimate knowledge of business gained at first hand. Its processes were known

[169]

to him mainly as the results of research and academic survey. With the details of business and all that they involve, he was not intimately acquainted. Details are of the essence of business. They are dominating and controlling, and sound processes and thinking based on them may conflict with deductions from premises based on an inadequate survey and grasp of them. Timothy Dwight, writing in 1802, had this to say:

"In the closet no man ever becomes acquainted with either the concerns or the character of men, or with the manner in which business ought to be conducted. The general principles of political science a scholar may understand equally with those of other sciences. But of business, which is necessarily done in detail if done to any purpose, the mere scholar literally knows nothing. He may be able to write a good political book, but he cannot do political business, because he never has done it. A plain man, educated in the business of a town, will easily show him that, in knowledge of this kind, he is an infant; and that, whatever may be his genius or his acquisitions.

"A large proportion of the citizens of this state have actually sustained one public office, and multitudes, several, and have of course been personally concerned in transacting public business. Hence they have already known by experience the difficulties incident to public concerns, and are, in a degree superior to what is usually found elsewhere, prepared to form judicious opinions concerning the measures of the Legislature. I have heard laws discussed by plain men with more good sense than any mere scholar could have displayed on the same subjects. By these men they were canvassed as to their operation on the actual interests of themselves, and others.

By a scholar they would have been examined as to their accordance with preconceived general principles. The former were certain means of determining on the merits of a law; the latter only probable, and very imperfect."

His lack of actual experience in business and of intimate contacts with its processes, details, and its managers, coupled with a suspicion of the plans and ideals of those in charge of big business—a suspicion which a generation ago had much foundation—led Mr. Wilson at times to use extreme expressions and to take courses of action which the whole present situation did not warrant, and it created in him a tendency unduly to distrust successful business men.

In view of his general capacity to assess things and to take stock of his own ability and peculiarities, it is somewhat singular that he did not more fully sense this disability. It is the more singular, when it is recalled that he pointed out that such knowledge and experience constituted one of Cleveland's greatest elements of strength. Writing of Cleveland in 1897, he said:

"His mind works in the concrete; lies close always to the practical life of the world, which he understands by virtue of lifelong contact with it. He was no prophet of novelties, but a man of affairs; had no theories, but strove always to have knowledge of fact."

I would not have it understood that I think this defect bulked large in Mr. Wilson's thinking and action; that it substantially marred his conduct and his usefulness as a leader; that I might give a higher rating to someone who had a mastery of business details and lacked Mr. Wilson's other tremendous, valuable powers; or that a, so-called, practical person could approximately as well have served the nation as he did, particularly in the great crisis during which he served. I have not been greatly impressed by the capacity of the average business man in his own line and I have been still less impressed by the capacity of the practical business man for the business of statesmanship. Experience in the Great War did not justify his being placed on a pedestal for his performance in governmental fields. The business man has his limitations—many of them—and one of them is to be quick to distrust those who have not been made as he was made and do not fully share his thoughts, and especially to distrust one who gets out of the beaten path, thinks new thoughts, and clothes them in unconventional phrases. No man is perfect. There are no supermen, not even the Germans. Mr. Wilson was not a superman and would have been the first to resent the intimation that he was.

There is a passage in Jowett's Plato which is illuminating. It has a very direct application to the matter under discussion:

"The question whether the ruler or statesman should be a philosopher is one that has not lost interest in modern times. In most countries of Europe and Asia there has been someone in the course of ages who has truly united the power of command with the power of thought and reflection, as there have been also many false combinations of these qualities. Some kind of speculative power is necessary both in practical and political life; like the rhetorician in the Phædrus, men require to have a conception of the varieties of human character, and to be raised on great occasions above the commonplaces of ordinary life. Yet the idea of the philosopher-statesman has never been popular with the mass of mankind; partly because he cannot

take the world into his confidence or make them understand the motives from which he acts; and also because
they are jealous of a power which they do not understand.
The revolution which human nature desires to effect step
by step in many ages is likely to be precipitated by him
in a single year of life.   They are afraid that, in the pursuit
of his greater aims, he may disregard the common feelings
of humanity.   He is too apt to be looking into the distant
future or back into the remote past, and unable to see
actions or events which, to use an expression of Plato's,
'are tumbling out at his feet.'   Besides, as Plato would
say, there are other corruptions of these philosophical
statesmen.   Either 'the native hue of resolution is sicklied
o'er with the pale cast of thought,' and at the moment
when action above all things is required, he is undecided;
or general principles are enunciated by him in order to
cover some change of policy; or his ignorance of the world
has made him more easily fall a prey to the arts of others;
or, in some cases, he has been converted into a courtier,
who enjoys the luxury of holding liberal opinions, but was
never known to perform a liberal action.   No wonder that
mankind have been in the habit of calling statesmen of this
class pedants, sophisters, doctrinaires, visionaries.   For,
as we may be allowed to say, a little parodying the words of
Plato, 'they have seen bad imitations of the philosopher-
statesman.'   But a man in whom the power of thought
and action are perfectly balanced, equal to the present,
reaching forward to the future, 'such a one,' ruling in a
constitutional state, 'they have never seen.'

"But as the philosopher is apt to fail in the routine of
political life, so the ordinary statesman is also apt to fail
in extraordinary crises.   When the face of the world is

[173]

beginning to alter, and thunder is heard in the distance, he is still guided by his own maxims, and is the slave of his inveterate party prejudices; he cannot perceive the signs of the times; instead of looking forward, he looks back; he learns nothing and forgets nothing; with 'wise saws and modern instances' he would stem the rising tide of revolution. He lives more and more within the circle of his own party, as the world without him becomes stronger. This seems to be the reason why the old order of things makes so poor a figure when confronted with the new, why churches can never reform, why most political changes are made blindly and convulsively. The great crises in the history of nations have often been met by an ecclesiastical positiveness, and a more obstinate reassertion of principles, which have lost their hold upon a nation. The fixed ideas of a reactionary statesman may be compared to madness; they grow upon him, and he becomes possessed by them; no judgment of others is ever admitted by him to be weighed in the balance against his own."

Wilson could not stoop to employ the arts which many men use to gain favour and popularity. He had little aptitude for the game of practical politics and resented its practices. He was weak in the technique of managing and manipulating men, and he had no desire to gain strength in this art. He relied on the strength of the cause in which he was interested.

Wilson was sensitive, shy, and reserved. He was a gentleman and could not and would not try to capitalize his personal advantages. There were intimacies to which he, like other true gentlemen, would not admit the public, and he naturally assumed that right-minded men would not seek to be admitted to them. These were inhibitions resulting from temperament and generations of good breeding. He could only with difficulty attempt to reveal himself, and when he did so, he had only moderate success. Evidently, he was speaking subjectively when, in the course of his Lincoln address, he said:

"I have read many biographies of Lincoln; I have sought out with the greatest interest the many intimate stories that are told of him, the narratives of near-by friends, the sketches at close quarters, in which those who had the privilege of being associated with him have tried to depict for us the very man himself 'in his habit as he lived'; but I have nowhere found a real intimate of Lincoln's. I nowhere get the impression in any narrative or reminiscence that the writer had, in fact, penetrated to the heart of his mystery, or that any man could penetrate to the heart of it. That brooding spirit had no real familiars. I get the impression that it never spoke out in complete self-revelation, and that it could not reveal itself completely to any one. It was a very lonely spirit that looked out from underneath those shaggy brows and comprehended men without fully communing with them, as if, in spite of all its genial efforts at comradeship, it dwelt apart, saw its visions of duty where no man looked on. There is a very holy and very terrible isolation for the conscience of every man who seeks to read the destiny of affairs for others as well as for himself, for a nation as well as for individuals. That privacy no man can intrude upon. That lonely search of the spirit for the right perhaps no man can assist. This strange child of the cabin kept company with invisible things, was born into no intimacy but that of its own silently assembling and deploying thought."

[175]

Wilson himself had no real familiars. He admired many men, had an affection for them and trusted them, but with only a few men did he seem to be at real ease. And these were men who had few angles and who seldom indulged in belligerent attitudes or stubborn opposition. I may be permitted to say that he seemed to have confidence in me, but if I were to judge by the times he sought to see me socially or outside official contacts, I should say that he was either highly indifferent to me or that he disliked me. But I understood the situation thoroughly and was entirely willing and content to have matters as they were. In fact, I strongly sympathized with him. The only time I came into such social personal relation with him, up to the close of the Administration, was when he invited me to play a game of golf with him. He took me out in his car. I beat him easily, which he did not in the least mind. He was courteous and considerate to the last degree, but we did not have a very easy time of it, possibly because both of us, being Scotch, were a trifle reserved and somewhat shy. The only time he ever showed a trace of intimate personal affection for me was when I lunched with him just before he went from the White House.

Just as Wilson had something in common with Lincoln, whom undoubtedly he had much in his thoughts, so also in these qualities of gentlemanly reserve and aloofness he resembled Robert E. Lee. In reading parts of Sir Frederick Maurice's recent book on Lee, I found myself thinking of Wilson, as, for instance, when he says:

"Lee was never what is called a man's man. He did not drink. He did not smoke. He had no taste for the ordinary amusements and weaknesses of the male sex.

While he had a limited number of professional friends and loved the companionship of service he opened his heart to no man. He needed some outlet for his natural reserve and it was to a woman he turned when he felt that need."

And again:

"Such, then, was one side of Lee's private life, but there was another at which I have as yet barely hinted, a side more dominant than even his love of wife, and children, and home, and that was his love of God. He believed in the living God, the Father, the Judge of the Earth. He had not the smallest doubt but that to God all things are possible, that by faith mountains might be moved. . . .

"If Robert E. Lee, soldier and Christian, was such 'as every man in arms would wish to be,' he was not a 'happy warrior.' At any time in his life it would have given him more joy to have won a soul to God than to have gained a victory. I agree with Mr. Gamaliel Bradford that Lee had one intimate friend—God."

The difficulty Wilson had in freely meeting people, aside from his temperament, was reinforced by a certain philosophy he entertained, by the stress under which he worked and by his physical state. He would not seek out men to consult with, but, within the limits of his time and strength, he did see people who sought him on business. He would play no favourites; and I think the fact that he could not see certain individuals, whom he might have liked to confer with more frequently without seeming to play favourites and creating ill feeling, caused him to limit his contacts; and on account of the fact that he was never very robust and that the demands on him were terrific, he felt it imperative to limit his social contacts to the minimum.

Wilson was undoubtedly aware of the popular impression that he was not approachable. In his address to the Press Club in New York in June, 1916, he touched upon this matter, saying:

"I have heard some say that I was not accessible to them, and when I inquired into it, I found they meant that I did not personally invite them. They did not know how to come without being invited, and they did not care to come if they came on the same terms with everybody else, knowing that everybody else was welcome whom I had time to confer with."

Wilson was a man of strong emotions, but he suppressed them. He had them thoroughly disciplined and rigidly kept them down. His inheritance and his philosophy combined to this end. His was the philosophy of self-mastery. His injunction to young men was to cultivate self-control. This philosophy he elaborated admirably in his lecture to students on "When a Man Comes to Himself." It was painful to him to let himself go and to show his feelings; and the only time I ever saw him lose his grip on himself was at the final Cabinet meeting, to which reference has been made.

If what has been said is substantially a correct analysis of Wilson's character and temperament, it will cause certain special cases of personal relation to fall into their proper perspective. It will not explain everything, but it will explain much. There are those who will see nothing in the picture I have given. They will continue to prefer to adopt a simpler theory and to picture him merely as an unfeeling, ungrateful, ruthless person. It is not infrequently said that he was an ingrate, that he used men and then dropped them, that men might act for him but not with him, and that most of those who had been

[178]

his friends had been repudiated by him or had voluntarily renounced him. Of course, I do not accept this verdict. Many men continued to work for him, and many men did work with him. I both worked for him and with him for eight years with increasing affection, respect, and admiration. My criticism, looking at the whole matter and the entire period broadly, was that he erred rather on the side of patience, loyalty, and generosity. The cases pointed to and played up largely from partisan motives are the exceptions and prove the rule.

The cases of George Harvey and McCombs present no difficulty to me. There was nothing in common between Wilson and Harvey. Wilson was a Liberal. Wilson was a Progressive—one of the greatest Progressives of the age, with a sense of direction, knowing where he was headed and how he proposed to get there. He differed in this respect from those Progressives who, like the beetle, mistake energy for progress, who in reality know nothing of history; who are, in fact, constantly seeking to promote programmes which have time and time again been demonstrated to be futile; and who are, therefore, merely out of date and behind the times, and whose chief asset is capacity for noise. I suspect that if Harvey had at the beginning understood Wilson and appreciated the fact that he was a sincere Liberal with a stern sense of duty, he would never have sponsored him. In the actual break, we have a typical illustration of Wilson's objective habit of thought. In his interview with Harvey, he discussed the point raised as to whether Harvey's constant activity was injurious publicly and personally, and when he gave his opinion frankly he had no thought that any offence was taken. His letters to Harvey afterward revealed his grief that any offence was given and also his eagerness to make amends. His first letter was as follows:

"Every day I am confirmed in the judgment that my mind is a one-track road and can run only one train of thought at a time! A long time after that interview with you and Marse Henry at the Manhattan Club, it came over me that when (at the close of the interview) you asked me that question about the *Weekly* I answered it simply as a matter of fact and of business, and said never a word of my sincere gratitude to you for all your generous support, or of my hope that it might be continued. Forgive me, and forget my manners!"

To this letter Colonel Harvey sent this reply:

"Replying to your note from the University Club, I think it should go without saying that no purely personal issue could arise between you and me. Whatever anybody else may surmise, you surely must know that in trying to arouse and further your political aspirations during the past few years, I have been actuated solely by the belief that I was rendering a distinct public service.

"The real point at the time of our interview was, as you aptly put it, one simply 'of fact and of business,' and when you stated the fact to be that my support was hurting your candidacy, and that you were experiencing difficulty in finding a way to counteract its harmful effect, the only thing possible for me to do, in simple fairness to you, no less than in consideration of my own self-respect, was to relieve you of your embarrassment so far as it lay within my power to do so, by ceasing to advocate your nomination. That, I think, was fully understood between us at the time, and, acting accordingly, I took down your name from the head of the *Weekly's* editorial page some days before your letter was written. That seems to be all there is to it.

"Whatever little hurt I may have felt as a consequence of the unexpected peremptoriness of your attitude toward me is, of course, wholly eliminated by your gracious words."

Mr. Wilson acknowledged this note, saying:

"Generous and cordial as was your letter written in reply to my note from the University Club, it has left me uneasy, because, in its perfect frankness, it shows that I did hurt you by what I so **tactlessly** said at the Knickerbocker Club. I am very **much** ashamed of myself, for there is nothing I am more ashamed of than hurting a true friend, however unintentional the hurt may have been. I wanted very much to see you in Washington, but was absolutely captured by callers every minute I was in my rooms, and when I was not there was fulfilling public engagements. I saw you at the dinner but could not get at you, and, after the dinner, was surrounded and prevented from getting at you. I am in town to-day, to speak this evening, and came in early in the hope of catching you at your office.

"For I owe it to you and to my own thought and feeling to tell you how grateful I am for all your generous praise and support of me (no one has described me more nearly as I would like myself to be than you have); how I have admired you for the independence and unhesitating courage and individuality of your course; and how far I was from desiring that you should cease your support of me in the *Weekly*. You will think me very stupid—but I did not think of that as the result of my blunt answer to your question. I thought only of the means of convincing people of the real independence of the *Weekly's* position. You will remember that that was what we discussed. And now that I have unintentionally put you in a false and embarrassing position, you heap coals of fire on my head by continuing to give out interviews favourable to my candidacy! All that I can say is that you have proved yourself very big, and that I wish I might have an early opportunity to tell you face to face how I really feel about it all. With warm regard," etc.

As far as Lansing is concerned, the only questions which are likely to give a reader of his book any trouble are these: Why did Lansing see fit to continue in service when he knew he was opposed to his chief on matters of fundamental importance, matters so near to Wilson's heart? Why did Wilson not ask for his resignation much earlier? When the President asked Lansing to resign he did not give the public the facts of the case, and in consequence Lansing for a time was regarded, especially by partisan people, as a martyr. When Lansing published the facts it became apparent that he should not have stayed in the Cabinet as long as he did.

I asked Mr. Wilson if he had read Lansing's book, and he replied with a smile, "No, I have not, but I am sure if it suits Lansing it would suit me."

The cases of Walter Page and Colonel House are essentially different. Nothing has been published as to the President's thought in either case. Page's letters and House's memoirs have revealed the extent of their lack of sympathy with the President's course from time to time. But the President, to the last, expressed his affection for both men. I heard him say more than once that Page was the best letter writer he knew, and that, when his letters appeared at the proper time, they would make the most interesting contribution to the story of the period.

Wilson belonged to the aristocracy of brains. He was an intellectual thoroughbred. His mind, which was of high quality, had been refined and disciplined by years of hard study and by years of teaching. His faculties were always thoroughly at his command. He did not have to labour and strain for results. He was quick to grasp the essential points in a complex problem or set of facts, to get to the heart of the matter under discussion, to see facts in their proper relation, and to arrive at a sound conclusion; and long and careful training, combined with natural talent, gave him the ability to express his thoughts tersely, artistically, and eloquently, without apparent effort and without prolonged preparation. In all the years in which I listened to him talking, informally, in Cabinet meetings, or elsewhere, I never detected a word or phrase out of place, or heard him use a bungling sentence. He was one of three men I have known whose conversation or address, taken down and reported by an intelligent stenographer, could be published without any real need of editing. The other two were his uncle, Dr. James Woodrow, and President Eliot. What this means, even the average well-trained man well knows. Most of them probably experience a feeling of humiliation when their spontaneous utterances are taken by stenographers and returned to them. They find more difficulty in straightening out their expressions than they would in rewriting the statement.

I had many opportunities to note the President's skill in expressing himself and to admire his command of his faculties. One which stands out in my mind clearly was

[183]

when he signed the Farm Loan Act. Two Congressmen, much interested in the measure, asked me if I thought the President would be willing to have them present when he signed the Act, if he would use two pens and give one to each. I told them I would ascertain the President's wishes. He promptly acquiesced. We joined him in his office. He signed the measure, using two pens, which he gave to the Congressmen. Then he stood up and said a few words. He had had little or no time to familiarize himself with the subject matter, but he dealt with it very intelligently and in very apt language. He said:

"I am very glad to have a modest part in this piece of legislation. It is high time that something were done to provide additional financial assistance for the farmer. Our existing banking machinery, while helpful to the farmer as to all other citizens, because it has secured and assured safe banking and provided a national currency and credit, has been adapted primarily to the needs of the manufacturer and the merchant. Their turnover is rapid, their assets are liquid. There has been a gap. There has been need of an agency, under understanding management, reaching out intimately and to the rural district, and operating on terms suited to the farmers' needs. The farmer is the servant of the seasons. The gap has now been filled."

This was the whole argument in a nutshell.

Certainly, in point of formal education, Wilson was the best trained man who ever occupied the White House. He had received the best training that American universities could furnish, and he had supplemented this by long years of study as a professor and as a lecturer. He was a student of history. He saw things in their perspective in

[184]

systematic, orderly fashion. He knew the limitations of things. He had been a profound student of American institutions and problems, and had developed knowledge of foreign governments and foreign history. Mr. Wilson was a pioneer among Americans in the study of foreign arrangements and governmental policies. His book, "The State," dealing with comparative governments, was the first in the field; and Wilson was instructing America about foreign matters before most of his critics had escaped from the bondage of provincialism.

It was a genuine pleasure to talk with Wilson, to engage in conference with him and to discuss light or serious, simple or complex matters with him. He could be light and gay. Nobody could or did tell so many good or apt stories as he; and yet he did not manufacture stories or lug them in by the ears. They appeared naturally, they came quickly; and his sallies, while seldom biting and never bitter, were keen and enlightening. He was witty rather than humorous, in this characteristic resembling the best English and New England thinkers and speakers rather than the typical American. His wit never verged on the doubtful or the vulgar. He naturally resented vulgarity and irreverence.

One reason why it was a pleasure to discuss matters with Wilson is that he was quick and did not have to be educated. One could assume more with him than with almost any other person I have known. And he was patient, very patient, patient even of dullness. He was much more patient than I would dream of being, or ever desired to be. I saw him many a time sit and listen with courtesy to long-drawn-out statements by men of mediocre capacity and little information, who had had scant opportunity to

[185]

form useful judgments, and who usually obscured the sub-ject at every turn. Not infrequently I almost writhed in agony and in ill-concealed irritation, but Mr. Wilson never gave a sign. I have, therefore, always been greatly amused by representations that he would not take counsel or listen to advice. Some of those, including one or more members of his Cabinet, who gave currency to this view, could only mean that he did not frequently take their ad-vice or heed their views; and he was wise, because their views, as a rule, were of little assistance, their knowledge was scanty and impressionistic, and their judgment bad, and yet they desired to seem to be in the President's in-timate counsel and to be in the limelight.

It is not true that Wilson did not consult his Cabinet on new departures and policy, or on important matters. He did; and he would have done so more freely had he not known that the very ones—and they were few in number —who criticized him for failure to do so made it difficult for him to do so by their persistent practice of heralding everything to the public, whether it was wise or timely or not.

And, Mr. Wilson was not what I would call obstinate. He was slow in arriving at conclusions. He took pains to get light and all the facts; and then, when he thought he had all he could get or needed, he made up his mind. Then he was difficult to move. This was as it should have been. I admired him for this trait. He was diffi-cult to move because it was not easy to give him better reasons for a different course than he had for the one he proposed to take, but he was not immovable. Better rea-sons and sound reasoning would alter his views, and changed conditions would modify them. A number of

[186]

times I witnessed him change his views quickly, views which he strongly entertained. He altered his views on preparedness. He altered his views on proposed statements, such as his notes to Germany; and he swung round completely on the proposal for a tariff commission. As I have pointed out, when a tariff commission was proposed, he resisted it. He stated that the old commissions had been futile and he thought that the new one might be. I argued for a commission not to take the tariff out of politics, which is a futile suggestion, but to give the public and the Congress information. He finally accepted the suggestion. I am now inclined to think that his first view was right and that I was wrong. The conception was a good one, and the law was well conceived; but it has been pretty well demonstrated that the Commission cannot get the facts to the public for its education and that Congress will pay little attention to its economic findings. Of course, it need not be emphasized that it was a mistake to give the Commission power, with the President's approval, to alter tariff rates. This radically changed its status from a fact-finding body to a piece of political machinery. It puts the whole body into politics. The flexible provision is a futile conception. With the average Republican administration in power, the flexing will always be upward or the rates will remain as they were. With the average Democratic administration, the flexing will be downward. This power ought immediately to be taken away from the body; and then, if it becomes clear that its findings cannot compel public attention, or that Congress will ignore them, the law creating the Commission ought to be repealed. In such case, the Commission will only be an expensive luxury.

[187]

Mr. Wilson knew, of course, that he was charged with being inflexible and unchangeable. On January 27, 1916, on his preparedness tour, referring to the matter, he said:

"Perhaps when you learned, as I daresay you did learn beforehand, that I was expecting to address you on the subject of preparedness, you recalled the address which I made to Congress something more than a year ago, in which I said that this question of military preparedness was not a pressing question. But more than a year has gone by since then, and I would be ashamed if I had not learned something in fourteen months. The minute I stop changing my mind with the change of all the circumstances of the world, I will be a back number.

"There is another thing about which I have changed my mind. A year ago I was not in favour of a tariff board, and I will tell you why. Then the only purpose of a tariff board was to keep alive an unprofitable controversy . . . But the circumstances of the present time are these: There is going on in the world under our eyes an economic revolution. No man understands that revolution; no man has the elements of it clearly in his mind. No part of the business of legislature in regard to international trade can be undertaken until we do understand it; and members of Congress are too busy, their duties are too multifarious and distracting to make it possible within a sufficiently short space of time for them to master the change that is coming."

Mr. Wilson, as I knew him, was not dictatorial, and I do not believe that the facts warrant any such view. Certainly, I did not find him so in my official relations with him. I was with him in two departments for eight years, dealing with many important matters. He did not, in the entire time, give me any order or make any substantial suggestion to me and he did not refuse to accept any recommendation I made to him or disapprove any course of action I proposed. Also, I saw no sign of a dictatorial spirit in my observation of his relations with any other of his subordinates or associates.

He was scrupulous in his observances of the proprieties and of the law and constitution in dealing with independent bodies and with the coördinate powers—Congress and the Supreme Court. He respected the independence of such bodies as the Interstate Commerce Commission, the Civil Service, the Federal Trade, and the Tariff Commissions. He instantly repelled any suggestion that any sort of pressure, direct or indirect, should be brought to bear on any of them. He knew too well that if they were not above suspicion their usefulness would be impaired.

But Wilson did conceive himself, as President, to be the leader of his party. In his address to Congress, on currency legislation, June 28, 1913, he said: "I have come to you as the head of the government and the responsibile leader of the party in power." A little later, on July 4th, at Gettysburg, he made the same claim, saying: "I have been chosen the leader of the nation. I cannot justify the choice by any qualities of my own, but so it has come about and here I stand." This was a novel note for a President to sound; and I have no doubt that it caused many in the opposition to prick up their ears and paved the way for partisan tactics. But it was not a new note for Wilson. Also, it was probably not news to the scholarly leader of the Senate minority, Henry Cabot Lodge. He knew, as other students were aware, that for more than a quarter of a century Wilson had been a critic of Congressional government and had urged changes in machinery, in attitude and in practices, which should bring about greater responsibility in our government and lodge responsibility for leadership in the President. Lodge, as editor of the *International Review*, had, in 1879, published the article by Wilson written when he was a Senior at Princeton, dealing with this subject at length. In fact, from the time Wilson was twenty years old until he was forty-seven, the defects of Congressional government and the desirability of developing responsible leadership were the main themes of his writings and addresses.

When one considers closely what is required to get a solution of any matter of consequence, one is always astonished to find that a reasonably good conclusion is reached, and when all the problems of a government or business are thought of, it seems miraculous that chaos does not reign. It takes lots of trouble to run any part of the world, but the world keeps moving and Congress even works after a fashion, and, on the whole, not so badly.

The main defect of Congress or Congressional government, Wilson insisted, is that it is leaderless or irresponsible. The remedy, he contended, is to adopt Cabinet government. In support of his contention, he set out the advantages usually claimed for responsible or parliamentary government. Perhaps his fullest exposition of this contention is that in his article in the *Overland Monthly*, January, 1884:

"In seeking an escape from the perplexity," he wrote, "manifestly the safest course is to content ourselves with travelling ways already trodden, and look to the precedents of our own race for guidance. Let, therefore, the

[190]

leaders of parties be made responsible. Let there be set apart from the party in power certain representatives who, leading their party and representing its policy, may be made to suffer a punishment which shall be at once personal and vicarious when their party goes astray, or their policy either misleads or miscarries. This can be done by making the leaders of the dominant party in Congress the executive officers of the legislative will; by making them also members of the President's Cabinet, and thus at once the executive chiefs of the departments of State and the leaders of their party on the floor of Congress; in a word, by having done with the standing committees, and constituting the Cabinet advisers both of the President and of Congress. This would be Cabinet government.

"Cabinet government is government by means of an executive ministry chosen by the chief magistrate of the nation from the ranks of the legislative majority—a ministry sitting in the legislature and acting as its executive committee; directing its business and leading its debates; representing the same party and the same principles; 'bound together by a sense of responsibility and loyalty to the party to which it belongs,' and subject to removal whenever it forfeits the confidence and loses the support of the body it represents. Its establishment in the United States would involve, of course, several considerable changes in our present system. It would necessitate, in the first place, one or two alterations in the Constitution. The second clause of Section Six, Article I, of the Constitution runs thus: 'No Senator or Representative shall, during the term for which he was elected, be appointed to any civil office under the authority of the United States which shall have been created, or the emolu-

[191]

ments whereof shall have been increased, during such time; and no person holding any office under the United States shall be a member of either House during his continuance in office.' Let the latter part of this clause read: 'And no person holding any other than a Cabinet office under the United States shall be a member of either House during his continuance in office,' and the addition of four words will have removed the chief constitutional obstacle to the erection of Cabinet government in this country. The way will have been cleared, in great part, at least, for the development of a constitutional practice, which, founded upon the great charter we already possess, might grow into a governmental system at once strong, stable, and flexible. Those four words being added to the Constitution, the President might be authorized and directed to choose for his Cabinet the leaders of the ruling majority in Congress; that Cabinet might, on condition of acknowledging its tenure of office dependent on the favour of the Houses, be allowed to assume those privileges of initiative in legislation and leadership in debate which are now given, by an almost equal distribution, to the standing committees; and Cabinet government would have been instituted." Additional amendments, he pointed out, would be necessary. The terms of the President and Congress would have to be lengthened. In closing this article he said:

"So long as we have representative government, so long will the Legislature remain the imperial and all-overshadowing power of the state; and so long as it does remain such a power, it will be impossible to check its encroachments and curb its arrogance, and at the same time preserve the independence of the Executive, without joining these two great branches of government by some link, some bond of connection, which, whilst not consolidating them, will at least neutralize their antagonisms, and, possibly, harmonize their interests. A Cabinet committee would constitute such a bond; for it would, as we have seen, be a body which, from its very nature and offices, would be at once jealous of the pretensions of the Houses and responsible for the usurpations of the Executive; interested, and, therefore, determined to yield not a jot of their lawful executive authority, and yet bound to admit every just claim of power on the part of their legislative colleagues.

"That must be a policy of wisdom and prudence which puts the executive and legislative departments of government into intimate sympathy and binds them together in close coöperation. The system which embodies such a policy in its greatest perfection must be admired of all statesmen and coveted of all misgoverned peoples. The object of wise legislation is the establishment of equal rights and liberties amongst the citizens of the state, and its chief business, the best administration of government. Legislatures have it constantly in charge, and specially in charge, to facilitate administration; and that charge can be best fulfilled, of course, when those who make and those who administer the laws are in closest harmony. The executive agents of government should stand at the ear of the Legislature with respectful suggestions of the needs of the Administration, and the Legislature should give heed to them, requiring of them, the while, obedience and diligence in the execution of its designs. An executive honoured with the confidence of the Legislature, and a Legislature confiding itself with all fullness of trust, yet

[193]

with all vigilance, to the guidance of an executive acknowledging full responsibility to the representatives of the people for all its acts and all its counsels; this is a picture good to look upon—a type of effective and beneficent self-government. The changes in our form of government which the establishment of such a system would involve are surely worth making if they necessitate no sacrifice of principle.

"It cannot be too often repeated that, while Congress remains the supreme power of the state, it is idle to talk of steadying or cleansing our politics without in some way linking together the interests of the Executive and the Legislature. So long as these two great branches are isolated, they must be ineffective just to the extent of the isolation. Congress will always be master, and will always enforce its commands on the Administration. The only wise plan, therefore, is to facilitate its direction of the government, and to make it at the same time responsible, in the persons of its leaders, for its acts of control, and for the manner in which its plans and commands are executed. The only hope of wrecking the present clumsy misrule of Congress lies in the establishment of responsible Cabinet government. Let the interests of the Legislature be indissolubly linked with the interests of the Executive. Let those who have authority to direct the course of legislation be those who have a deep personal concern in building up the executive departments in effectiveness, in strengthening law, and in unifying policies; men whose personal reputation depends upon successful administration, whose public station originates in the triumph of principles, and whose dearest ambition it is to be able to vindicate their wisdom and maintain their integrity.

"Committee government is too clumsy and too clan-destine a system to last. Other methods of government must sooner or later be sought, and a different economy established. First or last, Congress must be organized in conformity with what is now the prevailing legislative practice of the world. English precedent and the world's fashion must be followed in the institution of Cabinet government in the United States."

Thirteen years later, August 4, 1897, Wilson made Leaderless Government the subject of an address before the Virginia Bar Association. He gave the same picture of the shortcomings of our system. He again pointed out our leaderless situation. Congress, he contended, could not lead:

"The President cannot lead. . . . My studies have taught me this one thing with a definiteness which cannot be mistaken: Successful governments have never been con-ducted safely in the midst of complex and critical affairs except when guided by those who were responsible for carrying out and bringing to an issue the measures they proposed; and the separation of the right to plan from the duty to execute has always led to blundering and ineffi-ciency; and modern representative bodies cannot of them-selves combine the two. . . . If you would have the present error of our system in a word, it is this—that Con-gress is the motive power in the government and yet has in it nowhere any representative of the nation as a whole. Our Executive, on the other hand, is national; at any rate, may be made so, and yet has no longer any place of guid-ance in our system. It represents no constituency, but the whole people; and yet, though it alone is national, it has no originative voice in domestic national policy.

"The sum of the matter is, that we have carried the application of the notion that the powers of government must be separated to a dangerous and unheard-of length by thus holding our only national representative, the Executive, at arm's length from Congress, whose very commission it seems to be to represent, not the people, but the communities into which the people are divided. We should have Presidents and Cabinets of a different calibre were we to make it their bounden duty to act as a committee for the whole nation to choose and formulate matters for the consideration of Congress in the name of a party and an administration; and then, if Congress consented to the measures, what they are already—a committee to execute them—make them work and approve themselves practicable and wise. And that is exactly what we ought to do. We should have not a little light thrown daily, and often, when it was least expected, upon the conduct of the departments, if the heads of the departments had daily to face the representatives of the people, to propose, defend, explain administrative policy, upon the floor of the Houses, where such a plan would put them: and heads of departments would be happy under such a system only when they were very straightforward and honest and able men. I am not suggesting that initiative in legislation be by any means confined to the Administration—that would be radical, indeed—but only that they be given a free, though responsible, share in it—and that, I conceive, would bring the government back very nearly to the conception and practice of Washington. It would be a return to our first.models of statesmanship and political custom.

"I ask you to put this question to yourselves: Should we

[196]

not draw the Executive and Legislature closer together? Should we not, on the one hand, give the individual leaders of opinion in Congress a better chance to have an intimate part in determining who should be President, and the President, on the other hand, a better chance to approve himself a statesman, and his advisers capable men of affairs, in the guidance of Congress? This will be done when the Executive is given an authoritative initiative in the Houses. I see no other way to create national figures in the field in which domestic policy is chosen, or to bring forward tested persons to vote for. I do not suggest methods—this is not the place or the occasion; I suggest an idea—a way out of chaos: the nationalization of the motive power of the government, to offset the economic sectionalization of the country; I suggest the addition to Congress, which represents us severally, of a power, constituted how you will, which shall represent us collectively in the proposing of laws; which shall have the right as of course to press national motives and courses of action to a vote in the Congress. This will not subordinate Congress; it may accept the proposals of the Administration or not, as it pleases (it once took a scolding from Washington himself for not accepting them); but the country will at least have a mouthpiece, and not all of policy will lurk with committees and in executive sessions of the Senate."

By this time Wilson was apparently less confident as to the specific remedy or machinery that should be set up. He no longer suggested concrete amendments. I think his mind was beginning to take a slightly different slant. After this time, so far as I know, he did not again urge a change to Cabinet government. Certainly, after he went to Washington, I never heard him refer to the proposal. There were, however, two items of it left, which he emphasized and put into practice. One was the habit of appearing before Congress to deliver his messages, and the other was his assumption of leadership of his party and of the nation.

I think Wilson had never really thought through this problem which interested him for so many years. While exalting the power of leadership of the President, he was advocating changes in governmental machinery which would necessarily have made the President a figurehead. And he did not apparently recognize that, if his scheme were adopted, it would involve a complete breakdown of our Constitution and of our Federal form of government.

At one time I entertained, in even more extreme form, the views expressed by Wilson down to 1897. I was of the opinion that we should go further than he desired or anticipated we would go if we began with his scheme. I later undertook to revise the statement of my views, which I had written, to see if I could improve it, and only succeeded in convincing myself that I was wrong. This, if it proves nothing more, indicates that I have been open-minded in the matter.

It is very easy to draw an indictment, not only of Congress, but also of the relation existing between Congress and the Executive. In fact, it is easy to draw an indictment of our entire form of government. It has been frequently drawn. It is usually easier to criticize than it is to defend or construct.

It is charged that it takes too long to get an expression of the nation's will on important matters. Why did it take nearly three years to get a peace with Germany?

Why has the matter of our attitude toward the League been so long in debate? On these great matters, other nations quickly formed their decision and took their stand. Why did it take so many years to get tax legislation? Why has the policy of protection been in question for more than a hundred years? Why is it that it requires so much time for the will of the American people to get itself expressed? Who can say what the will of the American people is on a number of great public issues?

Why do we, who claim to be the most democratic people in the world, place so many restrictions on the expression of our will? Why do we almost alone among the nations preserve a system of checks and balances? Why is it that representatives elected in November do not take their seats until the fourth of March following at the earliest, and not until thirteen months after election in case no special session is called? Why has the Senate a complete check on the House? Why has the Executive a veto on the action of both? And why should the Supreme Court have power to declare what the Congress says is law to be no law?

No such checks exist in any other great constitutional country. Even Canada, our largest near neighbour, operates under a system in which the popular dominion assembly is dominant, both in legislative and executive matters. And all but two of her provinces proceed in ordinary fashion with a single legislative body popularly elected governing the state through their committees and cabinets.

It is charged that there is too much friction between the legislative and the executive branches and too much consequent waste and inefficiency. Why, during the war,

[199]

was it solemnly proposed to create a Congressional Committee on the conduct of the war? Why, during the war and immediately thereafter, were there created about ninety Congressional committees to find out what had happened? Why does Congress persist in hampering heads of departments by numerous narrow statutory restrictions? Why does it set up committees, such as those on printing and space, with power to administer law in relation to publications and working quarters? Why is it that, on important matters, the Executive attempts to go in one direction and Congress insists on going in another?

Obviously, the government has faults. Obviously, it is not a logically perfect scheme, and its parts do not operate with the perfection of a highly sensitive and delicate piece of well-oiled machinery. I recognize the faults; but I question the soundness of the chief representations made by Mr. Wilson. I dissent from his conclusion and am opposed to his remedy. The view is too academic. It overlooks the life of the government and the temper of our people.

I do not believe that Congress has lost its position as a predominant force in the government, or that the President has become the predominant force. I do not believe that it was intended that either should be predominant, or that either can become predominant, or should be permitted to do so. I do believe that, in the long run, if there is a tendency in either direction, it will be for the Congress more and more to become the controlling factor. Nor do I believe that the chief source of legislative evil is the lack of responsible contact between the executive and the legislative branches. And I feel reasonably certain that, when the matter is debated to a conclusion, it will not be decided that bringing the members of the Cabinet face to face in Congress for the purposes of discussion would accomplish anything of importance or would be regarded as desirable.

At present, heads of departments are accorded every opportunity through reports, through appearance before committees of Congress, and through frequent contacts with leaders, to present all matters or measures of consequence demanding Congressional action. They are always given courteous and full hearing and consideration. Such of their subordinates as they desire to have appear before committees of Congress are also accorded the fullest consideration and attention. In such manner, the Cabinet is in position, not only to educate large numbers of members of Congress, but also the leaders in their respective fields who by reason of full membership and constitutional standing in the Congress will, in the nature of things, be given a more sympathetic hearing than would an executive officer who is not a full and regular member of either House.

There is, as a matter of fact, vastly more executive and legislative contact than the public generally is accustomed to believe. When the same party is in control of all branches—and if it is not, there will be confusion under any set of conditions—if a Cabinet officer knows his business it is possible, as a rule, to secure coöperation in the framing of legislative measures and the execution of a programme. This has been demonstrated over and over again. When measures so framed and programmes so outlined come up before Congress for debate and determination, it seems reasonably clear that the handling of such matters by regular Congressional members, occupying positions of responsibility on terms normally of good fellow-ship even with their opponents, would be more effective than the attempt of heads of departments for whom the Congress is in no wise responsible and as to whom there would be much jealousy.

Cabinet members, merely with the status suggested, would be in an embarrassing position. They would re-semble more than anything else the traditional bumps on logs. They would be a target for heckling. Furthermore, members of the Cabinet, selected as heretofore presum-ably for administrative fitness or because of their com-manding position before the public, would not necessarily be particularly qualified to participate in Congressional debates or to assume legislative leadership. It would im-mediately become incumbent on the President in selecting his heads of departments to consider men more from the point of view of skill in parliamentary discussion and legislative leadership than of their qualities as administra-tors. It is seldom that the same man unites in high degree both the requisite qualifications, and it is a matter of common knowledge that many of the most competent administrative heads have not had aptitude for parlia-mentary business. It is also a matter of common knowl-edge that men who have ranked high among Congressional leaders who have been given Cabinet appointments have not demonstrated fitness for administrative positions. It is also obvious that if members of the Cabinet were ac-corded the privilege of taking full part in the transaction of Congressional business they would have little or no time for the supervision of the departments under their charge.

If we are to take any step at all in this direction with a

hope of accomplishing beneficent reforms and securing large results, we must, it seems to me, go the entire distance. We cannot eat our cake and have it also. We cannot retain the benefits of our Constitution and Federal form and at the same time secure in measurable degree the advantages of a parliamentary or responsible system of government. The question then arises whether we should go the entire distance.

Such a change would be revolutionary. It would mean a complete overthrow of our present scheme of government. To operate in its full perfection, it would be necessary for us to adopt the parliamentary system in its fullness. Briefly stated, this would mean: that the House of Representatives would become the dominant factor in our Federal Government both in legislation and in administration; that the Administration would be directed by a committee responsible mainly to the House of Representatives; that the Senate would lose, at least in part, its position as a coördinate body, just as has the House of Lords in England; that the President would become a formal executive, that is, in large measure, a figurehead, losing his veto power; that the Supreme Court would lose its power to declare laws unconstitutional; that there would be elections, not at stated intervals, but whenever the government seemed to lose the confidence of the country; and therefore, that our Constitution would cease to exist except as a variable and shifting force, its character to be determined in each instance at the will of the dominant body.

This is the picture of the only government in the world where it can be said that the parliamentary system exists in its full and satisfactory form, that is, in England.

Here, as is well known, the House of Commons is dominant. It governs through the Cabinet, in effect selected by the House. The House of Lords will not stand in the way of the House of Commons when the opinion prevails that the nation is behind the House. The general rule is that the House of Lords must, in matters of legislation, especially in financial matters, give way to the House of Commons. The King has no real executive functions. He is only the head of the dignified part of the Constitution. The real executive head is the Prime Minister, and the King has little option as to whom he shall ask to take the Premiership. He must send for the man, no matter how distasteful, who can lead the majority in the House and ultimately lead the nation. He has vetoed no measure of importance for generations, and could not do so. And as is well known, the British courts have no power to interfere with the measure passed by Parliament in the way of declaring it unconstitutional. They can only interpret the law.

It is claimed that this arrangement makes it easier for the will of the people to find expression. This, theoretically and logically, is true. In this respect, taking as a test of democracy the ease with which the will of the people can break through machinery and find expression, the English arrangement is more democratic than ours. It is claimed also that it leads to the presence and continuance in public life of abler men, promotes leadership, enables the people of the nation to have presented to them in more influential manner the pressing important problems, and that it is conducive to popular education.

That there is something in these contentions admits of little doubt. But that things are as they are in Great

Britain because of the piece of machinery called the responsible ministry or of the body of understandings supporting it, or that things would be here as they are in Great Britain, or on the whole that there would be marked improvements, I do not believe. Those who take the opposite view seem to me to overlook more essential factors and to overrate the value of machinery itself. They seem to me to attribute certain faults here to machinery whose explanation lies in other directions and to ascribe merits to machinery in Great Britain which are due to things deep down in the historical and social structure back of the frame of government. It has come to pass in this country that there is an inclination to place undue reliance on legislation and on machinery, and this warning uttered by Boutmy, the French publicist, to his countrymen, may well be heeded by us: "Constitutional mechanism has no value and efficiency in itself, independently of the moral and social forces which support it or put it in motion." Bryce, in similar vein, years ago, had this to say:

"All governments are faulty; and an equally minute analysis of the Constitution of England, or France, or Germany would disclose mischiefs as serious, relatively to the problems with which those states have to deal, as those we have noted in the American system. To any one familiar with the practical working of free governments, it is a standing wonder that they work at all. What keeps a free government going is the good sense and patriotism of the people, or of the guiding class, embodied in usages and traditions which it is hard to describe, but which find, in moments of difficulty, remedies for the inevitable faults of the system. Now, this good sense and

[205]

that power of subordinating sectional to national interests which we call patriotism exist in higher measure in America than in any of the great states of Europe. And the United States, more than any other country, are governed by public opinion, that is to say, by the general sentiment of the mass of the nation, which all the organs of the national government and of the state governments look to and obey."

Again, he says:

"The English Constitution, which we admire as a masterpiece of delicate equipoises and complicated mechanism, would anywhere but in England be full of difficulties and dangers. It stands and prospers in virtue of the traditions that still live among English statesmen and the reverence that has ruled English citizens. It works by a body of understandings which no writer can formulate, and of habits which centuries have been needed to instil."

Let us note some of the claims made for a responsible ministry system. Perhaps the leading claim is that it secures prompt expression of the will of the people and obviates delay in settling vexing questions. Too much is made of this, and too little is made of the fact that the delay is due to the failure of the people of the nation to make up their minds. This delay occurs in times of confusion, in countries where there are responsible ministries. It has occurred in Great Britain and in France since the Armistice. The nation has been in doubt. The policy has lagged. The main result has been frequent changes of government. Likewise, in the United States, in periods of confusion, until the people have made up their minds, there is delay. When they have thrashed a matter out and come to a conclusion, that conclusion finds expression.

The quarrel is rather with the people than with the machinery of government. And the need of delay for due consideration was recognized by the founders of the nation, and checks were accordingly provided. The illustrations in this direction are too numerous and too fresh in the minds of readers to justify citing.

A second and leading claim is that a responsible system of government attracts into public life and retains there a larger number of able and experienced men. England is cited as an illustration. Here again, too much is claimed for mechanism. The explanation in England largely is that there is a governing class of aristocratic origin, that it is not difficult for such men to secure access to public office, and that they have the leisure and the inclination to seek and to hold positions. It is by no means clear that, if we had a responsible system of government, we should secure and retain in public life an adequate number of our ablest men. I know of no reason for believing that constituencies would, in making their selections, vote from different motives from those which now actuate them. Democracy does not and will not necessarily seek its ablest men to hold political positions. They are rather inclined, on the whole, to seek men of an average quality whose thinking and motives run more nearly with their own. Democracy does not seem to be able to stand for very long the strain of living up to the thinking of men of the highest standards and the greatest intellects.

On the other hand, it seems more likely that the main effect would be a lower level of ability in the chief administrative positions of the nation. If the avenue to Cabinet positions were through the House of Representatives and the Senate, it is probable that very many men whom, un-

[207]

der our present arrangement, we could secure for heads of departments, would not offer themselves for Congressional seats with the possibility ultimately of being designated for the Cabinet, or if they did, that they would be elected. This may be unfortunate, but it is probably true.

Furthermore, if the heads of departments were selected from the leaders of the majority in Congress, unless more severe restrictions were imposed than we now have on the selection of departmental personnel, it is probable that the departments would be very much more political minded than they are.

In general, it would seem that this country has not reached the point in the growth of its habits and traditions where it would be willing to dispense with some checks on the expression of the public mind. It is one thing for a government of an old and settled country with well-defined traditions and habits to have greater freedom of action. It is one thing for a nation with ruling classes into the majority of whose population reverence has been instilled, and which is provincial and limited in its outlook, to have such a government. It is one thing for a nation whose area is less than that of the state of Oregon to have such a government. It would be interesting to see one of our states attempt the experiment. But it would be another thing for a country as big as the United States of America with its traditions in the course of rapid development, with large numbers of its people newly arrived, with greater similarity of economic conditions than exist in many smaller countries, with a more fluid state of mind, and more processes for the stimulation of impulses, to attempt the operation of a similar system.

And can it be said, after all, that our machinery, which is

pictured as so defective, has been an obstacle to progress? Are we behind any other nation in the world in the mass of legislation intended to accomplish reforms? Are our financial and economic policies less satisfactory? Are we suffering from too little legislation? Have we been backward in ministering through legislative programmes to the welfare of the masses of the American people or to any great class or section of them? It is common knowledge that we are in the forefront of progress, so far as legislation can affect it, in nearly every field of national activity. A better case should be made out before we undertake seriously to effect fundamental changes.

Certain things can be done which will result in bettering the relations of the legislative and the executive departments and in securing better results also in other directions. These things I shall briefly indicate.

In the first place, the Congress should promptly take two steps which are essential to the completion of a budget system. If it is legal, rules should be adopted by which the committees should not make changes in the estimates except by more than a majority vote and then when the committees have made their reports, the Congress, itself, should not make changes in the reports except by an abnormal majority. This is not without precedent in this country. At least one state has a provision of this sort. It goes without saying that the responsibility should also be placed upon the Executive for suggesting revenue changes to meet budget requirements. Unless these two things are done, we shall deceive ourselves into thinking that we have accomplished a great deal in the direction of budgetary practice.

A second thing which can be done and should be done,

to the relief both of the members of Congress and the Executive, is to place all except a very few officers and employees of every department of the government in the classified service. There is no reason why the personnel of every department should not be approximately as fully covered by the classified service and taken out of the hands of politicians as is that of the Department of Agriculture. This department is in many respects the best department of the government, and this is due in no small measure to the fact that only a few of its officers are not appointed for merit, such as the Secretary, the Assistant Secretary, and the Chief of the Weather Bureau. It is of the highest importance that such departments as the Treasury and the Interior be ordered in similar fashion. The results would be far-reaching.

Finally, the people must see to it that the government takes steps to secure and retain in certain positions of great responsibility individuals of the highest integrity, of exceptional ability, and of wide experience. Certainly, the people are entitled to as good service and to as high order of talent in the public business as are commanded by private enterprise. It is ridiculous for such a person as the Under-secretary of the Treasury, responsible for financial operations of enormous magnitude, to be called upon to serve the people for a smaller compensation than that received by many lesser subordinates in banks and other private institutions. The government does not need to pay salaries as high as those given in industry, but it should pay enough to retain able and experienced servants. It should pay them enough to live decently, to save something, and to work without undue apprehension as to the future of their families. It should pay enough to get the best talent and to keep it. The right men in government service, as in industry, are cheap at any reasonable price. The wrong men are expensive at any price. This great nation can amply afford to pay for the best talent to serve it. And it is very unjust and a little short of indecent for it to permit such conditions as the present to continue. It should not countenance a situation where men must serve it at a sacrifice, and where only the well-to-do can afford to hold office without sacrifice. It is undemocratic to permit the present situation to continue. Democracy for us, we believe, is the best form of government. It is a difficult one. It is being called upon to face increasingly complex problems. Its performance will depend in no small measure on the quality of its administrators. If these are mediocre, while our democracy may persist, its performance will be below the high standard which it should set and to which it aspires.

In the final analysis, whether a government is to succeed or fail, and whether it is to work well or badly, depends on the character of the population and particularly upon the capacity and standards of the electorate. In the past, our machinery of government has worked reasonably satisfactorily, not mainly because of the merits of the machinery but primarily because the people were competent. Whether our population with its recent large admixtures of people from countries with radically different habits of thought, states of mind, and backgrounds of experience, is as competent as it was formerly or will remain so is a matter for debate. There can be no debate, however, over the fact that with increasing complexities, economic and political, it is essential that it not only be as competent as it formerly was, but that its standards be constantly raised.

[211]

The right handling of problems implied in these remarks is now one of the most pressing problems confronting us. This involves the imposition of wise restraints on the admission of immigrants and the persistent employment of the best possible educational effort free from partisan bias and misrepresentation to educate our present population in the discharge of its civic tasks. The right kind of people can run any sort of government. The wrong sort of people cannot run any kind of government.

Wilson was, I think, wrong in picturing the earlier Presidents as leaders in the sense that they, as Presidents, moulded Congress to their ways of thinking. "Presidents," he said, in 1897, "were leaders intil Jackson went home to the Hermitage." If he meant they were leaders of the government rather than leaders of the people, he was mistaken. Washington had a great hold on the people, and for a long time was very influential with Congress, but when parties developed, it came about that he could not direct Congress, and in his last years Congress not only opposed him successfully, but in reality subjected him to insult. Jefferson was a great manipulator of men. He headed a small-sized popular revolution, and through his hold on the people, he had little trouble with Congress, in which his friends were dominant. Jackson, likewise, was for years a popular idol, but his political going was very rough, his fights with Congress were continuous, and his machinery finally went to pieces. Lincoln never really controlled Congress; and if he had lived, Congress, under Stevens and Charles Sumner, as I have before remarked, would have broken him. "Cleveland," Wilson said, "was, in the earlier years of his Administration, the type of the normal Constitutional Executive. He filled his messages with very definite recommendations, but thought it no part of his function to press his preferences in any other way upon Congress. . . . He has been the sort of President the makers of the Constitution had vaguely in mind: more man than partisan; with an independent executive will of his own; hardly a colleague of the Houses so much as an individual servant of the country, exercising his powers like a chief executive rather than a party leader." But Cleveland developed; according to Wilson: "Mr. Cleveland grew to the measure of his place. . . . The breath of affairs was at last in his lungs and he gave his party a leader."

But Wilson does not remind us that being a leader of a party is different from being the leader of the government, and especially of Congress; and leadership of Congress was the aim which he had in mind for so many years. And he could not then see that Congress would turn against Cleveland.

It is entirely proper and necessary for a President to have views and convictions. It is essential at all times that he urge them before Congress and the people. It is necessary that he do so at times, even though he may know that he will go down to defeat. If he can influence Congress and the people and secure their support, well and good. If he cannot, he must bide his time. He may be wrong. At any rate, the people must have time to make up their minds. Those favouring measures will continue to be impatient of delay; those opposing them will rejoice. Our forefathers figured out that delays might occur. They decided that delays in a democracy might not be detrimental, and, in the main, delays have not seriously impaired the fortunes of the nation. At times they have

[213]

worked to the nation's good. At any rate, Wilson, after he went to Washington, ceased to agitate for a change in government that would make the President the responsible leader in the government and of the government, and conceived himself only as a leader of his party and as a spokesman for the people.

While, according to Wilson, he was the leader of his party and, while he acted accordingly, with considerable effectiveness, incidentally stimulating partisan opposition because he set himself up as a partisan leader—opposition which he might otherwise have escaped in part—it cannot be said, I believe, that he did not recognize the place of Congress in our system and what was due it. On the contrary, he went even beyond the necessary bounds in observing its place and powers. He fought to get through Congress what he believed to be in the nation's interest, and, when necessary, sought to influence public opinion and to get its backing. But in all matters of national importance, particularly in the field of foreign affairs, in respect of which he, as President, was vested with great power, he went out of his way to keep Congress informed of developments and to reveal his thinking to it. Time and time again, although he knew that he had power to do things, he appeared before Congress to lay before it the situation and the essential things which lay in his thought. He did this for many reasons, particularly because, knowing that grave action might be necessary, and, knowing that Congress might be called upon to act, he desired it to know everything that he knew to enable it to register its dissent if it desired, and to have its backing and that of the country if the time came to strike.

This attitude he early revealed. On April 20, 1914,

when the trouble with Huerta became acute, in his first message after the Tampico incident, he said:

"No doubt I could do what is necessary in the circumstances to enforce respect for our government without recourse to the Congress, and yet not exceed my constitutional power as President; but I do not wish to act in a matter possibly of so grave consequences, except in close conference and coöperation with both the Senate and the House." During the war he did exercise vast powers. As President and Commander in Chief of the Army he had great powers given him by the Constitution. If he had not exercised them, his most active critics of what they pleased to call his dictatorial conduct would more savagely have criticized him for timidity and weakness.

Wilson also strikingly revealed his desire to keep Congress informed, both before the close of the war and afterward, in respect to his thinking as to the terms of peace and as to the machinery which should be set up after the war to maintain peace. Time and time again, he appeared before the Senate and revealed his full thought in these directions.

But perhaps some will say that, aside from war activities and functions, in the ordinary domestic affairs of the nation, there was under his guidance a deliberate policy of centralization and tendency to make the Federal Government an arbiter and controller of the life and destinies of the individual and the nation. There was a growth of legislation and activity of the Federal Government during Wilson's eight years. There was a striking growth before his time. The nation has steadily expanded. Its affairs have become vastly more complex. It was natural that the Federal Government's activity

[215]

should correspondingly increase just as the activities of states and municipalities have expanded. These will proceed. Of course, the tendency ought to be watched and controlled; we can easily go too fast and too far. But it is absurd to charge Mr. Wilson with a deliberate policy to exalt the Federal Government at the expense of the states.

Undoubtedly, we are too prone to assume that progress can be promoted or made by legislation. Of necessity, in the beginning of our national life, we had to lay broad foundations of organic law and had to place many laws on the statute books. We were pioneering a continent and we have attributed a large part of our progress to legislation. We have got in the habit every time a situation develops or any thought occurs to anybody, or to any group—and we have many men and women who are very busy and active—of passing a Federal or state law to remedy the situation or to uplift something or somebody. We have come too greatly to ignore the responsibility resting upon individuals for self and community improvement. Apparently we are beginning to recognize that there is a limit to what legislation can do, and to recognize that we can easily overload our state, Federal, and city governments.

But the people are responsible, and the people alone can apply the corrective. It seems to be difficult to get this thing into the heads of the people, viz.: That they, and they alone, are responsible for the expanding activities of government and for mounting expenditures. They are responsible both affirmatively and negatively, by aggression and by neglect. There is a general view to the contrary. It is the accepted opinion that

[216]

agencies in Washington—Congressmen or executive departments or both—are to blame. This is sheer nonsense. Congress reflects what appear to be the wishes of the people, and in no small measure is resistant to pressure brought to bear upon it. Heads of departments, as a rule, are constantly in the position of opposing requests for assistance in securing funds, coming from groups of interested outsiders. I know that, in two departments, I spent much more time in opposing demands for money than I spent in attempting to secure money for the services. There are not enough people in Washington to commit the American people to the enormous and rapid increase in governmental activities, and to consequent large expenditures. The actual outcome is partly the result of the growth of the nation in population and industry, with increasing economic complexities. We gain a nation of about twenty-five million people every twenty years; but the expansion in spending is greater than it should otherwise be, because of the prodigious energy of interested groups. Very many of the most vigorous critics of government extravagance are themselves members of groups and associations, or are interested in movements to extend the functions of the Federal Government and to increase its cost. This man or group demands a new department of public health or welfare; that one, a department of education; another, a department of aviation; another, of public works. This group fights fiercely fot the soldiers' bonus; that one, for an appropriation for maternity work; and another, for special aid to this or that class in society, particularly for the farmers. One association advocates a special appropriation for engineering research in the agricultural colleges, similar to

[217]

those granted for agriculture; another one agitates for agricultural-settlement appropriations or for larger military preparedness. Very few emergency situations of consequence arise in any part of the Union which do not result in offensives against the Treasury. Plant and animal disease outbreaks, floods, droughts, earthquakes, and sudden drastic economic changes, all lead to hurry-up calls for action from the Federal Government, and the appearance in Washington of groups of lobbyists. Let a bug, which is supposed to be destructive, appear in some state, and, in a short time, state commissioners of agriculture, accompanied by interested citizens and Senators and Representatives, are likely to put in their appearance, demanding Federal funds; and not infrequently they get them, even though the head of the department concerned makes an adverse report. Some time ago, the corn borer made its début in Massachusetts. The Department of Agriculture was promptly advised. Its experts began a survey; they reported that the pest was likely to spread, but, as I recall it, that it was doubtful whether it would be particularly destructive, and that, in any event, it could not be exterminated without such wholesale destruction of vegetation of all sorts as to make the undertaking impractical. They suggested that it might be worth while to secure funds with which to do some experimental work. In the meantime, the State Commissioners got active. A general meeting was called, and the Commissioners were about to go on record demanding a Federal appropriation of many millions of dollars, when the Federal experts interposed, with the result that the demands were greatly modified. The pressure for relief from various classes of farmers who are in trouble on account of reduced farm

[218]

prices, and for flood sufferers, is too fresh in the public mind to need more than passing mention. During the war, the President made available, from his special fund, $5,000,000, to be lent to farmers in certain states of the West where drought conditions had prevailed for three successive years. Many farmers there were in a critical situation, and it was desirable, for obvious reasons, that they be aided to save themselves and their homes. The relief was accorded as a war measure, and was a substitute for proposals in Congress involving appropriations of from twenty-five to fifty millions of dollars. In the spring of 1921, more than two years after the Armistice, pressure was exerted to secure a special fund from Congress. It was successful, and two billions of dollars were made available for loans mainly to farmers in the Northwest.

The people, even state officials, have come to look to the Federal Government for funds; in part, because of the difficulty of securing state support; at times, because the state legislature may not be in session and may not meet for several years; and in part, because it is normally more difficult to get money from near-by and financially hard-pressed local bodies. I am not now trying to pass judgment on the merit of such appeals: I am merely concerned with the processes by which the people themselves stand back of movements which cause increased Federal expenditures. Doubtless, this will continue. Groups will persist in their activities. The public, generally, will exhaust itself with criticism and with complaints of high taxes. The remedy lies with the public. The first thing for it to realize and accept is that it is responsible; that it can have what it wants. If it persists in its attitude of indifference while groups continue to be aggressive, it will continue to be victimized. The people can, if they wish, keep the groups under control. They can make it plain that the groups are not the American people, and that they usually make a noise out of all proportion to their numbers.

Wilson was keenly aware of the dangers of excessive or premature legislation and of overloading the government. He had a clear view of the nature and limits of laws and frequently emphasized the correct conception and practice. This was his definition of good legislation:

"Constructive legislation, when successful, is always the embodiment of convincing experience and of the mature public opinion, which finally springs out of such experience. Legislation is a business of interpretation, not of origination."

Again he said:

"It is in this spirit that we all ought to regard the laws, that we all ought to criticize the laws, and that we all ought to coöperate in the enforcement of the laws. Government, gentlemen, is merely an attempt to express the conscience of everybody, the average conscience of the nation, in the rules that everybody is commanded to obey. That is all they are. If the government is going faster than the public conscience, it will presently have to pull up. If it is not going as fast as the public conscience, it will presently have to be whipped up. Because the public conscience is going to say, 'We want our laws to express our character'; and our character must have this kind of solidity underneath it, the moral judgment of right and wrong. The only reason we quarrel with reformers sometimes is because they are, or suppose that they are, a little more enlightened than the rest of us, and they want us all of a sudden to be just as enlightened as they are, and we cannot stand the pace. That is all that makes us uneasy about reformers. If we could get our second wind, if we could keep up the pace as long as they do, we might be able to run as fast as they do, but we are more heavily weighted with clay than they are. We cannot go as fast. And we like companionship. We want to wait for the rest of them. We do not want to be in a lonely advance climbing some heights of perfection where there is no good inn to stop at overnight."

In July, 1916, he further elaborated his view before the Citizenship Convention in Washington, in these words:

"When you ask a man to be loyal to a government, if he comes from some foreign countries, his idea is that he is expected to be loyal to a certain set of persons like a ruler or a body set in authority over him, but that is not the American idea. Our idea is that he is to be loyal to certain objects in life, and that the only reason he has a President and a Congress and a Governor and a State Legislature and courts is that the community shall have instrumentalities by which to promote those objects. It is a coöperative organization expressing itself in this Constitution, expressing itself in these laws, intending to express itself in the exposition of those laws by the courts; and the idea of America is not so much that men are to be restrained and punished by the law as instructed and guided by the law. That is the reason so many hopeful reforms come to grief. A law cannot work until it expresses the spirit of the community for which it is enacted, and if you try to enact into law what expresses only the spirit of a small coterie or of a small minority, you know, or, at any rate, you ought to know, beforehand that it is not going to work. The object of the law is that there, written upon these pages, the citizen should read the record of the experience of this state and nation; what they have concluded it is necessary for them to do because of the life they have lived and the things that they have discovered to be elements in that life."

Wilson was a stern and stubborn fighter for the causes he believed in. He was as stubborn as "Old Hickory," whom he had much in his mind and whom he pictured as "a forthright man, who believed everything he did believe in fighting earnest"; adding, "In public life he is the only sort of man worth thinking about for a moment. If I was not ready to fight for everything I believed in, I would think it my duty to go back to Washington and take a back seat. . . . The United States had almost forgotten that it must keep its fighting ardour in behalf of mankind when Andrew Jackson became President."

Wilson did not seek a fight for its own sake, but he did not shirk it, and when he entered into it, he did so with great zest. "To judge by my experience," he said, "I have never been able to keep out of trouble. I have never looked for it, but I have always found it. If any man wants a scrap that is an interesting scrap and worthwhile, I am his man. I warn him that he is not going to draw me into a scrap for his own advertisement, but if he is looking for trouble that is the trouble of men in general and I can help a little, why, then, I am in for it." And Wilson always fought in the open and fought fairly. He was always ready to take the fight to the people and to drag any cause before them. He believed in letting the people know everything there was to know about the government. There were no secret recesses or dark corners in which he wished to hide things. "Nothing," he contended, "is so good for putrefaction as fresh air."

Wilson, as the President, was a partisan, in the sense that he set himself up as leader of his party, but not in the sense that he had a blind or unreasoning devotion to a party. He was interested in party only as a necessary agency in a constitutional democratic government, but, to him, it was not an end in itself. He always put the country high above party. He clearly recognized that neither of the great parties was normally in position to press its plans, regardless of men of independent minds.

Speaking in Indianapolis, on January 8, 1915, on Jackson Day, he said:

"My friends, what I particularly want you to observe is this: that politics in this country does not depend any longer upon the regular members of either party. There are not enough regular Republicans in this country to take and hold national power; and I must immediately add that there are not enough regular Democrats in this country to do it either. This country is guided and its policy is determined by the independent voter. . . . I am not an independent voter, but I hope I can claim to be an independent person, and I want to say this distinctly: I do not love any party any longer than it continues to serve the immediate and pressing needs of America. I have been bred in the Democratic party; I love the Democratic party; but I love America a great deal more than I love the Democratic party; and when the Democratic party thinks that it is an end in itself, then I rise up in dissent. It is a means to an end, and its power depends, and ought to depend, upon its showing that it

[223]

knows what America needs and is ready to give it what it needs."

Wilson thought clearly, and he had great capacity to express his thoughts. He was a literary artist by temperament and stern training. As an expositor of moral principles, he alone, among our other Chief Executives, can claim a place with Lincoln. Both of them fell upon times when great skill in exposition was of supreme moment; and it seems a little less than providential that this was so. Lincoln formulated for the nation, in imperishable words, the moral meaning of the struggle in which he was leader; and Wilson, in the Great War, fixed the thinking of his own country on high moral grounds and pitched the ideals of the Allies on a higher plane than even their own leaders had been able to do. And it is a matter of common knowledge that he powerfully affected the thinking of the people of the enemy powers and was instrumental in breaking their morale. If testimony of this were needed, it might be found in the complaints of no less an authority than Ludendorff. He complained bitterly that, not the armies of the Allies, but the mischievous propaganda of Wilson had defeated the German people. Wilson's thoughts and their expressions, therefore, were factors of enormous importance, not less by reason of the appeal which they made to the conscience of our people, the crusading spirit which they instilled into our boys and their heartening effect upon the Allies, than by their disturbing influence upon the minds of the people of the Central Powers.

But, as a writer for the untrained and undiscriminating reader and as a speaker, Wilson was not without a marked defect. He said too much in too few words and, when he had finished a thought, he let it drop. Several times I heard him laughingly remark in Cabinet meetings that he did not care how much any one said provided he said it in a few words. He studied his subject carefully, digested all the facts he could assemble, and then painted his picture with as few strokes as possible. His statements were based on wide knowledge and were the result of prolonged reflection. He uttered conclusions and did not take the trouble to reveal the steps he had taken or his mental processes. He wrote from a broad background of history and literature, and, not infrequently, his forms of expression were unconventional and not familiar to the average man, expressions whose origin and implication few of his half-educated audiences knew or could grasp. He habitually paid his audiences the compliment of appealing to their intelligence and of assuming that they knew more than they did.

Wilson coined very few phrases. Only a few of them struck the popular mind. Some of them were unfortunate. Some of them it would have been better if he had not used. Two of them, "Too proud to fight" and "Peace without victory," were the causes of violent criticisms, as was the sentence, "The objects which the statesmen of the belligerents on both sides have in mind are virtually the same, as stated in general terms to their own people."

The two phrases and the sentence given were used at a time of great emotional excitement, at a time when the Allies were in dire straits and making heroic efforts to sustain themselves. They exasperated many people, many ordinarily fair-minded people, whose feelings were deeply involved and who did not stop to consider the surrounding circumstances and just what Wilson had in mind. And,

[225]

of course, they were seized upon by partisans of all degrees and played up out of their context by a powerful partisan press. Certainly, it would have been better if Wilson had stopped to explain more fully what was in his mind. The phrases and the sentence did not disturb me at the time, or give me any concern, except for the fact that I knew that they would be misinterpreted. I knew what Wilson meant, and I agreed with his thought. It was particularly unfortunate that he used the phrase, "Too proud to fight" just when he did. At the time, he was being criticized for timidity and lack of understanding of the issues of the struggle. It was used in an address in Philadelphia, May 10, 1915, only three days after the sinking of the *Lusitania*, and three days before the first *Lusitania* note was sent. At this time, groups of people, particularly in a few Eastern cities, were greatly excited by the tragedy and were clamouring for immediate action. They instantly associated this utterance with the sub-marine controversy and saw in it a deliberate reference to the *Lusitania* incident, and a cowardly announcement that nothing could push Wilson into manly action.

Of course, Wilson, when he was speaking, did not have the *Lusitania* controversy in mind. With his customary single-track habit of thought, he was dealing, before foreign-born citizens after a naturalization ceremony, with the meaning of America and with their responsi-bilities. His mind easily dropped into an expression, a close parallel to which he was familiar with because of his long residence in the South. At the time he lived in the South, duelling was still practised. It survived until after 1880. I was familiar with the prevailing habit of thought and expression. I had frequently heard men

[226]

say that they had too much self-respect to be insulted by persons of a certain sort or to notice a challenge from them —they were too proud to notice or to fight such persons. Wilson's full thought he expressed as follows: "The example of America must be a special example. The example of America must be the example, not merely of peace because it will not fight, but of peace because peace is the healing and elevating influence of the world and strife. Is not there such a thing as a man being too proud to fight? There is such a thing as a nation being so right that it does not need to convince others by force that it is right." Very little of this utterance, except the phrase itself, was ever referred to or published. Partisans used the phrase out of its context for their own purposes. Neither was the trouble taken to point out that this same thought was not new with Wilson, and that he had employed it at least twice before.

In his special message on Mexico, August 27, 1913, he said: {

"Meanwhile, what is it our duty to do? Clearly, everything that we do must be rooted in patience and done with calm and disinterested deliberation. Impatience on our part would be childish and would be fraught with every risk of wrong and folly. We can afford to exercise the self-restraint of a really great nation, which realizes its own strength and scorns to use it."

And again later, on April 20, 1915, after his Philadelphia address, speaking before the Associated Press of New York, he said:

"My interest in the neutrality of the United States is not the petty desire to keep out of trouble. I am interested in neutrality because there is something so much

[227]

greater to do than to fight; there is a distinction waiting for the nation that no nation has ever yet got, that is the distinction of absolute self-control and self-mastery. Whom do you admire most among your friends? The irritable man? The man out of whom you can get a 'rise' without trying? The man who will fight at the drop of the hat, whether he knows what the hat is dropped for or not? Don't you admire, and don't you fear, if you have to contest with him, the self-mastered man, who watches you with calm eye and comes in only when you have carried the thing so far that you must be disposed of? That is the man you respect. That is the man, who, you know, has at bottom a much more fundamental and terrible courage than the fighting man. Now, I covet for America this splendid courage of reserve moral force, and I wanted to point out to you gentlemen simply this."

Wilson was soon to reveal strikingly to the nation and to the world just what he meant. He did this effectively before he decided that the time had come for us to fight. In speaking to the Railway Business Association of New York, January 27, 1916, he said:

"If there is one passion more deeply seated in the hearts of our fellow countrymen than another, it is the passion for peace. No nation ever more instinctively turned away from the thought of war than this nation to which we belong. . . . But, gentlemen, there is something that the American people love better than they love peace. They love the principles upon which their political life is founded. They are ready at any time to fight for the vindication of their character and honour. They will not at any time seek the contest, but they will not cravenly avoid it; because, if there is one thing that the individual ought to fight for and that the nation ought to fight for, it is the integrity of its own convictions. I would rather surrender territory than surrender those ideals which are the staff of life of the soul itself."

The use of the phrase "Peace without victory" also was unfortunate. Wilson recognized that it would be criticized and asked to be permitted to put his own interpretation upon it, but part of his interpretation did not help the matter. It was asking too much of human nature— of the Allies, facing a life-and-death struggle, not to seek a victory over the Germans. He pointed out that victory would mean peace forced upon the vanquished, accepted in humiliation, leaving a resentment and a bitter memory. Victory always leaves a sting in the vanquished, and the Allies proposed that there should be a sting. What Wilson, of course, had in mind was that the peace which should follow victory should be a just peace and, therefore, a permanent peace, and that it was of the utmost importance that when the victory was won the victors should be reasonable. He, of course, apprehended that they would not be reasonable; and what occurred in Paris and what has occurred since have demonstrated that his apprehensions were well grounded. Even with all his power, he could not get terms of peace which were wholly reasonable. He knew from the beginning that he was unlikely to succeed in attaining his aims in full; and for the further reason that he knew that peace must be organized and backed by civilized nations, when he felt the temper of the Allies in Paris, he insisted upon placing the Covenant of the League in the Treaty. Only now, after passion has somewhat abated and realities are being faced, is there prospect of a reasonably just and secure peace.   If one is attained, it will be substantially along the lines which Wilson indicated.

In declaring that the objects of the belligerents were virtually the same, as stated by their leaders to their own people, Wilson was unquestionably correct.   Leaders of nations, on both sides in every war, have always proclaimed the righteousness of their cause.   They did so in the late war, and, as they proclaimed them, their objects were virtually the same.   We need only remember the state of mind of people on both sides in our Civil War. But to say what Wilson did say and to say that the belligerents were actually fighting for the same principles are two utterly different things; and Wilson did not say and did not believe for a moment, at any time, that the objects of the two sides to the struggle were equally good. There was not a moment, from the time when the Germans first moved to the end, when he thought that their cause was righteous or justified and when he did not apprehend that we might have to step in.   It was because Wilson perceived this that, from the early days of the struggle, he embarked on his campaign of education to enlighten our own people, to secure unity when it would be needed, and a just peace when Germany was crushed, as he believed she would be.

It was pure tragedy that a man like Wilson, who knew what war means, who had witnessed the horrors of its aftermath, who detested it as a method of settling difficulties and thought it stupid, should have been called upon to lead this nation into war.   He spoke from his heart and experience when he said to Congress, in his War Message: "It is a fearful thing to lead this great nation into war"; and he held back more than two and a half years for many

[230]

reasons. I thought at the time, and still think, that he was right in his thinking and his action at each stage of the developments. At no point did I think the time had come for us to strike till we did strike; and I anxiously watched every step with utter sympathy for the Allies. I did not always agree with every part of Wilson's reasoning, but I accepted and endorsed his conclusions and course of action. I was influenced neither by the desires nor by the criticisms of the Allies of our course; and I was not disturbed by the mutterings of the pro-Ally Americans. I said frequently during the course of the developments that the Allies would continue to criticize us as long as we did not do exactly what they desired us to do, just as they would furiously applaud us if we did act according to their notions, and especially if we entered the war. My sole concern was what was our duty as Americans. Going in or staying out of the war and the time of it were matters solely for us to determine as American citizens, in the light of America's interests.

Naturally, the situation became tense when the *Lusitania* was sunk. Many citizens, especially in Eastern cities, were for immediate action. As I have already indicated, I was in California when the news of the sinking of the *Lusitania* came. I was in the West for five weeks following this tragedy. I realized clearly then that the majority of the people were not even thinking of this nation's entering the struggle. I was in most parts of the Union several times between 1915 and the spring of 1917, and at no stage, up to that time, were the masses of the people ready for this nation's participation. Wilson, too, had full knowledge of the state of mind of the great majority of the people. His attitude immediately after the sinking of the *Lusitania* is well pictured by Tumulty in his book, where he says:

"'I am bound to consider in the most careful and cautious way the first step I shall take, because once having taken it I cannot withdraw from it. I am bound to consider beforehand all the facts and circumstances surrounding the sinking of the *Lusitania* and to calculate the effect upon the country of every incautious or unwise move. I am keenly aware that the feeling of the country is now at fever heat, and that it is ready to move with me in any direction I shall suggest, but I am bound to weigh carefully the effect of radical action now based upon the present emotionalism of the people. I am not sure whether the present emotionalism of the country would last long enough to sustain any action I would suggest to Congress, and thus, in case of failure, we should be left without that fine backing and support so necessary to maintain a great cause. I could go to Congress to-morrow and advocate war with Germany, and I feel certain that Congress would support me, but what would the country say when war was declared, and finally came, and we were witnessing all of its horrors and bloody aftermath. As the people pored over the casualty lists, would they not say: "Why did Wilson move so fast in this matter? Why didn't he try peaceably to settle this question with Germany? Why could he not have waited a little longer? Why was he so anxious to go to war with Germany, yet, at the same time, why was he so tender of the feelings of Great Britain in the matter of the blockade?" Were I to advise radical action now, we should have nothing, I am afraid, but regrets and heartbreaks. The vastness of this country; its variegated elements; the conflicting cross-

[232]

currents of national feelings bid us wait and withhold ourselves from hasty or precipitate action. When we move against Germany, we must be certain that the whole country not only moves with us but is willing to go forward to the end with enthusiasm. I know that we shall be condemned for waiting, but in the last analysis I am the trustee of this nation, and the cost of it all must be considered in the reckoning before we go forward.'

"Then, leaning closer to me, he said: 'It will not do for me to act as if I had been hurried into precipitate action against Germany. I must answer for the consequences of my action. What is the picture that lies before me? All the great nations of Europe at war, engaged in a death grapple that may involve civilization. My earnest hope and fervent prayer have been that America could withhold herself and remain out of this terrible mess and steer clear of European embroilments, and at the right time offer herself as the only mediating influence to bring about peace. We are the only great nation now free to do this. If we should go in, then the whole civilized world will become involved. What a pretty mess it would be! America, the only nation disconnected from this thing, and now she is surrendering the leadership she occupies and becomes involved as other nations have. Think of the tragedy! I am not afraid to go to war. No man fit to be President of this nation, knowing the way its people would respond to any demand that might be made upon them, need have fears or doubts as to what stand it would finally take. But what I fear more than anything else is the possibility of world bankruptcy that will inevitably follow our getting into this thing. Not only world chaos and bankruptcy, but all of the distempers, social, moral, and industrial, that will flow from this world cataclysm. No sane man, therefore, who knows the dangerous elements that are abroad in the world would, without feeling out every move, seek to lead his people without counting the cost and dispassionately deliberating upon every move.'"

His attitude was frequently later revealed in public addresses. It was strikingly revealed in his statement at Los Angeles, September 20, 1919, on his Western tour, as follows:

"I remember how anxiously I watched the movements of opinion in this country during the months immediately preceding our entrance into the war. Again and again I put this question to the men who sat around the board at which the Cabinet meets. They represented different parts of the country; they were in touch with the opinion in different parts of the United States, and I would frequently say to them, 'How do you think the people feel with regard to our relation to this war?' And I remember one day, one of them said, 'Mr. President, I think that they are ready to do anything you suggest.' I said, 'That is not what I am waiting for. That is not enough. If they do not go in of their own impulse, no impulse that I can supply will suffice, and I must wait until I know that I am their spokesman. I must wait until I know that I am interpreting their purpose. Then I will know that I have got an irresistible power behind me.' And that is exactly what happened.

"That is what is now appreciated as it was not at first appreciated on the other side of the sea. They wondered and wondered why we did not come in. They had come to the cynical conclusion that we did not come in because

[234]

we were making money out of the war and did not want to spoil the profitable game; and then, at last, they saw what we were waiting for, in order that the whole plot of the German purpose should develop, in order that we might see how the intrigue of that plot had penetrated our own life, how the poison was spreading, and how it was nothing less than a design against the freedom of the world. They knew that when America once saw that, she would throw her power in with those who were going to redeem the world. And at every point of the discussion I was attempting to be the mouthpiece of what I understood right-thinking and forward-thinking and just-thinking men with regard to party or section in the United States to be purposing and conceiving, and it was the consciousness in Europe that that was the case that made it possible to construct the peace upon American principles."

Wilson's reasons for inaction were many and complex. He strongly felt that America alone could keep the balance of the world's thought and be prepared to succour the world and effect the necessary readjustments when the struggle ended. This was dominant in his thought for some time, in fact, even after we declared war and peace was concluded. He frequently expressed this view. In his Jackson Day speech at Indianapolis, January 8, 1915, he said:

"Look abroad upon the troubled world! Only America at peace. Among all the great powers of the world only America saving her power for her own people! Only America using her great character and her great strength in the interest of peace and of prosperity. Do you not think it likely that the world will some time turn to America and say: 'You were right and we were wrong.

[235]

You kept your head when we lost ours. You tried to keep the scale from tipping, and we threw the whole weight of arms in one side of the scale. Now, in your self-possession, in your coolness, in your strength, may we not turn to you for counsel and for assistance?' Think of the deep-wrought destruction of economic resources, of life, and of hope that is taking place in some parts of the world, and think of the reservoir of sustenance that there is in this great land of plenty! May we not look forward to the time when we shall be called blessed among the nations, because we succoured the nations of the world in their time of distress and of dismay? I, for one, pray God that that solemn hour may come, and I know the solidity of character and I know the exaltation of hope, I know the big principle with which the American people will respond to the call of the world for service. I thank God that those who believe in America, who try to seem her people, are likely to be also what America herself, from the first, hoped and meant to be—the servant of mankind."

In his address to the Associated Press in New York, April 20, 1915, he again touched upon this theme, saying:

"The world's affairs are drawing to a climax. We are the only great nation disengaged. The nations will turn to us for the cooler assessment. We shall some day have to assist in reconstructing the processes of peace. We are the mediating nation of the world. We mediate the blood and sentiments of the world. We are compounded of many nations. We understand all nations."

And in Chicago, on January 31, 1916, he again urged the point in these words:

"And those of us who are charged with the responsibility of affairs have realized very intensely that there

[236]

was a certain sense in which America was looked to to keep the balance of the whole world's thought.

"And America was called upon to do something very much more than that, even; profoundly difficult, if not impossible, though that be, she was called upon to assert in times of war the standards of times of peace. . . .

"We have believed and I believe that we can serve even the nations at war better by remaining at peace and holding off from this contest than we could possibly serve them in any other way. Your interest, your sympathy, your affections may be engaged on the one side or the other, but no matter which side they are engaged on, it is your duty even to your affections in this great affair to stand off and not let this nation be drawn into the war. Somebody must keep the great stable foundations of the life of nations untouched and undisturbed. Somebody must keep the great economic processes of the world of business alive. Somebody must see to it that we stand ready to repair the enormous damage and the incalculable losses which will ensue from the war, and which it is hardly credible could be repaired if every great nation in the world were drawn into the contest."

Whether Wilson's notion that we should and would be the succouring and mediating nation was his own idea or was first suggested by Walter Page, I do not know, but it is certain that Page, through 1914, strongly held this view and urged it on the President. On August 9, 1914, he wrote:

"Be ready, for you will be called upon to compose this huge quarrel. I thank Heaven for many things—first, the Atlantic Ocean; second, that you refrained from war in Mexico; third, that we kept our treaty—the Canal Tolls

[237]

victory, I mean. Now, when all this half the world will suffer the unspeakable mutilation of war, we shall preserve our moral strength, our political powers, and our ideals."

Wilson omitted no opportunity to make approaches as a mediator, but, of course, they had to be made with great care. Among other things he did, he sent the note asking both sides to state the terms on which they might consider making peace. This was a forlorn hope, but it served a useful purpose. It enabled the Allies to place themselves before our people in a favourable light. The Germans could say nothing which would not queer them further in America.

As matters developed, Wilson realized that the moment might come when efforts to protect our rights, to save our honour, and to effect mediation might fail, and that we would have to go in. He knew, however, the state of mind of the people and kept closely in touch with sentiment in all sections of the country and of Congress. He knew that the masses of the people, particularly in the South and West, were not really thinking about our getting into the war until after the beginning of 1917. He had in mind the difficulty which he experienced in getting Congressional support even for the army increases proposed in 1915. He actually did not succeed in getting the army bill through till August, 1916. He was confronted, too, until February, 1916, with a serious threat of the passage of the McLemore Resolution warning Americans off the high seas. He was, of course, aware of the large foreign elements which were naturally friendly to the Central Powers, and of the fact that large numbers of people, particularly in the South, had been especially

[238]

irritated with Great Britain because of her interference with the shipment of cotton to Central Europe.

In 1917, he said to Tumulty:

"Tumulty, from the very beginning I saw the end of this horrible thing; but I could not move faster than the great mass of our people would permit. Very few understood the difficult and trying position I have been placed in during the years through which we have just passed. In the policy of patience and forbearance I pursued, I tried to make every part of America and the varied elements of our population understand that we were willing to go any length rather than resort to war with Germany. As I told you months ago, it would have been foolish for us to have been rushed off our feet and to have gone to war over an isolated affair like the *Lusitania*. But now we are certain that there will be no regrets or looking back on the part of our people. There is but one course now left open to us. Our consciences are clear, and we must prepare for the inevitable—a fight to the end. Germany must be made to understand that we have rights that she must respect. There were few who understood this policy of patience. I do not mean to say this in a spirit of criticism. Indeed, many of the leading journals of the country were unmindful of the complexities of the situation which confronted us."

He, therefore, realized the need of educating the people and steadily pursued a definite course of laying issues before them and Congress. This was his broader objective in his Preparedness tour. In Pittsburgh, January 29, 1916, he said:

"While a year ago it seemed impossible that a struggle upon so great a scale should last a whole twelvemonth, it has now lasted a year and a half, and the end is not yet, and all the time things have grown more and more difficult to handle.

"It fills me with a very strange feeling sometimes, my fellow citizens, when it seems to be implied that I am not the friend of peace. If these gentlemen could have sat with me reading the dispatches and handling the questions which arise every hour of the twenty-four, they would have known how infinitely difficult it had been to maintain the peace, and they would have believed that I was the friend of peace. But I also know the difficulties, the real dangers, dangers not alone about things that I can handle, but about things that the other parties handle and I cannot control.

"It amazes me to hear men speak as if America stood alone in the world and could follow her own life as she pleased. We are in the midst of a world that we did not make and cannot alter; its atmospheric and physical conditions are the conditions of our own life also, and, therefore, as your responsible servant, I must tell you that the dangers are infinite and constant."

He returned to this topic at Milwaukee, January 31, 1916, saying:

"I feel that I am charged with a double duty of the utmost difficulty. In the first place, I know that you are depending upon me to keep this nation out of the war. So far I have done so, and I pledge you my word that, God helping me, I will if it is possible. But you have laid another duty upon me. You have bidden me see to it that nothing stains or impairs the honour of the United States, and that is a matter not within my control; that depends upon what others do, not upon what the government of the United States does. Therefore, there may at any moment come a time when I cannot preserve both the honour and the peace of the United States. . . .

"We want war, if it must come, to be something that springs out of the sentiments and principles and actions of the people themselves."

Wilson's position in the early stages of the war met with approval and support even from such pugnacious leaders as Roosevelt, who, of course, cordially resented and detested Wilson. Roosevelt's hindsight was quite different from his foresight. After certain events, and after the war fever spread, he was very vocal as to what he would have done, but in September, 1914, he was quite clear that nothing could be done about Belgium and preferred that we should so act as to be in position to mediate. In an article in the *Outlook* of September 22, 1914, he said: "Our country stands well-nigh alone among the great civilized powers in being unshaken by the present world-wide war. For this we should be humbly and profoundly grateful. . . . As regards the actions of most of the combatants in the hideous world-wide war now raging, it is possible sincerely to take and defend either of the opposite views concerning their actions. . . . When Russia took part, it may well be argued that it was impossible for Germany not to come to the defence of Austria, and that disaster would surely have attended her arms had she not followed the course she actually did follow as regards her opponents on her western frontier. . . . I wish it explicitly understood that I am not at this time passing judgment one way or the other upon Germany for what she did to Belgium. . . . I am merely calling attention to what has actually been done in Belgium, in accordance with what the Germans unquestionably sincerely believe to be the course of conduct necessitated by Germany's struggle for life. . . . It is neither necessary nor at the present time possible to sift from the charges, countercharges, and denials the exact facts as to the acts alleged to have been committed in various places. . . . I think, at any rate, I hope, I have rendered it plain that I am not now criticizing, that I am not passing judgment one way or the other, upon Germany's action. I admire and respect the German people. I am proud of the German blood in my veins. When a nation feels that the issue of a contest in which, from whatever reason, it finds itself engaged will be national life or death, it is inevitable that it should act so as to save itself from death, and to perpetuate its life. . . . The rights and wrongs of these cases where nations violate the rules of abstract morality in order to meet their own vital needs can be precisely determined only when all the facts are known and when men's blood is cool. . . . I am not at this time criticizing the particular actions of which I speak. . . .

". . . A deputation of Belgians has arrived in this country to invoke our assistance in the time of their dreadful need. What action our government can or will take I know not. It has been announced that no action can be taken that will interfere with our entire neutrality. It is certainly eminently desirable that we should remain entirely neutral, and nothing but urgent need would warrant breaking our neutrality and taking sides one way or the other. . . . Neutrality may be of prime necessity in order to preserve our own interests, to maintain peace in so much of the world as is not affected by

[242]

the war, and to conserve our influence for helping toward the reëstablishment of general peace when the time comes; for if any outside power is able at such time to be the medium for bringing peace, it is more likely to be the United States than any other. . . . Of course, it would be folly to jump into the gulf ourselves to no good purpose; and very probably nothing that we could have done would have helped Belgium. We have not the smallest responsibility for what has befallen her, and I am sure that the sympathy of this country for the suffering of the men, women, and children of Belgium is very real. Nevertheless, this sympathy is compatible with full acknowledgment of the unwisdom of our uttering a single word of official protest unless we are prepared to make that protest effective, and only the clearest and most urgent national duty would ever justify us in deviating from our rule of neutrality and non-interference. . . .

". . . Every public man, every writer who speaks with wanton offensiveness of a foreign power or of a foreign people, whether he attacks England or France or Germany, whether he assails the Russians or the Japanese, is doing an injury to the whole American body politic. We have plenty of shortcomings at home to correct before we start out to criticize the shortcomings of others."

Later, the spirit of partisanship got the better of Roosevelt, and during the remainder of the period he was a difficult factor, but Wilson gave little heed to him.

It was easy for people—Roosevelt, Page, and others—to say that if the President, when the *Lusitania* was sunk, had boldly declared that we should join the Allies, he would have carried the people with him; it is another thing to know this. I have a suspicion that he would have had hard sledding. It is possible that he would have had strong partisan opposition to such a course, a large element in Congress against him and no such unity in the Nation as he did have when we did enter the war.

Furthermore, we certainly struck at an opportune time. What might have happened if we had gone in in 1915 when Germany and the Central Powers were still strong? I do not know. The war might have dragged along for several years. War weariness might have overtaken this country as it had some of the Allies; the sacrifices of life and the financial burdens would have become staggering. We would certainly not have paused in our efforts to carry the load of fighting three thousand miles from home, but serious complications might have set up. On the other hand, Russia might have stayed in the war, Bulgaria might have joined the Allies, and the end might have been speedy. But such speculations are idle.

Wilson led the nation into war at the right moment—the moment when Germany abandoned all pretences, broke her promises, declared her intention to resume unrestricted submarine warfare, and undertook to dictate the course we should follow. Then Uncle Sam rolled up his sleeves and made it plain that he was "free, white, and twenty-one" and would see whether anybody could tell him what he could or could not do. From this moment. Wilson had back of him a united and determined people, and he knew it.

Wilson hated the thought of war. He knew what it meant, but he accepted the challenge with the same poise and calm courage that he had manifested in the more difficult former trial of maintaining peace.

Wilson's knowledge of the meaning of war and what the new task involved and his boldness were made manifest

[244]

at the outset and were evident at each stage of the development, from first to last. There was no hesitating. He did not waver for an instant, and he had at no time any doubt as to the issue. With him, it was a foregone conclusion. There was in him the spirit of the Crusader and of the Roundhead. He would have immediate and good execution of the enemy, for the good of their souls and for the glory of God.

In his war message, he said:

"It is a war against all nations. American ships have been sunk, American lives taken, in ways which it has stirred us very deeply to learn of, but the ships and people of other neutral and friendly nations have been sunk and overwhelmed in the waters in the same way. There has been no discrimination. The challenge is to all mankind. Each nation must decide for itself how it will meet it. The choice we make for ourselves must be made with a moderation of counsel and a temperateness of judgment befitting our character and our motives as a nation. We must put excited feeling away. Our motive will not be revenge or the victorious assertion of the physical might of the nation, but only the vindication of right, of human right, of which we are only a single champion."

And again he declared:

"There is one choice we cannot make, we are incapable of making: we will not choose the path of submission and suffer the most sacred rights of our nation and our people to be ignored or violated. The wrongs against which we now array ourselves are no common wrongs: they cut to the very roots of human life.

"With a profound sense of the solemn and even tragical character of the step I am taking and of the grave responsi-

[245]

bilities which it involves, but in unhesitating obedience to what I deem my constitutional duty, I advise that the Congress declare the recent course of the Imperial German Government to be, in fact, nothing less than war against the government and people of the United States; that it formally accept the status of belligerent which has thus been thrust upon it; and that it take immediate steps not only to put the country in a more thorough state of defence but also to exert all its power and employ all its resources to bring the government of the German Empire to terms and end the war.

"What this will involve is clear. It will involve the utmost practicable coöperation in counsel and action with the governments now at war with Germany, and, as incident to that, the extension to those governments of the most liberal financial credits, in order that our resources may so far as possible be added to theirs. It will involve the organization and mobilization of all the material resources of the country to supply the materials of war and serve the incidental needs of the nation in the most abundant and yet the most economical and efficient way possible."

He was glad that the matter had come out into the open:

"We are accepting this challenge of hostile purpose because we know that in such a government, following such methods, we can never have a friend; and that in the presence of its organized power, always lying in wait to accomplish we know not what purpose, there can be no assured security for the democratic governments of the world. We are now about to accept gauge of battle with this natural foe to liberty and shall, if necessary, spend the whole force of the nation to check and nullify its pretensions and its power. We are glad, now that we see the facts with no veil of false pretence about them, to fight thus for the ultimate peace of the world and for the liberation of its peoples, the German peoples included: for the rights of nations great and small, and the privilege of men everywhere to choose their way of life and of obedience. The world must be made safe for democracy. Its peace must be planted upon the tested foundations of political liberty. We have no selfish ends to serve. We desire no conquest, no dominion. We seek no indemnities for ourselves, no material compensation for the sacrifices we shall freely make. We are but one of the champions of the rights of mankind. We shall be satisfied when those rights have been made as secure as the faith and the freedom of nations can make them.

"Just because we fight without rancour and without selfish object, seeking nothing for ourselves but what we shall wish to share with all free peoples, we shall, I feel confident, conduct our operations as belligerents without passion and ourselves observe with proud punctilio the principles of right and of fair play we profess to be fighting for."

His closing paragraph was reminiscent of the days of the Revolution:

"It is a distressing and oppressive duty, gentlemen of the Congress, which I have performed in thus addressing you. There are, it may be, many months of fiery trial and sacrifice ahead of us. It is a fearful thing to lead this great peaceful people into war, into the most terrible and disastrous of all wars, civilization itself seeming to be in the balance. But the right is more precious than peace, and we shall fight for the things which we have always carried nearest our hearts, for democracy, for the right of those who submit to authority to have a voice in their own governments, for the rights and liberties of small nations, for a universal dominion of right by such a concert of free peoples as shall bring peace and safety to all nations and make the world itself at last free. To such a task we can dedicate our lives and our fortunes, everything that we are and everything that we have, with the pride of those who know that the day has come when America is privileged to spend her blood and her might for the principles that gave her birth and happiness and the peace which she has treasured. God helping her, she can do no other."

There will be no compromise:

"I accept the challenge. I know that you accept it. All the world shall know that you accept it. It shall appear in the utter sacrifice and self-forgetfulness with which we shall give all that we love and all that we have to redeem the world and make it fit for free men like ourselves to live in. This now is the meaning of all that we do. Let everything that we say, my fellow countrymen, everything that we henceforth plan and accomplish, ring true to this response till the majesty and might of our concerted power shall fill the thought and utterly defeat the force of those who flout and misprize what we honour and hold dear. Germany has once more said that force, and force alone, shall decide whether Justice and peace shall reign in the affairs of men, whether Right as America conceives it or Dominion as she conceives it shall determine the destinies of mankind. There is, therefore, but one response possible from us: Force, Force to the utmost, Force without stint or limit, the righteous and triumphant Force which shall make Right the law of the world, and cast every selfish dominion down to the dust."

[248]

Wilson's voice was like the voice of a prophet of old:

"The military masters under whom Germany is bleeding see very clearly to what point Fate has brought them. If they fall back or are forced back an inch, their power both abroad and at home will fall to pieces like a house of cards. It is their power at home they are thinking about now more than their power abroad. It is that power which is trembling under their very feet; and deep fear has entered their hearts."

And again he cried:

"For us there is but one choice. We have made it. Woe be to the man or group of men that seeks to stand in our way in this day of high resolution when every principle we hold dearest is to be vindicated and made secure for the salvation of the nations. We are ready to plead at the bar of history, and our flag shall wear a new lustre. Once more we shall make good with our lives and fortunes the great faith to which we were born, and a new glory shall shine in the face of our people."

And finally he exclaimed:

"It is because it is for us a war of high, disinterested purpose, in which all the free peoples of the world are banded together for the vindication of right, a war for the preservation of our nation and of all that it has held dear of principle and of purpose, that we feel ourselves doubly constrained to propose for its outcome only that which is righteous and of irreproachable intention, for our foes as well as for our friends. The cause being just and holy, the settlement must be of like motive and quality. For this we can fight, but for nothing less noble or less worthy of our traditions. For this cause we entered the war, and for this cause will we battle until the last gun is fired.

"A supreme moment of history has come. The eyes of the people have been opened and they see. The hand of God is laid upon the nations. He will show them favour, I devoutly believe, only if they rise to the clear heights of His own justice and mercy."

From the moment the country entered the war, Wilson took a stand which was of the first importance—that politicians should not hamper the army and the navy. This was unique in American history. It was obvious that politicians in Congress would attempt to meddle in military matters, as they had in all previous wars, particularly in the Mexican and Civil wars, causing unnecessary sacrifices of lives and property and endangering the nation itself. In no other directions in our history has Congressional action been so inefficient and baneful as in its interference with the direction of military matters, and in no other way has its stupidity been so strikingly exhibited. If an exception should be made, it would be made in its conduct during the periods of reconstruction which have followed our wars. At the outset, in the beginning of our last war, elements in Congress again set out to meddle and to control military policies, but Wilson opposed a firm front to the attempt and stopped it. Congress was then free to do its great part in making available for the struggle the resources of the nation. This part it played nobly. In stopping it from interfering with the conduct of war, Wilson saved Congress from itself.

One of his first notable actions was his calling upon the military experts to recommend a soldier to command the army. On their recommendation he selected General Pershing, and, having selected him, he left him free. His own part was to back up the leaders of the army and of the navy. What they wanted would be provided; whom Pershing wanted in France would be sent and no others.

Beyond this, the next thing Wilson did was to urge boldness and aggressiveness. One needs only to recall his letter to Admiral Sims and his address to the officers of the Atlantic Fleet. In this address, he said:

"Now, the point that is constantly in my mind, gentlemen, is this: This is an unprecedented war and, therefore, it is a war in one sense for amateurs. Nobody ever before conducted a war like this, and therefore nobody can pretend to be a professional in a war like this. Here are two great navies, not to speak of the others associated with us, our own and the British, outnumbering by a very great margin the navy to which we are opposed, and yet casting about for a way in which to use our superiority and our strength, because of the novelty of the instruments used, because of the unprecedented character of the war, because, as I said just now, nobody ever before fought a war like this, in the way that this is being fought at sea, or on land either, for that matter. The experienced soldier—experienced in previous wars—is a back number so far as his experience is concerned; not so far as his intelligence is concerned. His experience does not count, because he never fought a war as this is being fought, and therefore he is an amateur along with the rest of us. Now, somebody has got to think this war out. Somebody has got to think out the way, not only to fight the submarine, but to do something different from what we are doing.

"We are hunting hornets all over the farm and letting the nest alone. None of us knows how to go to the nest and crush it; and yet I despair of hunting for hornets all over the sea when I know where the nest is and know that

[251]

the nest is breeding hornets as fast as I can find them. I am willing for my part, and I know you are willing because I know the stuff you are made of—I am willing to sacrifice half the navy Great Britain and we together have to crush out that nest, because, if we crush it, the war is won. I have come here to say that I do not care where it comes from, I do not care whether it comes from the youngest officer or the oldest, but I want the officers of this navy to have the distinction of saying how this war is going to be won. The Secretary of the Navy and I have just been talking over plans for putting the planning machinery of the navy at the disposal of the brains of the navy and not stopping to ask what rank those brains have, because, as I have said before and want to repeat, so far as experience in this kind of war is concerned, we are all of the same rank. I am not saying that I do not expect the admirals to tell us what to do, but I am saying that I want the youngest and most modest youngster in the service to tell us what we ought to do if he knows what it is. Now, I am willing to make any sacrifice for that. I mean any sacrifice of time or anything else. I am ready to put myself at the disposal of any officer in the navy who thinks he knows how to run this war. I will not undertake to tell you whether he does or not, because I know that I do not, but I will undertake to put him in communication with those who can find out whether his idea will work or not. I have the authority to do that and I will do it with greatest pleasure. . . .

"We have got to throw tradition to the wind. Now, as I have said, gentlemen, I take it for granted that nothing that I say here will be repeated and therefore I am going to say this: Every time we have suggested anything to the

[252]

British Admiralty, the reply has come back that virtually amounted to this, that it had never been done that way, and I felt like saying: 'Well, nothing was ever done so systematically as nothing is being done now.' Therefore, I should like to see something unusual happen, something that was never done before; and inasmuch as the things that are being done to you were never done before, don't you think it is worth while to try something that was never done before against those who are doing them to you. There is no other way to win, and the whole principle of this war is the kind of thing that ought to hearten and stimulate America. America has always boasted that she could find men to do anything. She is the prize amateur nation of the world. Germany is the prize professional nation of the world. Now when it comes to doing new things and doing them well, I will back the amateur against the professional every time, because the professional does it out of the book and the amateur does it with his eyes open upon a new world and with a new set of circumstances. He knows so little about it that he is fool enough to try to do the right thing. The men that do not know the danger are the rashest men, and I have several times ventured to make this suggestion to the men about me in both arms of the service: Please leave out of your vocabulary altogether the word 'prudent.' Do not stop to think about what is prudent for a moment. Do the thing that is audacious to the utmost point of risk and daring, because that is exactly the thing that the other side does not understand, and you will win by the audacity of method when you cannot win by circumspection and prudence. I think that there are willing ears to hear this in the American Navy and the

American Army because that is the kind of folk we are. We get tired of the old ways and covet the new ones.

"So, gentlemen, besides coming down here to give you my personal greeting and to say how absolutely I rely on you and believe in you, I have come down here to say also that I depend on you, depend on you for brains as well as training and courage and discipline."

Wilson's determination and success in keeping the hands of the politicians off the army and the navy will be rated one of his great contributions to the nation in this time of stress. For it, Wilson is entitled to the gratitude of all the people. It is to be hoped that the precedent he set will be followed for all time.

Wilson habitually took the long view. He preferred to go down to defeat fighting for a cause which he knew some day would triumph than to gain a victory of an issue which he was confident would in time be shown to be false. He played for the verdict of history.

What history will say of Wilson, I do not know. That he will figure largely in it is obvious. It is unavoidable that he should. He was a central figure in this nation, and one of the central figures of the world in the period of its most colossal tragedy. Quoting him, I may say:

"We find every truly great mind identified with some special cause. His purposes are steadfastly set in some definite direction. The career which he works out for himself constitutes so important a part of the history of his times that to dissociate him from his surroundings were as impossible as it would be undeservable."

APPENDICES

APPENDIX I

The Achievements of the Democratic Party

Extracts from Speeches Delivered During the Campaign of 1916

THE Democratic party has now been in power for about three and a half years. Even its opponents admit that its record has been striking, and they do not dare to attack it specifically. The party's achievements in this short period have been greater than those of the Republican party during a period three or four times as long. It is impossible within the limits of your patience to give this record in any detail. I can review only a few of the larger accomplishments and indicate their significance. I shall deal mainly with what the Administration has done for the farmer and shall, I believe, demonstrate that the farmer, in simple justice, should support the Administration. It has kept its promises. It has kept faith with the farmers, and they will keep faith with it.

"You recall the political situation before the fourth of March, 1913. For years the tariff had been a dominant issue. There was a general demand for its revision. The Republican party, in their platform of 1912, had declared that some of the schedules were too high and should be reduced. The Progressive party charged that the Payne-Aldrich tariff was unjust, especially to labour, and demanded that it should be so reformed that some of its benefits should reveal themselves in the pay envelope of

[257]

the labourer. The Democratic party promised prompt revision downward. It faithfully kept this pledge, as it has numerous others. You know the outcome. In response to an overwhelming demand from the American people, the Democratic party promptly attacked the problem and passed the Underwood Tariff Law. Its action was conservative and wise and was in the interest of the masses of the American people. This action was coincident with a great expansion of American manufacturing and a new era in American trade.

"I shall not weary you with a discussion of the tariff in its relation to existing conditions. You are not seriously concerned about it. It is obvious that this nation was never more prosperous than it is to-day, and that never before were more labouring people at work with higher wages.

"But there is one point which deserves comment. Republican leaders, finding themselves embarrassed in trying to raise the usual alarms, have looked to the future, have attempted to frighten you by what may happen when the war closes, and demand that the old high protection party be returned to power to safeguard this nation against the fierce competition of Europe. I am amazed at their audacity. I can conceive no greater insult to the intelligence of a great people. That Europe at the close of this war should be in condition to compete with this country, especially on more favourable terms than before, is unthinkable. Some would have you believe that, while the conflict rages and while trade barriers exist, the industries of Europe, especially of the Central Powers, are pouring out masses of products, which, when peace comes, will flood this nation. Could anything be more unlikely? Do you realize that from twenty-two to twenty-five million men in Europe are under arms? Do you not know that from 55 to 60 per cent. of the artisans of Europe are at the front, and that the people who are not fighting are working to supply those who are? Never before has there been anything like this war. This is a war of nations, of whole peoples, a war in which the entire economic and industrial life of the people is redirected for purposes of destruction. It is impossible that there should be in any of these nations a great reservoir of useful commodities which the nations themselves have not long ago consumed.

"By what process do they arrive at the conclusion that stricken Europe will be a more formidable foe? Is war a blessing? Is it the path to national economic supremacy? Would they advise this nation to start a war in order to get ready to meet competition? If they mean what they say and are interested mainly in profits, as they are, certainly, they should urge war. Consider what this war is doing. Think of the demoralization of industry, the destruction of property, the waste of capital. What gain accrues from the slaughter of millions of working men and of alert industrial leaders, from many more millions of wounded and maimed, of widows and helpless children? Bear in mind the burden of debt piling up, greater than anything ever imagined in the history of the world. Even now the interest charge on the war debt in each nation must equal its former entire national budget. When peace comes, will not the process of re-direction of industry, of recovery and reconstruction, be slow and painful, covering generations? Clearly the thought of this great people will be engaged, not in planning to resist fierce and brutish competition, but to extend aid and succour. The most hopeful sign now visible to thoughtful men is the growing appreciation of the folly of international selfishness and a determination to effect an adjustment on another basis. The old plan spelled war and is doomed. Is it not a sorry figure our opponents cut when they try to frighten the people of this great nation, increasing in efficiency, with the danger of competition from invalid Europe, and in urging them to renewed and more aggressive selfish enterprises? Those who do so have no vision and are no friends of humanity and permanent peace. . . .

"Already the American farmer is the most efficient farmer in the world. He does not produce more per acre. It is not necessary for him to do so. And it would be unwise for him to undertake to do so. But he does produce from two to five times more per man, or per unit of labour and capital, than any other farmer in the world. He is still pioneering a continent with immense undeveloped resources before him. He is more alert and uses more and better machinery and has more powerful instrumentalities at his service than have the farmers of any other nation. He now masters his rivals in the field of competition, and will more and more easily hold his own in the race for agricultural supremacy.

"And yet the protected interests have attempted to convince the American farmer that he is in danger from competition abroad, even in his own market. Those who raise this alarm do not pay a compliment to the intelligence of the American farmer. There is and has been no substantial competition in competitive agricultural commodities. The greatest and most impartial expert authority on the American tariff has asserted without qualification that, for the most part, tariff duties levied on agricultural imports were simply dust in the farmer's eyes and a sop to him to get his support for protective rates on manufactured products. In none of the three years from 1914 to 1916, inclusive, did the percentage of imports of corn to the domestic production exceed $\frac{1}{2}$ of 1 per cent., of wheat $\frac{7}{10}$ of one per cent., of oats 2 per cent., and of potatoes $1\frac{1}{10}$ per cent. And in each of the three years from 1914 to 1916, inclusive, the exports of corn exceeded the imports by from 34,000,000 to 40,000,000 bushels, the exports of wheat by from 140,000,000 to 331,000,000, the exports of oats by from 98,000,000 to 100,000,000, and the exports of potatoes by from 2,750,000 to 4,750,000. Further illustrations are furnished in the statistics of meat imports and exports. In none of the three years did the percentage of imports of meat (beef, mutton, and pork) to the total domestic production exceed $1\frac{2}{10}$ per cent., while, at the same time, the exports of these products exceeded the imports by from 900,000,000 to 1,800,000,000 pounds.

"These achievements [outlined on pp. 257-270] would have done credit to three or four administrations in normal times with nothing unusual to harass the President and Congress. The astounding thing about it is that this record was made, not in normal times, but in time of the greatest upheaval the world has known, when the thought of your Chief Executive and your representatives was absorbed by many difficult and delicate foreign problems.

"This record would amply justify at the hands of the fair-minded voters of the nation a favourable verdict.

But even a greater service has been rendered by the President to the farmers and the whole nation in the field of foreign affairs.

"From the outset there were grave foreign questions to be dealt with. Our memory is short. Have you forgotten Japan and the delicate controversy extending over many months? You know the outcome. An adjustment was reached and our friendly relations with Japan have persisted. Mexico I need not remind you of. We inherited that situation, and it has been with us to the present time. The exact final conclusion no human being can predict. But you do know several things. You recall the declaration of the President that, in dealing with the nations to the south of us, this great Republic would refuse to give its moral countenance to any individual who undertook to promote revolution for his selfish ends. You remember his announcement of the humane and just policy 'that the people of small and weak states had the right to expect to be dealt with exactly as the people of big and powerful states would be,' and that in dealing with the people of Mexico he has acted on that principle. You do know that he has saved this republic from the shameless disgrace of a war with the downtrodden, hapless, and helpless people of Mexico. You do know that he refused to give the moral support of this great nation to a selfish, drunken despot who was trying to fasten his tyrannical rule on the Mexican people; and you approve his action. You recall the difficult problems presented in the European field because of the new instrumentalities of war employed. You remember the submarine controversy. The President of these United States demanded of Germany that the lives of passengers on merchantmen should not be jeopardized, and that their method of using this instrument of destruction should be changed. She has promised compliance.

"These are the large results. They have been secured without the sacrifice of national honour, and millions of people applaud Woodrow Wilson for saving this nation the horrors of war. In this foreign field, Woodrow Wilson has expressed the will of the overwhelming masses of American people. He has preserved neutrality with such an even balance that he satisfies none of the extremes at home or abroad. Under him, democracy has expressed itself in diplomacy; and it is interesting to contemplate what might have been the course in Europe if democracy had been given all the facts and had had an opportunity to express its will.

"But apparently this outcome does not please the opposition. Nothing that the President has done is right; everything is wrong. At best, if what he has done is right, his way of doing it has been wrong. And yet what definite alternatives have they offered or do they offer? Do they suggest anything except that Wilson is wrong in everything? Their candidate promises absolute and adequate protection to property and life abroad. How? He neglects to say, by the use of force, the effective alternative.

"After many months Mr. Hughes says that he would have recognized Huerta. After many months Mr. Taft says he would have recognized Huerta. Do the American people agree that this government should have recognized him? Another leader says that he would have kept out of Mexico entirely or would have intervened. Is it not likely that, if he means what he says, he would have intervened? They criticize the taking of the Custom House at Vera Cruz. Do you remember what caused it? Do you recall the seizure of our seamen from a naval boat carrying the American flag? Admiral Mayo did in this instance what American admirals have done since our flag was first hoisted. There were other incidents— the imprisonment of a seaman from our fleet at Vera Cruz and the withholding of an official dispatch. It was clear that Huerta was bent on retaliation for non-recognition, and that there could be no headway as long as he occupied his usurped position. The President said he must go. The Vera Cruz Custom House was seized and he went! What would the critics have said if the President had failed to sustain Admiral Mayo? Can you not imagine the ravings of the martial gentleman from Oyster Bay? Mr. Elihu Root, in his recent Union League Club speech, reviews the history of this business and criticizes it. Has he not a short memory? Does he recall an incident in Washington following the occupation of Vera Cruz and the tender of good offices of the A. B. C. Powers? Does he not remember that with emotion he called attention to the unhappy conditions in Mexico and concluded with these words: 'Thank Heaven, we have a President in whose lofty character, in whose sincerity of purpose, in whose genuine desire to do what is right, wise, patriotic, and what is best for the country and humanity, we can all trust absolutely. I trust in it. . . . I have confidence in the character and purpose of the President of the United States. He is my President, and I will stand behind him in his leadership.' That was Root the international lawyer.

"In the submarine matter, they appear to reveal the

[264]

wisdom of hindsight. From the outset, they assert, they would have made the German Emperor keenly aware of the American spirit. Of course, the German Emperor was sitting up nights trying to analyse the American spirit. They would have prevented the sinking of the *Lusitania*. Ample warning, they cry!—warning given through an advertisement in a New York paper immediately before the vessel sailed! One would have sent for the German Ambassador! Another would have seized German ships which enjoy the courtesy of our harbours! What would England have said to the holding up of one of her government vessels because of a newspaper advertisement? What would Germany have said if the merchant marine of her citizens had been seized? Such vapouring is childish!

"There is no part of the foreign policy which they do not attack, and yet many matters pertaining to it are still under negotiation. How amazing, then, it is that their candidate should have proclaimed that he would not discuss the recent exploits of the German submarines near our own coast because he might embarrass the Administration. How consistent this is and how difficult to explain, except on the theory that what he conceives to be a present problem should not be mentioned by him for fear he might be asked to say what he would do about it—a thing he dreads apparently above all things.

"What is his foreign programme? You have a right to know. He tells you he will not meddle with things that do not concern us. Does anybody propose the contrary? He does say that we will not merely talk about the rights of small states but will observe them. Is this not the Democratic policy which he attempts to appropriate?

Does he succeed in convincing you that any alternative to the President's course might have been effectively attempted except one involving bluster and perhaps force? What conclusion can you draw from the utterances of their candidate and of his trusted lieutenants?

"Mr. Roosevelt, whom Mr. Hughes endorses by telegram, tells us that Mr. Hughes must be elected and that there must be a direct reversal of the policy of the President. This administration, 'these false servants of the people,' he shrieks, 'have taught the people to enjoy soft ease and swollen wealth.' This, incidentally, reveals his interesting conception of who the people are. Certainly, the people cannot be the masses of the United States; for they are not conscious of enjoying 'soft ease or swollen wealth.'

"What would constitute a direct reversal of the policy of the President? Have you not a right, in these grave issues, to know the specifications? If these men get into power and are men of conscience, they must make a change. In what direction, they do not reveal. . . .

"They tell us that you have been humiliated, that 'the conscience of the people has been seared,' that 'ignominious infamy' has been heaped upon the nation. Is it true? Are you conscious of humiliation and dishonour? Are your consciences seared? Are these gentlemen better judges of the honour of the American nation than you are, or more ready to vindicate it? They tell us that each belligerent despises us. For what? Must it not be in the last analysis because we are not at war on its side? How quickly the enthusiasm and admiration of any one of them for us would manifest themselves if we should join

[266]

"The partisan critics and the belligerents may despise you for not wanting war, if they wish, but this is your country. The war raging abroad is not your war. You are vitally interested in many of its issues, but you are not responsible for it. Your will in these matters should pre; vail, and on these foreign issues you have a clear right to a specific statement from the opposition and to express your will on their proposal. The present policy is morally right, and the conscience of the people is clear. 'No man is so well informed or wise who can, without wicked presumption, impose on a hundred million people his opinion of the right and wrong of the European war and found a policy on it.'

"What do they offer you in any direction? What specific thing does the Republican platform propose? I recall one: the proposal in favour of woman suffrage by state action; and it their candidate has cast aside. Nor in the speech of acceptance of their candidate can you find any specific recommendation on any controversial matter. The only issue which he has succeeded in partially retaining, the eight-hour issue—the strike issue— has arisen since he resigned to save the country. . . .

"Is there not general surprise and disappointment over Mr. Hughes? Did you not expect from him a clear and specific announcement of issues and proposals, and are you not entitled to it? Only one thing is clear: The whole programme of the Republican leaders is this—anything to beat Wilson. They are bent on trying to get into power by pursuing the course of least danger, by taking the least chance of offending anybody. They are pursuing the policy of 'stalling,' of trying to back into power, as it were, to get the support of people whom they would offend if they declared their purpose. Was the President not right in asserting that they cannot go in any direction for the reason that they would have to go in many directions at the same time? They assume that, if the people are not informed, there will be votes to place them in power. This is not complimentary to the American voters. They cannot be fooled on everything all the time.

"Really, how can they make a programme? Whom will they satisfy? How can there be an effective adjustment of affairs between Mr. Roosevelt and Mr. Hughes, between Mr. Roosevelt and Mr. Taft, Mr. Gifford Pinchot and Senator Smoot, Mr. Raymond Robbins and Senator Warren, Mr. William Allen White and Mr. Penrose, and the belligerent pro-Ally and the equally belligerent pro-German? Contemplate their candidate's plight! Are you not reminded of the chameleon? You remember the experiment of the man who placed it first on a piece of red cloth and it turned red; on a piece of green cloth and it turned green; on a piece of yellow cloth and it turned yellow; on a piece of blue cloth and it turned blue; and then on a piece of plaid and it was paralyzed. Mr. Hughes has the impossible task of attempting 'to coördinate the incongruous' or to harmonize the contradictory and irreconcilable. What can the country expect from a party with such elements and such leaders? I have sympathy for the great rank and file of the Republican party. They are as patriotic and as honest as other American citizens. But I am concerned with those in positions of leadership. Their party split and went on the rocks before 1912. It is more motley and irreconcilable to-day. . . .

"What about his associates? The present more unmanageable aggregation is in the hands of the same old leaders. The men who controlled the Republican Convention of 1912 controlled the Republican Convention of 1916, and are in immediate control of the candidate's campaign. If the Republicans should capture the Senate these same men will control it. What is their programme? Where are they going? You know what the Democrats have done and in what direction they are headed. Have you any doubt where the reactionary Republican leaders are headed? Do they not remind you of the darkey whose friend met him and asked: 'Whar yo' gwine?' He replied: 'I'm not gwine nowhar. I done been whar I gwine.' The Republican party under these leaders has been where it is going, has only one aspiration, and that is to go back to where it was, to the good old days of government by special interests, to the days of Mark Hanna. . . .

"Woodrow Wilson quickly dispersed the lobby and rid the executive and legislative offices of the government of the presence of gentlemen who attempt to use 'influence instead of argument.' I recall my own experience during the first weeks in Washington. How difficult it was to transact business without interference—without the nuisance of the presence of the attorneys of special interests! And I recall that, after the notice of their activities was issued to the American people by the President, I have been able each day to attend to my duties without interference. If the American people could fully realize just what this means, 80 per cent. of them would vote to return Woodrow Wilson to the White House. He has declined pressure to sacrifice money and men in Mexico, secured the revision of the tariff without dictation, and given the nation a sound banking system. These things indicate one reason why Woodrow Wilson is hated. He cannot be controlled. . . .

"I have appealed to you as to a jury. I have presented the case. You know the record, and now, may I ask what is your estimate of the man who, under the American people to whom he has appealed, is primarily responsible for what has occurred?

"Is there any great business enterprise anywhere on earth that would for a moment dream of displacing a manager who had done as well by it as Woodrow Wilson has by this nation? From just and fair-minded, intelligent men, there can be but one answer, and I confidently expect an overwhelming verdict of approval from the voters of this nation the seventh day of November."

APPENDIX II

WHY WE WENT TO WAR*

I. SUBMARINE WARFARE AND THE PRUSSIAN AUTOCRACY

WHY is the United States at war with Germany? Why all this preparation, expense, and jeopardy of thousands of American lives? Are we fighting the battles of England, France, Italy, and Russia? Are we in the war to pull the chestnuts of the Allies out of the fire? Are we fighting to help them recover lost territory or to acquire new possessions? Why do we fight at all? Why not employ peaceful means? Why not negotiate?

These questions are now being asked not infrequently, especially by German propagandists, by a few disloyal natives, and by some unintelligent and unpatriotic pacifists. Such people imagine that the time is opportune. They imagine that many Americans are astounded and resentful over the prospect of enormous expenditures, burdens of taxation, and sacrifice of life. They assume that there is, or will be, a reaction; that the people have short memories. They place reliance on the fact that the scene of conflict is remote, that our people cannot appreciate that a defensive war can be waged by forces at a distance, and that aggressive action may be in the highest degree defensive.

*Statements prepared in June, 1917, for the Committee on Public Information.

The main answer to these enemies of America within and without is simple. We are at war with Germany primarily to assert and to defend our rights, to make good our claim that we are a free nation, entitled to exercise rights long recognized by all the nations of the world, to exercise these rights without restraint or dictation from the Prussian autocracy and militarists, to have the kind of institutions we wish, and to live the kind of life we have determined to live. We are at war with Germany because Germany made war on us; sank our ships, and killed our citizens who were going about their proper business in places where they had a right to be, travelling as they had a right to travel. We either had to fight or keep our citizens and ships from the seas around England, France, and Italy, or to have our ships sunk and our people killed.

We did not make this war. Germany made war on America, and only after exercising great patience and enduring grievous wrongs did we formally declare this to be a fact. For more than two years Germany had committed hostile acts against our sovereignty, destroying the property and lives of our citizens, acts which, if committed by any smaller power or power nearer home, would have led to a quick demand from our people for a belligerent response. By turns, as it suited Germany's needs, she was apologetic and contemptuous, conciliatory and dictatorial, full of promises and heedless of them, finally repudiating her most solemn obligations. In the meantime, while we were extending hospitality to her diplomats here and representing her abroad, she was carrying on a hostile propaganda within our own borders as well as abroad, promoting plots to destroy our plants, and attempting to sow dissension among our people. Recall the history of our negotiations with Germany, of our attempts to secure justice by diplomatic, peaceful means.

February 4, 1915, Germany declared that on and after February 18, 1915, she would regard the waters around Great Britain and Ireland, including the Channel, as a war zone, and that "every enemy merchant ship would be destroyed without possibility of avoiding danger to crew and passengers." She pointed out that it would not always be possible to prevent neutral vessels from becoming victims of submarine attack. This action was without the colour of justification in international law. Her only legitimate course was to declare and to effect a blockade and then, having done so, to intercept enemy vessels, discriminating between enemy and neutral vessels, enemy and neutral cargoes, in the case of neutral ships captured to take to prize courts only those carrying contraband, to sink vessels only in extraordinary circumstances, and in every case to give safety to crews and passengers and to preserve all papers of ships sunk or captured. Because of the Allied fleets, it was impossible for Germany to do these things by the use of instruments heretofore employed. She could attempt them only with a new device—the submarine.

Unquestionably, new conditions of war had arisen and new means of waging it had come into existence; and just as it was recognized that fleets could not be held to a close blockade of ports, the old three-mile blockade, so it was tacitly admitted that a submarine could not be expected to capture and take a ship into port, but might sink it, provided it practised visit and search for purposes of discrimination, safeguarded the lives of crew and passen-

[273]

gers and therefore gave ample warning to vessels and did not sink them in places or under conditions in which non-combatants could not secure safety. These things, under international law, it was necessary that Germany have her submarine commanders do, or that she set aside international law and make necessity the only law, make law to suit herself and the desperate conditions into which she had brought herself by her own aggressive action.

The justification Germany attempted to give was that England had declined to respect in full the Declaration of London, had extended unnecessarily the list of contraband, had brought unfair pressure on neutrals, had declared the North Sea a seat of war, and was warring, not only on the military forces of Germany, but on the whole civilian population as well. She ignored the fact that England and her allies had fleets which, by the use of practices recognized by law, could maintain a blockade and which up to this time they have maintained without sinking ships or killing non-combatants. Germany could not do these things and had no right to whine because the Allies could. She is certainly the last nation in the world to demand that only military forces be considered as involved in the war. For centuries, Prussia had recognized clearly, more clearly than any other government, that a whole nation makes war, had proceeded early to organize herself on that basis, and had gone out to extend and had repeatedly succeeded in extending her possessions by force against laws of right and morality. Her tender consideration for the civilian population, and her view of the extent to which it should be exempted from the pressure and horrors of war are amply illustrated by her dealings in Belgium, northern France, Poland, Serbia, and on the high seas. Certainly, Germany ought to have thought of England's fleet and the possibility of being cut off before she so recklessly embarked in war. She did not establish, and has not yet established, even an approximately effective blockade. She impertinently warned neutrals to keep their citizens off merchant vessels and out of the war zone. Neutral citizens had, and have, a perfect right to travel on unarmed or even defensively armed enemy merchant vessels and to go where they please on the high seas. To have acceded to such insolent dictation from Germany would have amounted to a waiver of international law and right and to the doing of an unneutral act against the Allies, just as would compliance with the suggestion made by Germany on February 16th and frequently repeated, that neutrals cease to ship arms and munitions to the Allies. Germany knew that neutrals had a perfect right to do this. She herself had exercised the same right more than once. She knew the dealers in this country would have filled munitions orders for her and that it was no fault of ours that she could not secure them. These things, too, she ought to have thought of before she provoked hostilities.

On February 11th, this government replied, contesting Germany's position and warning her that it would hold her to a strict accountability and take every necessary step to safeguard American lives and property and to secure a full enjoyment of their rights on the high seas.

March 12, 1915, the Allies issued a decree in which they declared that it was necessary to prevent merchandise from reaching Germany directly or through neutrals. They, however, asserted in taking this step that they would not follow Germany in her cruel and barbarous

[275]

methods, and would not in their intention endanger neutral vessels or the lives of non-combatants; that they would act in strict conformity with the laws of humanity. On March 28th, a German submarine sank the *Falaba*, drowning an American citizen; on May 1st, the *Gulflight*, drowning two American citizens; and on May 7th, the *Lusitania*, drowning 114.

These acts were followed by a protest from this government on May 13th in which a demand was made for disavowal of the action of the commander of the submarine in sinking the *Lusitania* and for reparation. This government informed Germany that it would omit no word or act necessary to the performance of its sacred duty of maintaining the rights of the United States and of its citizens and of safeguarding their free exercise. On May 28th, Germany replied, placing the responsibility for the sinking of the *Lusitania* on Great Britain and the British shipping company, asserting that the *Lusitania* was an auxiliary cruiser, which was false; that it was armed, which was equally false; and that the company permitted it to carry munitions, which it had a right to do. On the 1st of June, the German Government asserted that the attack on the *Gulflight* was an unfortunate accident, that the submarine commander was in no wise to blame, and expressed regret and stated that it would pay damages.

On the 9th of June, the government of the United States replied to Germany's *Lusitania* note, denying the statements, as to the character of the *Lusitania* and as to her armament, asserting that it was sunk without warning, solemnly renewed its representations, and asked assurances that American ships and the lives of American citizens be not put in jeopardy. A month later, Germany answered, saying that she was compelled to meet the British blockade, and that if her submarine commander had practised visit and search, the submarine would have been destroyed. She cynically added that in any event it was to have been expected that a mighty ship like the *Lusitania* would remain above the water long enough for its passengers to get off. The sinking of this ship, she hypocritically represented, revealed with horrible clearness to what jeopardy of human lives the manner of conducting war employed by her adversaries led. American ships, she promised, would not be hindered from their legitimate business, and lives on neutral vessels would not be jeopardized. This was promise number one. She decreed that neutral vessels must be properly marked, sufficient notice be given in advance, and a guaranty be furnished that they would not carry contraband. She impudently informed us that she would agree to a proposal to increase by instalments the number of vessels available for the passenger service by placing a reasonable number of neutral ships under the American flag. She informed us that American citizens did not need to travel to Europe on enemy vessels and that she was merely following England's example in declaring a part of the high seas an area of war. In her singular psychology, a mere declaration by her was to be given the same regard and weight as an established fact. With her lack of a sense of humour, she apparently could see no difference between an effective blockade maintained by England and a paper blockade announced by her. Accidents suffered by neutrals on enemy ships in such an area could not be judged differently from those suffered in a war zone on land. If this country could not secure a sufficient number

[277]

of neutral ships, then the German Government would permit it to place four enemy vessels under its flag.

Of course, the Secretary of State answered that Germany's reply was unsatisfactory. It did not indicate how the principles of international law and humanity could be applied. It proposed a partial suspension of them, which in effect set them aside. This government noted Germany's assurance, made once more, as to the freedom of the seas, that the character and cargoes of merchant vessels would be first determined and that lives of non-combatants would not be jeopardized. The United States demanded the disavowal of the fact of the commander of the submarine, and reparation for injuries. It renewed the warning to Germany and advised her that the repetition of such an act against the rights of the United States affecting her citizens would be regarded as deliberately unfriendly.

Less than a month after this definite representation, Ambassador Page sent notice from London of the sinking of the *Arabic*, with a loss of three American lives. Five days later, the German Ambassador expressed the hope that the United States would await full information before acting, and asserted that, if American lives were lost, it was not in accordance with the intention of the German Government. A week later, he gave this assurance: "Liners will not be sunk by our submarines without warning and without safety of non-combatants provided that they do not try to escape or offer resistance." This was promise number two. He added that this policy was decided upon by his government before the *Arabic* was sunk. This was followed, on September 7th, by word from the German Government through Ambassador

[278]

Gerard that the *Arabic* was sunk because it planned to attack the submarine; that the government could not admit indemnity even if the commander was mistaken; and that if he was, the government would be willing to submit the case to The Hague. On the fourteenth, after receiving the facts, Mr. Lansing wrote that the *Arabic* was not warned and did not try to ram the submarine. On October 5th, Bernstorff replied that the German Government rules had been made so stringent that no repetition of the *Arabic* case was possible, admitted the validity of the evidence against the *Arabic's* attempt to ram the submarine, expressed regret at the occurrence, disavowed the act, and offered indemnity. This was promise number three.

On January 7, 1916, the German Ambassador gave notice that German submarines in the Mediterranean would destroy any vessels, passenger as well as freight, but only after the safety of passengers and crew had been assured. Three months later, Germany reopened the whole subject, rehashing the old arguments, and, with obvious insincerity, expressed the conviction that the United States would appreciate her point of view. Germany was evidently getting ready to break all her promises.

On March 27th, the State Department sent Ambassador Gerard word that there was much evidence that the Channel passenger steamer *Sussex* was sunk by a torpedo, March 24th, with 328 passengers on board. It asked for information concerning the following ships which, with Americans on board, were sunk: The *Englishman*, the *Manchester Guardian*, the *Eagle Point*, and the *Berwindale*, all sunk within a comparatively short time. The German

Government replied on April 11th, saying either that it did not have sufficient information to form an opinion, or that it was doubtful if the sinking was traceable to a submarine, or that the ship attempted to escape. It asserted that the *Sussex* was not torpedoed, and frivolously represented that the German commander made a sketch of a vessel torpedoed at the time in question and that this sketch did not look like the picture of the *Sussex* in the London *Graphic*. If, however, the commander was mistaken, Germany would be willing to submit the case to The Hague. In other words, she made a false statement about the matter and agreed that if her statement was proven to be false she would arbitrate. Within a week, this government replied that the *Sussex* was torpedoed; that this was not an isolated case; that it was clear Germany had made indiscriminate destruction a deliberate policy, contrary to assurances given again and again; that the United States had been willing to wait till the course of Germany was susceptible of only one interpretation; and that that time had been reached. It added: "Unless the Imperial German Government should now immediately declare in effect an abandonment of its recent methods of submarine warfare against passenger and freight carrying vessels the government of the United States can have no choice but to sever diplomatic relations with the German Empire altogether." The next day the President addressed the Congress to the same effect.

On May 4th, Germany replied that she was alive to the possibility that the *Sussex* was torpedoed, admitting, in effect, that she was caught in having made a false statement. Her commanders, she asserted, had orders to conduct warfare in accordance with visit and search except in the case of enemy trade with enemy ships in the war zone. As to these she gave no assurance and claimed that she had never given any. She regretted that the United States did not extend the same sympathy to the German civilian population that it did to the victims of submarine warfare. However, she was willing to go the limit: "In accordance with the principles of law German submarines will exercise visit and search before sinking merchant vessels recognized by law if they do not attempt to escape or resist." This was promise number four. The United States, however, must make England restore the freedom of the seas; that is, make her surrender her naval advantage. If she did not succeed, then Germany would be facing a new situation. The United States replied, expressing satisfaction that Germany had abandoned her indiscriminate destruction of merchant vessels and her expectation that there would be a scrupulous execution of the altered policy. She could not even discuss the suggestion that respect by Germany for the rights of the United States should depend on the conduct of any other government affecting the rights of neutrals. Responsibility in such matters was absolute, not relative.

In the latter part of the year there were rumours that Germany would make suggestions concerning peace. It was suspected that her action would be insincere and would be intended to affect the public sentiment of neutrals, especially that of a portion of the population of the United States. On December 12th, the German Chancellor indicated that Germany might be willing to discuss peace. A few days later, the President sent substantially identical notes to the powers, suggesting the desirability of a statement of terms on the basis of which they would be willing to discuss peace. This thought, of course, had long been in the President's mind and had no connection with the utterances of the German Chancellor. Germany replied, declining to state terms and proposing direct negotiations. On January 13, 1917, England and France complied with the suggestion of the President and stated their terms.

Germany's insincerity was made clear. She was posing as a victor and wished to enter into peace negotiations only provided she was regarded as a victor and on the basis of her retention of conquered possessions. Previously her preparations, including her submarine fleet, had not been matured. She drew the negotiations out interminably to gain time. It was also now made obvious that her aim in proposing peace was to create a favourable attitude among certain parts of the American people, to throw the responsibility on the Allies for prolonging the war, and to lay a predicate for her policy of submarine ruthlessness.

On January 31st, on the pretext of acknowledging receipt of the President's address to the Senate, Germany expressed regret that the attitude of the Allies, their lust for conquest, made peace impossible. This, she proclaimed, created a new situation, to which reference was made in a former note, and called for a decision. That decision was nothing less than to violate all her solemn pledges, to extend the submarine zone to Great Britain, France, and Italy, and to sink all ships. She was confident that this action would lead to a speedy termination of the war and would be understood by the United States. As a favour to this country, she would permit it to send one steamer a week each way to a particular port, Falmouth. She fixed the day for arrival, Sunday, and the day for departure, Wednesday. The ship must be striped with three stripes each a meter wide, white and red alternating, and a guaranty must be given that it carry no contraband.

The President promptly executed his warning to Germany, severing diplomatic relations with the German Empire on February 3d. Immediately the President laid the matter before Congress and informed it of his action. American ships, however, remained in port as they arrived, as did those of other neutrals, and Germany was achieving her ends by menace. On the same day, the *Housatonic*, an American steamer, was sunk, and on February 13th the *Lyman M. Law*. It was obvious that a further step must be taken, or this country would be impotent and would be playing into the hands of the Prussian autocrats. Therefore, on February 26th the President asked Congress for authority to arm merchant vessels and even then said that war, if it came, could come only by the act of Germany.

In the period from February 26th to April 2d, six American ships were sunk with loss of many lives. Ships of other neutrals were destroyed and Americans were murdered. In this whole period, 226 American citizens, many of them women and children, were killed. Armed neutrality obviously was ineffective. The country was experiencing all the disadvantages of war without any of the rights or effectiveness of a belligerent. Only one alternative was left.

On April 2d the President appeared before Congress and recommended that a state of war be declared against the

German Government. The Congress accepted the recommendation by a vote of 373 to 50 in the House of Representatives and 82 to 6 in the Senate.

If we had not accepted the challenge of the war-mad, desperate, dictatorial, contemptuous, hypocritical, and mediæval Prussian militarists, we would have had to admit that we were not a free nation, that we preferred peace at any price and were interested only in the fleshpots. This country either had to swallow its own words, abdicate its position as a free sovereign power, concede that it had no rights except those which Germany accorded it, hold its citizens and ships away from Europe, or to recognize the plain fact that Germany was acting in a hostile manner against it, fight to defend its rights, fight for humanity and the cause of civilization and free peoples everywhere, joining its power with the other free nations of the world to put an end to autocratic and brute force. There was one choice we could not make—we were incapable of making. We could not "choose the path of submission and suffer the most sacred rights of our nation and our people to be ignored or violated."

Does not this review make it plain what it would mean to the world if Germany should win, and if free, democratic, law-supporting nations like Great Britain and France were destroyed, if Europe should fall under the domination of Germany, headed by the Prussian military autocrats who know no right except might, who believe that small and peace-loving nations have no standing, and who attach no sanctity to a pledge, no matter how solemn? If Prussian militarism should be permitted to dominate, then the Anglo-Saxon fight for free institutions and liberty, persisting from Runnymede to Yorktown, its

[284]

fight against the absolute rights of kings and barons, with its Magna Charta, its Bill of Rights, its Declaration of Independence, and the heroic fight of the French people for liberty, would have been made in vain. Has it not become patent that Prussia is the last great stronghold of feudal absolutism; that in fighting Prussian autocracy the modern nations are truly assisting the Germans, who are only in part conscious of their servitude, to gain what England, France, and America have had for generations; and that we are surely finally about to make the world safe for democracy and humanity?

II. THE PRUSSIAN MILITARY AUTOCRACY

What is this Prussian military autocracy against which is arrayed four fifths of the world? How has such an influence persisted in a nation which many have regarded as foremost in science, in sociology, and in some respects in community living? Does it really exist? Many Americans find difficulty in believing that there is such a force to-day in Germany. This is natural. They have, for the most part, until recently, thought almost exclusively in terms of German art, education, science, including medicine, and industry. For many generations Americans went to school in Germany. German university training was considered almost a prerequisite for academic advancement. German industry was known to be making giant strides. Germany was assumed to stand for the maximum of efficiency in everything. It was the home of science, the final expression of modernism.

In respect to all these things, the world's impressions contained a large amount of error. Germany has never been supreme in science. In discovery, in creative science, and in invention she has lagged behind England and France and has been inferior to this country. Her peculiar merit has been that she has made a system of science, organized it back of industry and especially back of those industries which are fundamental to military pursuits, and has applied it intelligently and persistently. Especially in applied chemistry has her achievement been marked. In industry her chief performance has been to organize it through every possible form of state aid or support. Prussia in particular has been highly organized at the top. She is really a great public corporation for military and industrial purposes. She is a feudal estate writ large and, as such, well administered. She has been overorganized and organized on an unsound basis; and there is truth in the assertion that much of her dissatisfaction with pre-war conditions was due to the unwholesomeness of her economic situation. In a measure she was trying to lift herself by her bootstraps. She was strong at the top and weak at the bottom. Taking it by and large, Prussia is not and never has been as efficient as the United States or Great Britain. These have been insufficiently organized at the top, but they have been immensely strong in their foundations; and what organization they have had has been in the main for peace and not for war.

Americans, even those who travel and read much, have not concerned themselves deeply about foreign political institutions. They have taken note of what lay on the surface and have not always carefully examined it. They have observed that German cities are orderly and clean, that Germany is a confederation, and that suffrage for the

Reichstag is universal. It was not unnatural for them hastily to assume that German institutions are modern, as her science is, and that they were therefore democratic. It is not uncommon for people to be deceived by names and appearances, especially in politics.

To understand Germany politically, we must examine her history and fix our attention on Prussia. There are two Germanies to-day: Modern Germany, Germany of the masses, kindly, orderly, and industrious; political Germany, governmental Germany, mediæval, absolutist, militarist, aggressive. The latter is passing; the former is the Germany of to-morrow.

About the time of the discovery of America, the Hohenzollern family ruled over an insignificant tract surrounding the village of Berlin. In 1611, its power was extended by the union of the Mark of Brandenburg and the Duchy of Prussia. In 1640 a strong character, Frederick William, came into power. He exercised despotic rule, but put his house in order and developed a relatively strong standing army with which to make further headway by force, as opportunity might offer. In 1688, the date of the Restoration in England, and the beginning of her orderly constitutional government, Frederick the Third, an ambitious individual, became head of the house. His title was Elector of Brandenburg and Duke of Prussia. He was anxious for recognition—for the title of king. The War of Spanish Succession was about to begin. His overlord, the Holy Roman Emperor, needed assistance. Frederick was prepared to trade and promised the aid of his army in exchange for the title of Elector of Brandenburg and King of Prussia. This he secured in 1701. Here was the first phase of the contact with Austria, the last of which is seen in our own day in the complete sub-ordination of Austrian to Prussian influence.

In 1713, a violent, brutish person, Frederick William the First, began to reign. Like his ancestors, he kept his eye on the main chance, husbanded his resources, and added to his army, which at his death numbered 80,000, an immense trained force for that day and time. He, too, was ready by force to add to his patrimony at the expense of any convenient neighbour. It was left to his successor to make use of what he had prepared. In 1740 the Emperor of Austria, Charles the Sixth, the last of the male line of Hapsburgs, died. He had bound the leading powers by solemn pledge to recognize as his successor his daughter, Maria Theresa. Frederick, the Great Frederick, promptly gave Maria Theresa strong assurance of friendship and support, having it in mind at the very time to commit a crime against her. He suddenly moved his army against her province of Silesia, and after eight years of desperate warfare appropriated it. He at least made no pretence of virtue, and is reported to have said: "Ambition, interest, and the desire of making people talk about me carried the day and I decided for war."

Prussia was defeated and humiliated by Napoleon in a quick campaign in 1806, but the liberal movements of the period scarcely affected her. She bided her time and laid her plans. Her next considerable advance was made in 1864, when she induced Austria to join her in taking Schleswig and Holstein from Denmark. Austria received Holstein; and in 1866 Prussia picked a quarrel with her and quickly vanquished her, appropriating Holstein and annexing Hanover, Hesse, Nassau, and Frankfort, which had taken sides with Austria. Thus she rounded out her territory. When the Prussian Parliament protested that force was not a sufficient justification for what had been done to Denmark, Bismarck replied: "Our right is the right of the German nation to exist, to breathe, to unite." The claim of a place in the sun, the doctrine of necessity, and the right of might are not of recent appearance in Prussian history. They have been the outstanding characteristics of her thinking and practice since she emerged from mediæval obscurity.

The next step was the crushing of France in 1870–71, the annexation of Alsace-Lorraine, and the imposition of Prussian leadership on Germany under the guise of a confederation. No wonder Bernhardi wrote: "The lessons of history confirm the view that wars which have been deliberately provoked by far-seeing statesmen have had the happiest results." No wonder Prussia believes that a great army is the corner stone of her well-being as a nation and that war is a positive good if it succeeds.

So Prussia has come to dominate Germany. She now seeks to dominate the whole of Central Europe and a part of Asia; and if she gains what she wants in this war, she will persistently lay her plans for the next great aggressive move.

Prussia is Germany. She has three fifths the area and five eighths the population. The German Empire is a federation only in name. Bismarck's aim was to make Prussia supreme in Germany and Germany supreme in Europe. He knew how to do the job. This is the underlying fact: Prussia is Germany, and Prussia politically is feudal. In such a system, sovereignty is the private right of rulers. The prince may deal with his people as private individuals do with their lands. Recently, we had a clear

[289]

practical illustration of this in Germany. The ruler of Waldeck got into debt. He could not raise the money to equip his army. He therefore sold his rights, his possessions, and his peoples to the King of Prussia and went to Italy to live on his income. The people exist for the government and not the government for the people. Frederick William was not joking when he wrote: "Salvation belongs to the Lord and everything else is my affair"; or again, "We are lord and king and can do what we will." Neither was the present Kaiser when he asserted: "We Hohenzollerns take our crown from God alone and to God alone are we responsible in the fulfilment of our duty." He was simply revealing the true inwardness of his royal mediæval mind and of Prussian politics, speaking from the background of centuries of feudal traditions. Prussia is a feudal state. It practises paternalism on a large scale in this modern day, as did the Duchy of Prussia on a small scale centuries ago. It asserts the divine right of the king and of aristocrats to rule.

Prussian governmental arrangements to-day of all grades are the legal expression of the economic interests and domination of the large landowners and of their recent allies, the great industrial leaders. Feudal estates still persist in the kingdom, with their principal strongholds in East Prussia, Posen, and Pomerania. In Prussia 31 per cent. of the land is in estates of more than 250 acres, large holdings for central and western Europe; in Posen 55 per cent. and in Pomerania 52 per cent. The average size of 8,365 estates in East Prussia is 1,132 acres; of 2,793 in Pomerania, 1,380 acres. Many of these are very large and are owned by descendants of feudal lords. The great landholder, the junker, is an individualist independent, militaristic, conservative, in favour of armed strength, condescending to inferiors, with a feeling for power, and with the instincts of a soldier, a supporter of monarchy as long as monarchy has a strong arm and supports him and his interests. At first, the junker fought the new industrial class, but a reconciliation was effected, and recently the powerful leaders of the two classes have coöperated. The caste system prevails everywhere. Society is stratified and the individual in each stratum is trained for his duties in his particular sphere. Education and society, as well as the army, are organized on this basis; and there is no small truth in the witticism that "every Prussian is satisfied because he has somebody below him to kick." Royalty, the junkers, and the great industrial leaders run Prussia, and Prussia runs Germany.

"But," it may be asked, "how can this be? The Reichstag is the popular house of the Imperial Parliament, and its members are elected by universal suffrage. Is this not conclusive evidence of popular participation and control?" Let us see. In the first place, the electoral districts for the Reichstag have not been changed since they were formed in 1871, when Germany was dominantly agricultural, rural. The great increase in population has been in the cities, and these are the homes of the Liberals and Radicals. It would have been dangerous to change the districts. This would have given the Liberals and Radicals full representation. To-day Berlin should have at least twenty representatives, and elects only eight. The number of voters in agricultural districts equal to those of Berlin returned forty-eight members. In 1907 twenty seats were won by the Conservatives with an average vote of 10,500, and six by Socialists with an average vote of 77,500. The average vote for all Socialist members was 67,000 and for all Conservatives 25,680. The significance of this can readily be seen when it is stated that out of 12,260,000 votes cast in 1912, 1,662,000 were National Liberal, 1,996,000 represented the strength of the Centre party, 1,126,000 that of the Conservative, and 5,750,000 that of the Socialist and Radical parties.

But in reality this makes very little difference. The Reichstag is little more than a debating society. It was intended to be nothing more, to be a "sop" to the progressives. Its powers are great on paper, but exceedingly small in reality. It has the constitutional function of passing on the budget, but the principal revenue laws are permanent. The Reichstag can neither increase nor decrease the schedules, nor make any change in the existing situation unless the King of Prussia wishes it. This comes about in this way: The Bundesrath is the upper house of the Imperial Parliament. Its members are delegates from the various states, representing several state governments and not the people. They vote according to instructions, and one member may cast the vote for any delegation. Fourteen members can defeat any measure, and the Government of Prussia—that is, the King of Prussia—controls twenty votes.

The Reichstag does not really initiate legislation. Important measures are first discussed in the Bundesrath, then they go to the Reichstag, and back to the Bundesrath for approval. The initiative for the most part comes from the Chancellor, who is also Prime Minister of Prussia. The ruler, as Emperor, may instruct the Chancellor to prepare a measure, as King he may order him to introduce it and may direct amendments to be made and prevent changes. As Emperor he may promulgate the law, and as King he administers it in Prussia. There is no imperial cabinet. The Chancellor is the only minister. The other heads of departments act independently of each other but under the supervision of the Chancellor. The Chancellor is not in the slightest degree responsible to Parliament or to the people, but solely to the Emperor, and this by reason of the fact that he is also Prime Minister of Prussia and represents the King of Prussia in the Bundesrath. When Von Bethmann-Hollweg became Chancellor he emphasized this fact, asserting, "I do not serve Parliament," adding that he would not play the rôle of servant of the people's representatives. The Chancellor does not sit in the Reichstag as such, but as Prussian delegate to the Bundesrath, all members of which have a right to sit in the lower house and there to support their measures.

Of the 397 members of the Reichstag, Prussia sends 236. The body can be dissolved at any time by the Bundesrath, with the consent of the Emperor. This power has been used effectively three times to break down the resistance of the Reichstag: in 1878, when it refused to pass the bill to suppress the Socialists; in 1887, when it would not agree to fix the size of the army for seven years; and in 1893, when it declined to change the military system. In each case, the new body did what the government demanded. Since the principal financial arrangements are matters of standing law, if the Reichstag refuses to pass a new budget increasing allowances, or passes one reducing them, the government can be carried on on the old basis without any action on the part of Parliament.

We find a parallel for this in English history in the days of the Stuarts.

The upper house, the Bundesrath, consists of 61 instructed delegates, usually officers of state, frequently ministers, voting under instruction and appointed without fixed tenure. Of this number, Prussia controls twenty. This body and the King of Prussia dominate the Reichstag.

By the constitution, the presidency of the confederation belongs to the King of Prussia. He appoints the Chancellor and most other officers, directs foreign affairs, commands the army and navy of the whole empire, inspects and disposes of troops, appoints all officers whose commands include the contingent of the state, and the selection of all general officers is subject to his approval. Prussian military regulations are enforced throughout the empire. The Emperor declares defensive war, and there is no authority to determine what war is defensive and what offensive. Bismarck's principal aim was to create a powerful military state. All the world knows how well he succeeded.

Many of the foregoing important direct powers belong to the Emperor. Obviously larger powers accrue to him by virtue of the fact that he is King of Prussia and that Prussia is Germany. The Emperor, as such, has no material rights in legislation, no authority to appoint or to disapprove laws, yet he constantly does these things. He has no power to issue decrees, yet here also, says Zorn, the German publicist, "The monarchical principle, without legal provisions, and indeed contrary to them, has forced recognition. . . . We, Wilhelm, by grace of God, German Emperor, order with the consent of the

[294]

Bundesrath." Again Zorn says, "The inspiring forces of the world's history and the magnitude of his actual power have given the Emperor a position wholly different from what was legally intended and places him on a par with monarchical emperors—we see how formally inspired and even constitutional provisions lose their force in face of the constraining necessities of national life." So the Prussianizing of Germany is complete. There is normally a higher law in Germany than the constitution. That law is the law of necessity or might.

Let us take a more intimate view of Prussia and ascertain what are the arrangements of this dominant member, what chance is afforded the people for expression. Take her Parliament, the Landtag. What does it represent? Is there a government responsible to the people? The Landtag has two chambers, the house of lords and lower house. The former is a mediæval body composed of princes of royal blood, members who are independent princes of the Holy Roman Empire, or hereditary members designated at will by the King, and others designated by him at will or on nomination of landholders. The King can control it at any time by appointing new members. It now has a membership of 300, one third hereditary nobles with large estates—junkers—and one third dominated by landholders—junkers. It is a class assembly, far removed from the people.

The lower house is composed of members elected indirectly by an electoral body. One member is selected in each district. The electoral body is selected in this fashion: One third of it is designated by the large tax-payers who pay the first third of the taxes, one third by those who pay the second third of the taxes, and the remainder by the rest of the voters. From 3 to 5 per cent. of the voters choose one third of the electors; from 10 to 12 per cent. a third, or about 15 per cent. of the voters choose 213 of the electors. In 2,200 districts one man selects a third of the electors. In 1908 the number of votes cast was 2,215,000. The Social Democrats, with 601,000 votes, elected seven members. They should have secured 105. The Conservatives, with 356,000 votes, elected 152. They were entitled to 62. The Clericals, with 502,000 votes, won 104 seats, instead of 88, their proper number. The Liberal party secured 28 instead of 40. In East Prussia the number of inhabitants to a representative was 63,000; in Berlin 170,000. Berlin secured nine votes and should have had 24. One fourth the population in agricultural districts selected 161 members; one fourth in the cities elected 41. Remember, too, that the ballot is not secret, and that pressure is consistently brought to bear on the lower-class voter. The municipal councils are selected in the same way. The classes rule.

The province is the highest subdivision of Prussia. Its chief executive is appointed by the King. Its legislative body is not elected by the people but by legislative bodies of the next lowest subdivisions, the circles and the municipalities. The president may veto the action of the body if it goes beyond its jurisdiction. Its measures must be approved by the King, who may dissolve it at will.

The circle is the chief local subdivision. Its principal administrative officer is appointed by the president of the province. The members of its legislative body, the Kreistag, are divided between the cities and the rural districts, not more than one half to the cities. The mem-

[296]

bers assigned to the cities are not elected directly by the
people, but by the municipal assemblies, which represent
property.   The rural members are divided into two equal
groups: The great landowner and large taxpayer of the
rural community elect half; the other half are elected
indirectly by a body composed (1) of those who pay a
small tax, (2) of proprietors of manors, and (3) of electors
selected by rural communal assemblies.   To be a voter
even for one of these electors who shares the doubtful
privilege of joining larger taxpayers and owners of
mediæval manors in selecting half the rural members of
the local assembly the other half of which is controlled
absolutely by wealth, the individual himself must be a
small taxpayer.   This is certainly placing the individual,
the man, politically at the vanishing point.

There is no manhood suffrage in Prussia, in Germany,
where it counts for anything.   It does not count for anything so far as the Reichstag is concerned.   Evidently,
in Prussia, it is non-existent.   Landowners and men of
industrial standing are strongly intrenched.   They have
dug themselves in and made their administrative and
legislative trenches of reinforced concrete.   The junker is
not only on top; he is pyramided, Autocracy, absolutism,
is supreme.

Granted that the ruling class does its paternalistic job
for the people as well as such a job can be done by a few
for the many, at best it must be inadequately done; for no
part of the people can understand the needs of all the
people and satisfy them as well as all the people can.
Granted, I say, that the job, for a paternalistic job, is well
done, still the essential nature of the régime is unsound,
unmodern, mediæval, and out of tune with modern tenden-

cies. This governing class, believing in expansion by armed force, provoked war, violated the neutrality of Belgium, directed the submarine campaign, sweeping aside international law and custom built up through the centuries, sinking great passenger and freight vessels like the *Lusitania*, the *Arabic*, and the *Sussex*, slaughtering women and children. It ordered the deportation of Belgian civilians, planned and executed the campaign of spying and violence in this and other neutral countries, and directed the submarine negotiations with all its evasions, cynicism, and duplicity, again and again making solemn promises, constantly violating them, and, finally, brazenly breaking their most solemn pledge to a great, patient, peaceful power. These people entertain the mediæval notion that one nation's prosperity is another nation's menace, that it is to the interest and happiness of one nation to dominate other peoples and areas, and that small nations have no rights which strong nations need to protect and have no justification for existence.

The President told us that, for a little while, he was unable to believe that such things would, in fact, be done by any government as have been done by Germany during this war. It was difficult for the American people to credit it. It is yet difficult to believe that the great masses of the German people, if they were fully informed, would sanction it. It is only through a knowledge of the character and mediæval ideals of the few who dominate Prussia and Germany that we can begin to understand it. With such information, we can more easily appreciate what was in the President's mind when he said: "We have no quarrel with the German people. . . . It was not upon their impulse that their government acted in entering the war. It was not with their previous knowledge or approval. It was a war determined upon as wars used to be determined upon in the old unhappy days when peoples nowhere were consulted by their rulers and wars were provoked and waged in the interests of dynasties or by little groups of ambitious men who were accustomed to use their fellow men as tools. . . . A steadfast concert for peace can never be maintained except by a partnership of democratic nations. No autocratic government could be trusted to keep faith within it and to observe its covenants. . . . We are accepting this challenge of hostile purposes because we know that in such a government, following such methods, we can never have a friend; and that in the presence of its organized power, always lying in wait to accomplish we know not what purpose, there can be no assured security for the democratic governments of the world. We are now about to accept the gage of battle with the natural foe of liberty and shall, if necessary, spend the whole force of the nation to check and nullify its pretensions and power. We are glad now that we see the facts with no veil of false pretences about them, to fight thus for the ultimate peace of the world and for the liberty of its peoples, the German people included; for the rights of nations great and small and the privilege of men everywhere to choose their way of living and obedience." Was he not clearly right when he asserted in his answer to His Holiness the Pope: "We cannot take the word of the present rulers of Germany as a guaranty of anything that is to endure unless explicitly supported by such conclusive evidence of the will and purpose of the German people themselves as the other peoples of the world would be justified in accepting.

[299]

Without such guaranties, treaties of settlement, agreements for disarmament, covenants to set up arbitration in the place of force, territorial adjustments, reconstitutions of small nations, if made with the German Government, no man, no nation can depend on. We must await some new evidence of the purposes of the great peoples of the Central Powers"?

APPENDIX III

STEPS TO VICTORY*

THIS is a day of big things, of staggering questions, of unprecedented undertakings, and of incredible happenings. It is almost true that the incredible is the only believable and the impossible the only attainable. One cannot be shocked or surprised or diffident any more. Therefore, I entertained with complacency the suggestion that I meet you here and discuss the theme of the evening.

It is unnecessary for me to confess that I am not wise enough to dispose of this subject to your satisfaction or to my own. I am not equal to it; but I have the satisfaction of knowing that all of you are not, and even all of us at this head table are not. Perhaps a unified allied council may discover, indicate, and take all the necessary steps, but I am reasonably certain that nothing less will suffice.

There is one thing I like about the subject. It evidences the right spirit, the requisite determination, and a commendable and justifiable optimism. It assumes that we must and shall win, and win without undue delay. It implies that, having put our hand to the plough, we will not turn back, or even look back, and that we refuse to entertain the suggestion of possible failure.

---

*This subject was suggested by the officers of the Economic Club of New York City, and it will be noted that the address was delivered before the club on December 6, 1917.

FIRST AND LAST STEPS TO EARLY VICTORY

A clear, fixed, unalterable purpose to attain the ends we had in mind in accepting Germany's challenge, based on a thorough appreciation of the meaning of this struggle and a willingness to make all necessary sacrifices, I regard as the first and last most essential steps to an early victory. This war is a test of the spirit of nations, even more than of their material resources and strength. The issue of it depends on the relative intelligence, moral qualities, and attitude of the people engaged. Never before has there been a war which so effectively demanded the highest exhibition of intellectual capacity and also the unfaltering display of will power and moral courage. No more important duty confronts the leaders of thought everywhere than that of informing the national mind and of sustaining and confirming its spirit and purpose. Public opinion must be anchored, and the motive for terrible sacrifices be firmly fixed. No matter what the difficulties, no matter what the seriousness of the strain, there can be no faltering. Civilization cannot afford to entertain the thought of defeat. The challenge of Germany went to the roots of freedom and of national existence. There is no halfway house. Proposals to parley with an unbeaten enemy, who proclaims himself victor, indicate nothing less than a willingness to admit defeat. They spell relaxation of effort and demoralization. They mean assent to Prussia's century-old policy of extending her mediæval patrimony by force and of gradually imposing her will on the world. They mean nothing more than a truce, "a truce with usury," a mere interruption of the strain and its assumption at a later day with interest compounded. All history points to this conclusion.

THE PACIFIST A CONSTANT MENACE

No greater dangers confront democracy than those which may arise from drifting, from mental or moral fatigue, from confused advice, from entertaining dangerous fallacies, and indulging in friendly optimistic sentiments toward an implacable enemy. These are the dangers which extreme partisanship and pacifism breed. The pacifist is a constant menace; the mere partisan a criminal; and especially obnoxious is the vain omniscient partisan to whom the future is an open book, who alternately rags the public and assaults its enemies, censures everybody and everything except himself, indulges in irresponsible criticisms and misrepresentations, causing unwarranted popular confusion and unrest, generally giving aid and comfort to the enemy. These things must be abated through force of an educated public opinion if possible, but, in any event, must be abated.

PEOPLE WILLING TO MAKE SACRIFICES

The indications to date are numerous that the people of this nation as a whole have an effective appreciation of the meaning of the struggle and a willingness to make large sacrifices. It is only necessary to go among them to realize the strength of their sentiments and determination. Everywhere I have been impressed with the sound sense and fine spirit of the great majority of our citizens. In respect to patriotic attitude, I have confirmed my suspicion that there were no geographical boundaries to it, no North, no South, no East, no West, and that no section has a monopoly of intelligence or patriotism.

We may also judge conclusively the state of mind of the

people by the action of Congress. This body represents public opinion. It does not adopt and pursue a course of action if the people are hostile. In six months, that body has given to popular sentiment an expression without parallel in parliamentary annals. The first great step toward winning this war was taken when the President of the United States, on April 2d, in advising Congress to declare the existence of a state of war with Germany, pointed out what war would involve and demand. The striking thing about that historic address was not so much the advice it contained, momentous as that was, but rather the clear perception it revealed of the magnitude of the task before the nation.

RESPONSE OF CONGRESS

The response of Congress was prompt and adequate. It authorized and directed the President to employ the entire naval and military forces of the Union and pledged to the government all the resources of the nation to bring the conflict to a successful termination. The task of making good this pledge was entered upon and discharged in such manner as to startle many at home and to amaze even foreigners who had become habituated to prodigious operations.

THE FEDERAL RESERVE LAW AND THE WAR

Clearly Congress for the time being had taken the necessary steps to make good its pledge of placing the resources of the country at the disposal of the government. At the same time, it created or authorized the creation of essential administrative agencies. In respect to administrative

[304]

agencies, important developments had already taken place. Most striking and significant of all was the enactment of the Federal reserve law and the creation of the Reserve Board and banks. This action obviously was taken without suspicion that the world was on the verge of war and that we would soon be involved. It was taken to insure better banking conditions in time of peace, and especially to enable us to weather financial storms. Before the reserve act was passed, the nation, as you well know, had no adequate banking system. Its financial arrangements had never been able to withstand strain either in peace or in war. In each of our considerable struggles, we had promptly suspended specie payments, with all its attendant disabilities and burdens. But now, after four years of world financial strain, such as no financier dreamed it possible for the world to bear—I might say for six years, because there was a world-wide financial chill for at least two years before 1914, due to apprehension of war and to the undoubted financial preparations made by the Central Powers—after this long strain and the shock of the last six months, our finances are sound and we are proceeding in orderly fashion. For this reason, and because of our obligation to extend liberal credits, it is not extravagant to say that no greater contribution to the winning of this war has been or will be made than through the passage of the Federal Reserve Act in 1913 and the successful establishment of the system well in advance of trouble.

ORGANIZATION OF CONSULTING BOARDS

Steps toward preparedness in respect to other highly essential interests were taken much before war was declared. Their significance was not grasped by the public at the time. For the most part, they have been over-looked. Pursuant to an act of Congress of March 3, 1915, two years before the war, the President appointed the National Advisory Committee for Aëronautics, composed of the most eminent students of the subject. In connection with the work of this committee, and in part through its labours, has been developed our enormous aviation programme and expansion. Likewise, during the summer of 1915, the Secretary of the Navy organized the admirable Naval Consulting Board with Edison as chairman and 2 representatives elected by each of 11 great engineering and scientific societies. Furthermore, on September 7, 1916, after a long and unfortunate delay caused by unintelligent opposition, the shipping act was passed, creating a board with large powers and appropriating fifty millions of dollars for the construction, purchase, charter, and operation of merchant vessels suitable for naval auxiliaries in time of war. This was the beginning of the present huge shipbuilding programme whose speedy execution is of paramount importance.

THE COUNCIL OF NATIONAL DEFENCE

But that is not all in the way ot early preparedness. On August 29, 1916, the Council of National Defence, consisting of six heads of departments and of an advisory commission of seven, nominated by the council and appointed by the President, was created. The council was charged with the duty of mobilizing military and naval resources, studying the location, utilization, and coördination of railroads, waterways, and highways, increase of domestic production for civil and military purposes, the furnishing of requisite information to manufacturers, and the creation of relations which would render possible the immediate concentration of national resources.

The creation of the Council of National Defence was not the result of sudden inspiration. It was directly suggested by the activities of two very important groups of individuals. In March, 1916, a committee from the five great medical and surgical associations, having an aggregate membership of from 70,000 to 100,000, was formed. It met in Chicago on April 14, 1916, and tendered to the President the services of the medical men of the nation. In March, also, representatives of five engineering organizations, with a membership of 35,000, met in New York and formulated a plan to make an inventory of the country's producing and manufacturing resources. The thought and purposes of these two bodies were brought to the attention of the President, and their consideration resulted in recommendations for the creation of the Council of National Defence.

NEW AGENCIES CREATED

Thus, a number of months before war was declared, agencies had been created covering, at least in outline, many of the essential new activities. Seven of these of peculiar importance had begun to find themselves and to chart their course. I refer to the Shipping Board, the aviation, the medical, the manufacturing, the transportation, the munitions, and the labour committees. When war came these bodies greatly speeded up their work. Others were created—among them, the Food Administration, the Fuel Administration, the War Trade Council, the War Trade Board, and the War Industries Board.

THE WAR INDUSTRIES BOARD

The last is of unique importance, and yet its work is little understood. Its members are the direct representatives of the government and of the public interest. The tasks of the board are stupendous. It acts as a clearing house for the war industries' needs of the government, determines the most effective ways of meeting them, the best means of increasing production (including the creation of new facilities), the priority of public needs and also of transportation. It considers price factors, the labour aspects of industrial operations, large purchases of commodities where market values are greatly affected, and makes appropriate recommendations to the Secretaries of War and Navy. Judge Lovett is in immediate charge of priorities, Mr. Baruch of raw materials, and Mr. Brookings of finished products. These three constitute a commission for the approval of purchases by the Allies in this country from credits made through the Secretary of the Treasury. I need only remind you of the items of the appropriations for supplies, ordnance, and other things to impress you with the magnitude of the board's task. Its machinery is not yet perfect, but it is working, and I am sure that no step will be omitted to make it as nearly adequate as possible. If a better scheme can be devised, it should be promptly adopted. It is obviously of the highest importance that the resources of the nation, made available by Congress, should be administered with the utmost skill and effectiveness.

MOBILIZATION OF TALENT

No machinery is of great value unless it is properly manned. The right sort of men is the first requisite of any kind of successful enterprise. I believe this requisite has been satisfied and that the Nation is mobilizing for this emergency additional men of as high character and fine talent as it possesses. Where so many are involved special mention is invidious, and I cite the names of the following merely as samples: Willard, Gompers, Baruch, Rosenwald, Coffin, Martin, and Godfrey; Hoover, Garfield, Vanderlip, Davison, Vauclain; McCormick, Thomas D. Jones, Lovett, Brookings, and Frayne; Dr. Anna Shaw, Mrs. Philip Moore, Mrs. Cowles, Mrs. Catt, Miss Wetmore, Mrs. Lamar, Mrs. Funk, Mrs. McCormick, and Miss Nestor; and Doctors Simpson, Crile, Janeway, Flexner, Vaughn, Mayo, and Welch—all fine types of American citizenship, only a few of the hundreds working in their respective spheres in the nation and in the states, having no selfish end to serve, working with an eye single to the public interest and to the winning of this war, giving freely their services in as fine spirit as the nation ever witnessed, revealing the real strength of democracy.

So much, and perhaps more than enough, as to the Congressional pledge of resources and the creation of machinery. Let us turn to other matters which I am sure you have in mind. I know you are asking what is being accomplished. What are the results? Obviously, some of them it would be inadvisable to indicate. Others I can only hint at. For the most part they have been detailed to the public through one agency or another from time to time. I shall try to summarize.

THE ARMY CANTONMENTS

The nation has to-day in all branches of its military services under arms and in training more than 1,800,000 men, some in France, some on the ocean, and others in camps or at their posts of duty at home. Approximately ten and a half millions of men have been enlisted in the regular army, incorporated in the National Guard, or registered under the draft act. Those registered but not yet called out are being classified on the basis of national need. Rapid headway has been made in training subordinate officers, and the gigantic undertaking of providing suitable quarters or camps for the men in training has practically been finished. The nation now has 35 army cantonments—16 for the National Army, 16 for the National Guard, 2 at points of embarkation, and 1 for the Quartermasters' Training School—all complete in respect to buildings or tents, lighting, sanitary arrangements, and temporary roads. The National Army cantonments were completed within the time set by the General Staff. What this involved cannot easily be set forth. It entailed the selection of sites, the planning of buildings, the securing of responsible contractors, the mobilization of labor, the assembling of materials, and the construction of modern hospitals and roads. These camps alone cover 150,000 acres and called for the use of 75,000 carloads of materials, including 500,000,000 feet of lumber. Their cost was approximately $128,000,000. The work was begun June 15th and the finishing touches were put on by December 1st. In addition 16 canvas camps for the National Guard were completed at a cost of approximately $48,000,000. Thus local habitations were quickly provided for the new army, superior in respects to ventilation and conveniences to the best practice of Europe.

Five instrumentalities or factors highly necessary for victory, it may be asserted without hesitation, are destroyers—the enemies of the submarine—airplanes, ships, medical service, and food. What of these?

TO FIGHT THE SUBMARINE

Of the first, the torpedo-boat destroyers, all I may say is that the construction programme of the navy contemplates 787 ships of all types, at an estimated cost of $1,150,000,000, including additional destroyers costing $350,000,000. The latter are to be of uniform standard model, large and fast. Some are to be built within 9 months and all within 18 months. This vast and urgent undertaking required a great extension of building facilities, and as private capital was unable or unwilling to make the extensions, the government had to do so. When completed, these plants belong to the nation. I may add that these destroyers will require thousands of men to man them, but that they are being trained, and when the vessels are completed the crews will be ready.

CONTROL OF THE AIR

The work for the control of the air grows apace. Of the great aviation training fields, 17 in number, 2 are old, 1 is rebuilding, 7 were practically completed by September 1st, and 7 others will be finished within two weeks. In addition there are in operation to-day at leading universities 10 ground schools giving preparatory instruction in flying. Finishing courses are being given to our students in most of the Allied countries, and more than 30 experienced foreign air service veterans have been loaned to us for duty in Washington and elsewhere. The building programme calls for 20,000 machines. It will be expedited by reason of a great and interesting achievement, that of a standardized engine, something which no European nation has developed even after three and a half years of war. This accomplishment is in line with the best American traditions and was made with unique speed. What standardization of the engine and of its parts means in respect to speed and quantitative production, in repairs and economy of materials, need not be dwelt upon. It has been estimated that the service, when in full strength, will require a full force of 110,000 officers and enlisted men, an army greater than our regular military force of a few months ago.

PROVIDING MORE SHIPS

All agree that the enemy submarine must be destroyed. In the meantime, shipping sunk by them must be replaced. England must not be starved. Supplies to all the Allies must go forward without interruption. Our own troops must be transported and provided with everything essential for effectiveness and comfort, and domestic transportation of men and commodities be maintained and greatly increased. Furthermore, commodities must be brought here from many distant places. Therefore we must have ships, more ships, at once. Nothing more urgent. How is this matter proceeding? In the first place, the Shipping Board, on August 3d, commandeered 426 vessels either in course of construction for domestic or foreign account or contracted for, with a tonnage of more than 3,000,000. Thirty-three of these ships, with a tonnage of 257,000, have been completed and released. Ex-German and Austrian ships with a capacity of 750,000 tons have been taken over for government use. The Fleet Corporation has contracted for 948 vessels with a total tonnage of 5,056,000, of which 375, with a tonnage of one and a third million, are wooden; 58, with a tonnage of 270,000, are composite; and 515, with a capacity of 3,500,000, are steel. All these ships have an aggregate tonnage of 8,835,000, or nearly a million and a half tons greater than that of the regular merchant marine of the nation in 1916. Contracts for 610,000 tons additional are pending. The total building programme calls for more than 10,000,000 tons, and it is proposed that a considerable part of it shall be executed by the end of 1918. The nature of this task may be more easily appreciated when it is remembered that the construction in the United States for 1916 did not exceed 400,000 tons, and that the average for the five years preceding was 350,000. At present, there are 100 yards building ships, exclusive of 20 building the commandeered vessels, and of these 100, 70 are new. The policy of standardization has been pursued and five classes of ships have been adopted.

MEDICAL ORGANIZATION

I have already referred to the preliminary steps toward medical organization. Further action was promptly taken. An inventory was made of the medical resources of the nation, of doctors, nurses, and others who could be called by the Surgeon General, and of hospitals and supplies. Courses in modern military medicine and surgery for third- and fourth-year students were formulated and adopted by 75 of the 95 medical schools in January, 1917.

It was known that 80 per cent. of the instruments used in this country were made in Germany. It was necessary to develop their production here, and to facilitate this, the first essential step was to introduce standardization, to resort to staple articles. More liberal standards were authorized, and the variety of types was greatly reduced. Instead of scores of kinds of scissors, a dozen were agreed upon. Instead of many sorts of needles, forceps, and retractors, two, three, or four types were adopted. Manufacturers were given priority of materials and consequently full military orders will be delivered in less than eight months. It is illuminating that one concern, taking its chances, had manufactured according to specifications, by the time it was awarded a contract, enough material to require 10 carloads of lumber for packing. This was the result of the efforts of 75 of the most eminent medical specialists of the nation, working with the military staff in contact with 250 leading manufacturers.

The peace strength of the medical forces of the army was 531 and of the navy 480. Now the Surgeon General of the army has in his regular force and in the new enrollment of physicians actually accepting commissions 16,432, a number sufficient for an army of two and one third millions and a dental force of 3,441, adequate for an army of 3,400,000. The navy now has 1,795 medical officers, a number in excess of present needs. The Red Cross has enrolled 15,000 trained nurses, organized 48 base hospitals with 9,600 doctors, nurses, and enlisted men, 16 hospital units with smaller staffs to supplement the work of the base hospitals, is furnishing supplies to 35 hospitals of all sorts in France, and since May has raised more than $100,000,000.

[314]

ORGANIZATION OF AGRICULTURE

What shall I say about the organization of agriculture for the production of food, clothing, and other materials? It is unnecessary to dwell upon the need of an adequate supply of food for the civilians and soldiers of this nation and also for those of the nations with whom we are associated. When we entered the war, this country was and had been facing an unsatisfactory situation in respect to its supply of foods and feedstuffs. The production in 1916 of the leading cereals was comparatively low, aggregating 4.8 billions of bushels as against 6 for 1915, 5 for 1914, and 4.9 for the five-year average. The wheat crop had been strikingly small, and it was certain that, on account of adverse weather conditions, the output for 1917 would be greatly curtailed. The situation was no better in respect to other conspicuously important commodities, such as potatoes and meats. The need of action was urgent and the appeal for direction insistent. The nation looked for guidance primarily to the Federal department and to the state agencies which it had so liberally supported for many years. It was a matter of great good fortune that the nation had had the foresight, generations before, in another time of national stress, in 1862, to lay soundly the foundations of agriculture. In respect to agencies working for the improvement of rural life, the nation was prepared. In point of efficiency, personnel, and support it had establishments excelling those of any other three nations combined, and a great body of alert farmers who were capable of producing two or three times as much per unit of labour and capital as the farmers of Europe.

Steps were quickly taken to speed up production. In a two-day session at St. Louis, the trained agricultural officers of the country conceived and devised a programme of legislation and organization, the essential features of which have not been successfully questioned, and the substantial part of which has been enacted into law and set in operation. Initiative was not wanting in any section of the Union. Effective organizations quickly sprang up in all the states, and the services of experts everywhere immediately were made available. The response of the farmers was prompt and energetic. Weather conditions for the spring season were favourable and the results are that crop yields have been large and that the nation is able, not only to feed itself, but in considerable measure to supply the needs of those with whom we are coöperating.

That the farmers of the nation have generously responded to the appeals for increased production, and that much has been done to insure a large supply of foods and feedstuffs, justifies no let-down in their activities or in those of all agricultural agencies. On the contrary, even greater efforts must be put forth in the coming months, if we are to meet fully the civilian and military demands. There must be no break-down on the farms, no failure of foods, feedstuffs, or clothing. Especially must we have a more abundant supply of meats and fats to replenish the stores of the long-suffering Allies.

DIFFICULTIES CONFRONTING AGRICULTURE

Many difficulties confront the agricultural forces. Fertilizers are scarce, farm machinery has advanced in price, and transportation is burdened. To secure an adequate supply of labour everywhere will demand our best energies. Especially serious to the farmer is the task of retaining on his farms his regular year-round help. An army could not be raised without taking men from every field of activity, and it would have been unfair to any class to have proposed its complete exemption. The problem is a constructive one. Mere complaint is useless. Our aim is to secure even greater production from the labour on the farms; and it must be attained. Farmers in the same community must coöperate with one another more actively. Forms of labour not heretofore regularly or fully utilized must be employed, and plans for the shifting of labour from places where the load has passed to communities where there is urgent need must be perfected. Whether more drastic action will be needed remains to be seen. General conscription would present many difficulties. Several things are certain. Relatively nonessential industries must be prepared to release labour and capital for essential undertakings; and, either through state or Federal action, any able-bodied individuals who can but will not do useful work must be pressed into the service.

UNITY IN ACTION

It would appear, then, that the courses we must follow, the directions we must take to win victory, have been indicated and charted. While corrections and extensions will be made, I am confident that the important essential steps have been taken and that success will come rather through steadying and expediting these than through any novel enterprises. Unquestionably the coördination of all domestic agencies, governmental and private, must be perfected so that the Nation may direct its great energies and resources with full effect against the enemy. I am equally confident that the most "practicable co-operation in counsel and action with the governments now at war with Germany" must be secured. What specific form that shall take I am not wise enough to suggest; but that there must be unity of policy and effort, the wisest utilization of our combined resources, and the most skilful strategical handling of military and naval forces on the basis of international and not of particularistic interests under an unhampered, common control seems to admit of no manner of doubt. Mistakes may be made even then, but not so many or as fateful ones as may be made if there are as many programmes as there are nations involved. Campaigns cannot otherwise be successfully conducted and battles won against great powers having the advantage of interior lines and of a single, absolute directing mind. The solution of this problem is the present pressing need for victory now or later.

FINANCIAL BURDEN BORNE NOW

Furthermore, we must keep in the forefront of our thinking the imperative necessity for maintaining the integrity and soundness of our finances. To this end, it seems to me the people of the nation, after adjustments have been made to changed industrial conditions and to the new revenue legislation, must be prepared increasingly to meet the burdens of this war through just and equitable taxation. If they can be convinced of the plain truth, that the easiest way temporarily and ultimately to bear the financial burdens of war is to meet them as they rise,

[318]

as largely as possible through taxation, the task will be relatively simple. This is a fact, but not an obvious one. Centuries of unsound traditions and many delusions stand in the way. There is the singular misapprehension that, by borrowing, the burden of waging a war to that extent can be shifted to future generations. If this were true, there would be no definable limit to the extent and variety of war the present generation could wage. The truth is that in a nation like ours, not borrowing abroad, whether control of wealth is secured through taxes on all or in part through loans from the few, the people pay for the war as it proceeds, and that if the books were closed at the end of the war, the nation would have paid for it. The iron, the steel, the coal, the clothing, the shoes, the lumber, the ammunition, the guns, and the ships secured by the government are used and destroyed at the time, and, for the most part, cannot later be enjoyed. By borrowing, a burden, it is true, is placed on the people after the war, but it is a burden of restitution. A credit relation is set up, and an obligation on the part of all is incurred to pay back with interest the wealth the nation has used. The main fact is that the wealth is taken and consumed by the nation at the time. The burden is borne while the war is on. As I see it, there are only two really plausible arguments that may be made for resorting mainly to loans— one a psychological argument, namely, that the people do not effectively appreciate the necessity for the war, and would be impatient or resentful; the other, a physical one, that it is difficult in time to devise an equitable measure, to administer it, and to secure revenue promptly. The former argument should appeal more strongly in an autocracy than in a democracy, and especially in one which so quickly perceived the justice and need of a conscription of men. The second applies with diminishing force as the war is prolonged and time is afforded for action.

PRODUCING AND SAVING

If it be true that the burden of war is actually borne at the time, then it follows that the capacity of a nation to wage war is measured by its ability to maintain production and especially to save—to abstain from luxuries, and to stop waste. Hence the importance of our many appeals in this direction.

And let us not be deluded by inflated reports of the rapid growth of our wealth into thinking that we can meet the burdens of this war without further increased production and economy. There is danger of this when figures come from responsible sources without proper interpretation and explanation. In such times as these, statements of wealth in terms of dollars may mean relatively little. The nation, for instance, has been informed that the value of the 1917 output of farm products is twenty-one billions of dollars, whatever that is—a sum equal to the total appropriations and authorizations made by Congress in its last session for war purposes. Newspapers have written editorials about it. We are told that no land ever before produced so great farm values, that it is providential that these blessings are heaped upon a worthy people, and that America has the will to place this unexampled treasure at the service of the world. These statements are true, and very misleading. The simple fact is that the actual volume of agricultural things produced, bushels of cereals, bales of cotton, number of hogs and sheep, and some other things, is smaller than in 1915, and that consumers simply generally get much less for a dollar. The same statement may be made in a measure as to the reported statistics of industrial production. It is highly important that these things be seen in the right light, and that they are not permitted to impair the motive for saving.

Now, taxes have this advantage over loans: They more directly enforce economy. It is true that, whether we part with our wealth through taxes or the loan of our savings, we shall have less to spend on ourselves, but it is not always true that we make our loans from our realized savings. Just there is the difficulty. To pay our subscription, we not infrequently resort to borrowing beyond our willingness to save, and thereby set in operation processes which may result in undue expansion of credit. Taxation, especially on consumption, more particularly on luxuries, tends more directly to enforce saving, to keep the general level of prices steady, to check investment in non-essential directions, and to release capital and labour for urgent needs. But, after all, large sums must be secured through loans. Borrowing in itself will not necessarily bring about an undue expansion of credit and an advance in prices. It may promote saving. It will do so if payments are made from funds on hand or with savings from current income. It is, therefore, of the first importance to the successful prosecution of the war that the disposition of the people to economize be stimulated. The conception of the war savings certificate plan was, for this purpose, a peculiarly happy one, and its promotion must receive the cordial support and indorsement of financial leaders everywhere.

PATRIOTISM AND PROFITS

That we have the physical resources to win this war, if they are properly conserved, I entertain no doubt; that we have these in larger measure than any other nation in the world is a matter of common knowledge. We have not yet fully realized the enormous power of the country. If in the 'sixties, when we were a simple, crude, undeveloped nation, doing things, relatively speaking, on an "ox-cart" basis, with the question yet undetermined whether we were to be one nation or two, we could wage the mightiest war up to that time and issue from it with unrivalled power, what can we not do to-day, with a united people and with immeasurably greater resources, if our spirit is right and our purpose is steadfast? Unless the descendants of the men who followed Grant and Lee are degenerate, there can be no question of the ultimate outcome. It is time for each individual to search his heart and to purge his mind and purpose of selfish motives and for each class in society to think in terms of the nation rather than in terms of its own interest. It is no time for any class to hug to its bosom the delusion that it possesses a monopoly of patriotism. Human nature is pretty evenly distributed, and no little selfishness manifests itself in every direction. Unfortunately, there are self-seekers in every group, men who assume the attitude that, if they are to make additional efforts to increase production or to serve the country, the nation must pay them the price. Their patriotism, it is implied, needs to be stimulated. This is impossible because there is no foundation to work upon. I have heard many manufacturers solemnly assert that if the government wished them to speed up their operations, to extend their plants, or to take additional trouble in any direction, it must guarantee to them an abnormally large profit in addition to the requisite allowance for amortization. One of them recently suggested to me that he was getting weary of the burdens he had assumed, and that if the government wished him to continue or to undertake new tasks, it would have to induce him to do so by permitting him greatly to increase his profits. What would he or others say of a soldier, of the man drafted into the army, who protested that for so much he would go to the seaboard, but if the government wished him to go abroad, it must stimulate him with a 25 per cent. increase in his pay, or, if he went to the front trenches, with 50 per cent?

In the words of the President, "Patriotism has nothing to do with profits in a case like this. Patriotism and profits ought never in the present circumstances be mentioned together. It is perfectly proper to discuss profits as a matter of business . . . but it would be absurd to discuss them as a motive for helping to serve and save our country. . . . In these days of our supreme trial, when we are sending hundreds of thousands of our young men across the seas to serve a great cause, no true man who stays behind to work for them and sustain them by his labour will ask himself what he is personally going to make out of that labour. No true patriot will permit himself to take toll of their heroism in money or seek to grow rich by the shedding of their blood."

THE INDIVIDUAL'S DUTY

I can conceive that each individual, no matter what class in society he belongs to or what service he renders, whether he be a manufacturer, a farmer, a labourer, a lawyer, a scientist, or a soldier, will take pains to see that he attains for himself and his operations the highest degree of efficiency and give the maximum service or product to the nation at the lowest cost consistent with efficient operation and effective standards of living; but it is inconceivable to me that any citizen who dares to call himself a patriot should aim to do less or to seek mere selfish advantage. It is obviously the duty of each civilian to reveal by his conduct the same standards of patriotism, devotion, and sacrifice, if necessary, either of life or property, that we expect from the men whom we send to the front directly to bear the brunt of battle. I am confident that it is in this spirit that most of the people of the nation are viewing their obligations and that the great body of public sentiment will permit no other attitude to manifest itself in those who are less right-minded. There can be no slacking, no turning back. The rights of the nation must be vindicated and its institutions preserved. Those who would keep the people of the world from going about their business in orderly and decent fashion must be taught a lesson, once for all. Guaranties that there shall be no recurrence of such a world calamity as the present must be enforced. A finish must be made once for all to all things feudal, humanity be safeguarded, democracy impregnably intrenched, and the lesson be forced home that the worthy and tolerable national aspiration is to have a clean national household from cellar to attic, and a durable and righteous peace must be secured, in accordance with the recent history-making declaration of the President, in itself a great step toward victory—a peace on the basis of reparation, justice, and security.

[324]

APPENDIX IV

ADDRESS DELIVERED AT FORT WORTH, TEXAS, IN MARCH, 1918

THERE is no man who has always regarded the prospect of engaging in a great war with greater reluctance or with greater repugnance than I have done during the whole of my life. There is no man more convinced than I that we could not have avoided doing so without national dishonour. I am fully alive to the fact that every nation which has ever engaged in any war has always invoked the sacred name of honour. Many a crime has been committed in its name. There are some being committed now. All the same, national honour is a reality, and any nation that disregards it is doomed."

These are not my words, but they might well be—they exactly express my views; and, if I may judge from your applause, they express yours also. They have a familiar ring and appeal to our deepest instincts and convictions. They are the words of the foremost champion of democracy in Great Britain, the present great Prime Minister, Mr. Lloyd George, and were uttered a short time after Great Britain entered the Great War.

Nine years ago, I had the singular good fortune to sit in the House of Commons and witness this great leader's struggle to carry the British people a few stages further along the road of democracy through his striking economic proposals; but, before his task was completed, he was compelled to turn aside from it, for the time being, to defend and safeguard the very foundations of democracy. To-day, we find him devoting all his energies to this new, unexpected, and more momentous undertaking, labouring valiantly to preserve democracy against the assaults of its last great foe, from the last great stronghold of autocracy and feudalism.

Now aligned with him and his European colleagues in this great struggle is the foremost spokesman of democracy in the world, our own President, Woodrow Wilson. How long and patiently he laboured to keep this nation at peace and to preserve its neutrality without sacrificing its honour is too well known to justify emphasis. Such patience and forbearance have never before been exhibited by the head of any great state. You do not need to be reminded of the bitter criticism to which he was subjected at home and abroad. You know that he yielded only when failure to act would have meant the sacrifice of every principle which the American people hold sacred and for which they have always been willing to fight, and would have involved the submission of this great nation to the dictation of an arrogant power.

I shall not offend your intelligence by entering into an extended exposition of the reasons which led this country into this war, or by attempting a detailed justification of its participation. Still, it is well to bear the record in mind and keenly to perceive the issues involved; for it is true, as someone has said, that the last word of the theory of war is that the strength of a nation in battle is measured by the hold which the causes and purposes of war have on the minds and hearts of the people. What is the record?

On February 4, 1915, Germany declared a war zone around Great Britain and said that every merchant ship would be destoyed without possibility of avoiding danger to crew and passengers. She pointed out that it would not always be possible to prevent neutral vessels from becoming victims of submarine attack.

This action was without the colour of justification in international law or practice. Germany's only legitimate course was to declare and effect a blockade and then, having done so, to intercept enemy vessels, discriminating between enemy and neutral vessels, enemy and neutral cargoes; and, in the case of neutral ships captured, to take to prize courts only those carrying contraband, and in every case to give safety to crews and passengers. Because of the Allied fleets, it was impossible for Germany to do these things by the use of instruments heretofore employed. She could attempt them only with a new device —the submarine. Unquestionably, new conditions of war had arisen and new means for waging it had come into existence; and such recognition of changed conditions as was consistent with international law and the laws of humanity was tacitly granted.

The justification Germany attempted to give was that England was using her fleet to the detriment of the whole civilian population of Germany. She should have thought of this possibility before she recklessly involved the civilized world in this catastrophe. She is certainly the last nation in the world to demand that only military forces be considered as involved in the war. For centuries, more clearly than any other nation, Prussia had recognized that a whole nation makes war, and had proceeded to organize herself on that basis. Her tender consideration for

[327]

civilian populations, and her view of the extent to which they should be exempted from the pressure and horrors of war are amply illustrated by her dealings in Belgium, northern France, Poland, Serbia, and on the high seas. Her representations had only one intention and that was to deceive the neutral nations of the world. She impertinently warned us to keep our citizens off merchant vessels, on which they had a right to be, and out of her war zone, into which they had a perfect right to go. To have acceded to such dictation from Germany would have amounted to a waiver of international law and right and to the doing of unneutral acts against the Allies. Our government protested.

Then came the sinking of ships, including the *Lusitania*, and the drowning of American citizens. You recall the false representations made by Germany. She asserted that the *Lusitania* was an auxiliary cruiser, which was false; that it was armed, which was equally false; and that the company permitted it to carry munitions, which it had a right to do. She cynically added that, in any event, a mighty ship like the *Lusitania* ought not to have sunk in twenty-one minutes. It ought to have remained afloat long enough for its passengers to get off. The sinking of this vessel, she hypocritically represented, revealed with horrible clearness to what jeopardy of human lives the manner of conducting war employed by her adversaries had led. But she promised that American ships would not be hindered from legitimate business and that lives on neutral vessels would not be jeopardized. This was promise number one. Next came the sinking of the *Arabic* and the promise of the German Government that liners would not be sunk by submarines without warning and without safety of non-combatants. This was promise number two. Later, she added that rules had been made so stringent that no repetition of the *Arabic* case was possible. This was promise number three. Then followed the torpedoing of the *Sussex* with 328 passengers on board; and many other merchantmen were sunk. The German Government first pretended that she had not torpedoed the *Sussex*. She frivolously represented that the commander had made a sketch of the vessel torpedoed at the time in question and that this sketch did not look like the picture of the *Sussex* in the London *Graphic !* She finally admitted in effect that she had made a false statement; but assured this country again that, in accordance with the principles of law, visit and search before sinking would be exercised in the case of merchant vessels recognized by law, if they did not attempt to escape. This was promise number four.

Early in 1917, the German Government suddenly repudiated all her solemn pledges and declared that she would extend the submarine zone and sink all merchant vessels. She insolently informed this country that she would permit it to send one steamer a week to a particular port. She fixed the day for arrival as Sunday and the day for departure as Wednesday. This ship had to be striped with three stripes a meter wide and a guarantee given that it carried no contraband.

"Keep your people at home," she ordered. "Tie up all your ships except one. Stripe it as I dictate; let it sail on the day I fix; send it to the port I designate. Tell your manufacturers to keep their products in their warehouses. Let your surplus foodstuffs go to waste. Tell your farmers to keep their millions of bales of cotton, their grain, and their meat at home till I order otherwise. Set aside international law and accept my law of necessity till I crush the great modern free states of Europe. Stand by till I finish with them and then maybe I will attend to you. Although our spies are operating among your people in Mexico, Japan, and elsewhere, even while you give hospitality to our ambassador, and although our agents are destroying your plants and our submarines are killing your citizens, stand aside. These things are necessary for our economic and military well-being. These are my orders. This is my law of necessity—I made it."

Such were the commands of the military overlords of Prussia to one hundred millions of free people, in defiance of every rule of international law and of every principle of humanity. They were the final expression of Prussian whim, the arrogant assertion of the law of necessity set up and interpreted exclusively by her, to be changed as she might see fit, the assertion of the supreme right of might. What would we do about it? What answer would we make?

What answer was there except one? Life is precious; but not at the sacrifice of everything that makes it worth while. National peace is desirable; but not at the cost of everything that makes a nation worth saving. No man worthy of the name of American citizen in such a situation could fail to exclaim with Patrick Henry: "Is life so dear or peace so sweet as to be purchased at the price of chains and slavery? Forbid it, Almighty God. I know not what course others may take, but as for me, give me liberty or give me death," or fail to say, with the Archbishop of York: "We must be free or die who speak the tongue that Shakespeare spoke and faith and morals hold that Milton held." What would Washington have said? And Jefferson, and Samuel Adams, and Andrew Jackson? What Lincoln and Davis? Lee and Grant? Sherman and Stonewall Jackson? What Albert Sidney Johnson, Hampton, Gordon, Wheeler, Sheridan, Hancock, and hosts of men who died that the nation might live? What did you say then? What do you say now? For my part, I would rather see this nation gloriously fail fighting for freedom with great England, heroic France, Italy, and Belgium, and see it pass from the pages of history than see it survive in the greatest ease and luxury submissive in any respect to the dictation of Germany.

So, at this late day, this stupid, wicked challenge came from the last great stronghold of feudalism in the world to the world's greatest free nation. It was the last of a series. It must be the last forever.

It had first been issued to little Serbia. You remember the circumstances. An Austrian prince had been slain in a neighbouring province stolen by Austria. The blame was fixed on Serbia. Demands which would have been unthinkable in connection with any of the great nations of the earth were made on her, touching the very roots of her sovereignty. England and Russia advised her to make every concession short of her independence. Serbia complied. She would press punishments for incitements against Austria, suppress demonstrations in educational institutions, remove officers proved to be guilty of acting against Austria, institute proceedings against persons suspected of being engaged in the plot, stop illicit traffic in arms, report her action to Austria, accept collaboration of Austrian officials to see that these things were done, and submit any doubtful matters to arbitration. But all this was without avail. It became clear, as Sir Edward Grey asserted, that Austria, backed by Germany, was not aiming at settlement or adjustment. She intended to crush a small state and to open the road to Bagdad. Serbia resisted, flung back two Austrian armies, and then, facing both Austria and Germany, paid for her love of liberty by martyrdom.

Russia mobilized to stop the outrage. Germany, knowing the conditions in Russia, was not afraid of her, but she was concerned about her great ally on the West. She turned to France and challenged her to state her intentions. France did not desire war. She was in her most pacific mood and unprepared, but she replied that a treaty with her was a sacred thing and that she would keep her word and preserve her honour. How she has done so, the whole world knows.

Belgium was next assaulted. She was informed by Germany that she would be invaded by France and could not repel the invaders, and that it was "necessary" that she should anticipate any hostile attack. Germany would feel the deepest regret if Belgium regarded as an act of hostility against herself the fact that Germany would be forced to enter Belgian territory! If Belgium maintained a friendly neutrality, Germany would guarantee her possessions. Should she oppose the German troops and throw obstacles in the way of their march, she would be compelled to consider Belgium as an enemy!

Belgium replied that France had pledged herself to respect Belgian neutrality. If France should fail to fulfil her obligation, she would be resisted. The treaties of 1839, confirmed by those of 1870, vouched for the independence of Belgium under the guarantee of powers, notably

[332]

of the government of Prussia. The attack on her independence would constitute a flagrant violation of international law and no strategic necessity could justify such violation. "The Belgian Government, if they were prepared to accept the proposals submitted to them, would sacrifice the honour of the nation and betray their duty toward Europe. Conscious of the part which Belgium has played, they refuse to believe that the independence of Belgium can only be preserved at the price of the violation of her neutrality." In short, the Belgian Government replied that she would respect her pledged faith and that Belgium "was a nation and not a military highway."

Great Britain was the next on the list. Germany attempted to seduce and deceive her and did not have sense enough to see that she was asking Great Britain to disregard and set aside her most sacred convictions and most deeply rooted habits, the very foundations of her national life, securely laid through the centuries. England had asked Germany and France to state their intentions with reference to Belgium. France had replied that she had pledged her faith, and that, of course, she would keep her word. Germany temporized. Finally, England fixed a limit of time. Her ambassador at Berlin was instructed to secure a definite answer. On the fourth of August, he saw the foreign minister, who stated that German troops had that morning entered Belgium, that they had to advance by the quickest and easiest way so as to be able to get well ahead with their operations and strike some decisive blow. The southern line had too few roads and too many strong fortresses. Rapidity of action was the great German asset. It was "necessary" for her to go through

Belgium. It was a matter of life and death. To get at great France she must destroy little Belgium and murder her women and children! It was "necessary"!

The English Ambassador remarked that this was very serious and he would see the Chancellor. The Chancellor was excited and harangued the Ambassador for twenty minutes, saying that England's action was terrible to a degree. Just for a word, "neutrality," which in war had so often been disregarded—just for a scrap of paper, Great Britain was going to make war on a kindred nation. It was like striking a man from behind while he was fighting for his life. He held Great Britain responsible for all the terrible events that might happen.

Nothing in history is finer than the reply of the British Ambassador. "If for strategical reasons it was a matter of life and death for Germany to advance through Belgium, violate her solemn pledge and the latter's neutrality, so it was a matter of life and death for the honour of Great Britain that she should keep her solemn engagements." "But at what a price!" exclaimed the Chancellor. "The fear of consequences," the Englishman replied, "could scarcely be regarded as an excuse for breaking solemn engagements." The German Chancellor, in his speech before the Reichstag the same day, announcing that German troops had occupied Luxembourg and invaded Belgium, admitted that it was contrary to the dictates of international law, but that the Germans were compelled to ride roughshod over legitimate interests of the governments of Luxembourg and of Belgium. "For the wrong which we are thus doing we will make reparation as soon as our military object is attained." In other words, to get at a strong nation, the German Government, on the

[334]

plea of necessity, deliberately made up her mind to wipe out a nation small in territory but great in spirit.

And then came our turn.

Even now these things sound incredible. Can you explain them on rational grounds, or on any theory of morals or justice? Is Germany simply crazy? Or is she merely four or five centuries behind the times, a belated exponent of a mediæval state of mind and of outworn doctrines? What is this fateful force which has so disturbed mankind and against which is arrayed four fifths of the world? How is it to be accounted for? What are its purposes?

To understand Germany politically, we must first of all fix our thoughts on Prussia and consider her history; for Prussia is Germany, having three fifths of her area and five eighths of her population. By slow degrees, Prussia has come to dominate all Germany. Prussia is Germany and also Austria, and now seeks immediately the control of the whole of Central Europe and part of Asia. If she gains what she wants in this war, she will again quietly lay her plans and prepare for the next great aggressive move.

About the time of the discovery of America, the Hohenzollern family ruled an insignificant tract surrounding the village of Berlin. In 1611, its power was extended by the Union of Brandenburg and the Duchy of Prussia. In 1640, when England was dealing with arbitrary force, giving the finishing blow to feudalism, uprooting the law of necessity, of whim, of divine right, cutting off the head of its king, Charles Stuart, a strong and forceful character assumed the direction of Prussia. He inaugurated a dynastic policy which has been relentlessly pursued to the present moment. He put his house in order, developed a strong standing army, and stood ready to expand his dominions by force, as opportunity might offer. In 1688, the date of the beginning of orderly constitutional government in England, a more ambitious individual, Frederick, became the head of the house. He was anxious for recognition, for the title of king. The war between his overlord, the Holy Roman Emperor, and Spain, was about to begin. The Emperor needed assistance. Frederick was prepared to trade and promised the aid of his army in exchange for the title of King of Prussia. This he secured in 1701, and this date marks the beginning of a series of steps which in our own day has led to the vassalage of Austria to Prussia. In 1713, a violent, brutish person, Frederick William the First, ascended the throne. Like his ancestors, he organized the whole nation, husbanded his resources, and developed an army of 80,000 men, an immense trained force for that day and time. He, too, stood ready to expand his mediæval estate by force at the expense of any convenient neighbour. It was left to his successor, Frederick, so-called "The Great," to make use of what had been prepared, to invoke the law of necessity, to make of a solemn obligation a scrap of paper, and, on a large scale, once more to "do the bandit stunt." In 1740 the Emperor of Austria, the last of the male line of Hapsburgs, died. He had bound the leading powers by solemn pledge to recognize as his successor his daughter, Maria Theresa, and to confirm her in her possessions. Frederick promptly gave Maria strong assurance of friendship and support, having it in mind at the very moment to commit a crime against her. Suddenly moving his army against her province of Silesia, after eight years of desperate warfare, he appropriated it.

Prussia was defeated and humiliated by Napoleon in 1806; but she bided her time and laid her plans. Her next considerable piece of robbery was in 1864, when she induced Austria to join her in taking Schleswig and Holstein from Denmark. She then turned upon Austria, took from her her part of the booty, and in addition annexed four of her considerable possessions. The Prussian parliament still had some conscience left and protested that force was not a sufficient justification for what had been done to Denmark. Bismarck replied: "Our right is the right of the German nation to exist, to breathe, and to unite." And so, at this early time, necessity as a rule of law and the right of might were formally announced as the guiding principles of this government.

The next step toward domination was the annexation of Alsace-Lorraine in 1871 and the imposition of Prussian leadership on Germany in the guise of a confederation. In these transactions, we plainly see the leading characteristic of Prussia as a government and the guiding principles of her politics. "Stand ready at all times with overwhelming force to take advantage of every opportunity and to secure control of peoples and territories by force." Is it any wonder that her writers hold that the lessons of history confirm the view that wars which have been deliberately provoked by far-seeing statesmen have had the happiest results? Is it surprising that the Emperor asserts that the German sword is his best protection, that a great army is the corner stone of his well-being, and that war is a positive good? Prussia believes that it is "necessary" for her welfare and happiness increasingly to dominate areas of the world by force and to subject people to her military and economic supremacy. To the ruling family, and to its immediate associates, Germany is a mediæval estate, to be extended by every conceivable device, without reference to equity or law.

To-day Germany's governmental arrangements of all grades are the legal expressions of the economic interests and domination of big landowners and of great industrial leaders. There is nowhere in the Empire any real recognition of the right of the great masses of the people effectively to participate in government. In the Imperial arrangements, the upper house is the controlling body, but it can do nothing without the assent of the King of Prussia, because he has a veto on its action. The lower house, elected by universal suffrage, is simply a sop to the masses. It is not even a free debating society. It has no initiative in legislation. If it does not do what the King of Prussia desires, he can carry on the government on the existing basis without its assent. If he wishes to extend his powers the Reichstag must assent or he will dissolve it; and in every case where it has differed from him and been dissolved, the new body has done his will.

In Prussia itself, which is the controlling force, in the legislative bodies from the highest to the lowest, the junker and the industrial magnates are intrenched. Less than 15 per cent. of the voters have the controlling voice in selecting the members of the Prussian Diet. There is no manhood suffrage in Prussia, in Germany, anywhere where it counts for anything. It does not count for anything in the Reichstag. In Prussia it is non-existent. The junker is not only on top; he is pyramided. Autocracy, absolution, culminating in the Kaiser, is supreme.

Since the formation of the Confederation, the Emperor's powers, instead of being restricted, have steadily expanded and, with or without legal sanction, constitutional restrictions have been thrown aside. "The monarchical principle," says a leading German publicist, "without legal provisions and, indeed, contrary to them, has forced recognition. The inspiring forces of the world's history and the magnitude of his actual powers have given the Emperor a position wholly different from what was legally intended. We see how even constitutional provisions lose their force in the face of constraining necessities of national life."

The state of mind of the ruling classes is hopelessly mediæval and out of harmony with the modern world. Witness its expression in the recent address of the Kaiser to his troops: "Remember that the German people are the Chosen of God. On me, the German Emperor, the Spirit of God has descended. I am His sword, His weapon, and His vicegerent. Woe to the disobedient and death to cowards and unbelievers." What blasphemy! The Spirit of God descending on the man who decorates naval commanders responsible for the drowning of hundreds of women and children! The Spirit of God descending on the man whose military commanders sanction the mutilation of children and the rape of women in Belgium, France, Serbia, and Poland!

Here we still see mediævalism stupidly strutting before the offended eyes of men and of God! And so it is that, in its final analysis, the great issue that has been joined is the issue between mediævalism and modernism, between the rule of necessity and might and the rule of right, between the rule of whim and the rule of law. We people of the modern world had thought that we had made an end to such things and freed ourselves from them for ever: that

England had given the finishing touch to the rule of divine right and of whim when she cut off the head of the Stuart; and that France had done the same when, two centuries later, she acted in similar drastic fashion. But we had been blind to the realities of central Europe and had failed to take note of the fact that modern means of transportation and electricity had made the Western world of our day much smaller than the Thirteen Colonies were a hundred years ago, when they proclaimed their independence.

We have discovered that there is truth in Jefferson's assertion that liberty is a tender plant and that, as it grows from more to more, it has to be watered by the blood of patriots. We have discovered that independence in this world is not a thing which can for all time be secured by what is done at a given place on a particular day. We have learned that the process of civilizing the world and of subjecting the disorderly to the rule of law is a slow one. There must be another Fourth of July for all the world, and we are now in the midst of making it good. But I verily believe that, when we this time set the world free from Germany, its independence will not again be seriously menaced; for Germany is its last great foe.

We are now engaged in this task. Will you complete it? Can you stand the test? It is "up to you." This is your fight and not merely that of the boys at the front. It is the fight of every man and woman in America. It means that all of us must be on our toes and pull together. This war is a test of the spirit of nations even more than of their material resources and strength. In the words of the Archbishop of York: "Force will fail unless there is moral conviction behind the nation," and every individual proclaims in historic language: "Here I stand; I can do no other. So help me God." A clear, fixed, unalterable purpose to attain the ends we had in mind in accepting Germany's challenge, I regard as the first and most essential step to victory. Never before has there been a war which so effectively demanded the highest exhibition of intellectual capacity and also the unfaltering display of will power and moral courage.

The way through this grim business is the only way out. There can be no turning back, no faltering, and no hesitation. This war will not be won by a miracle or by enchantment. The quickest way to win it, the cheapest way if you please, is to put into the struggle every ounce of our will, intelligence, and power as quickly as possible where it will be most effective.

It will not be won by the soap-box orators. It will not be won by professional pacifists. If the soap-box orators and professional pacifists could win a war against the Germans, the Russians would have been in Berlin long ago. There is only one man in the nation to whom we should look for guidance amidst the confusion of tongues, and his is the most potent figure in this field in the world.

This war will not be won by the omniscient, irresponsible critic or by pestiferous persons whose chief aim is to keep in the limelight. They rarely have enough sense to do constructive work, and like the beetle, mistake energy for efficiency. They simply add additional elements of confusion and unrest.

This war will not be won by the pin-headed politician who has his eye on the next election, or by the extreme partisan who alternately rags the public and assaults its enemies, criticizing everything and everybody except himself. He is afraid of nothing so much as he is of losing his office. He seeks to profit by "patrioteering" and omits no opportunity to hamper the President and the people.

This war will not be won by those individuals of loose, dispersed, and confused minds who preach a cult of internationalism and profess to see nothing in our life and institutions different from what they find in the mediæval countries of Europe. They deceive themselves by phrases and have never caught the meaning of the American spirit. It will not be won by those who spread the doctrine of class consciousness, promote the theory of class struggle, and who really mean to secure the dominance of their class. Their plans will not prevail. The world has not been working in vain for centuries to develop a common consciousness, a world opinion. It would gain nothing by tearing down an old dominant class and setting up a new one. Government by classes and class interest is passing from the earth. It is the German plan and is the antithesis of democracy. The American people will have none of it. I need scarcely add that German agents and German sympathizers in this country will not win this war for America and democracy. They are present and active and will ceaselessly labour to play on the hopes and prejudices of the masses of the people.

This war will not be won by those timid people who fear, or who pretend to fear, that the President seeks to be a dictator and demands a grant of unnecessary arbitrary powers, or by those who indulge themselves in refined and hair-splitting disquisitions on the Constitution, unduly obstructing the passage of measures necessary for the safety of the nation. The President desires no power which is not essential for the prosecution of this struggle against the Kaiser, and he desires it only so long as it is necessary to do this job.

All these persons, the people and the government must attend to at the proper time in orderly ways. They are obstructing the national will and are endangering the nation's safety. They are giving aid and comfort to the enemy. They are endangering the lives of more of your sons, brothers, and husbands, and involving you in immense unnecessary additional financial burdens.

We have undertaken the biggest task of our lives. Our work is cut out for us. We must see it through to a successful end. We shall not fail.

We are aligned with the free forces of the world and have back of us the conscience of civilization. I agree with the Archbishop of York that, in the ultimate analysis, there must be some power that can change the hearts of the German people which alone can make them fit associates for free and self-governing peoples; but in the meantime we must keep our powder dry and go through. This German plan of world empire will fail as other similar plans have failed. It is not the first time that it has been tried. The Persians tried it and were halted at Marathon and Salamis. Alexander attempted it and did not even get back home; Rome sought it and was finally overwhelmed by barbarians; Napoleon played for the same stake and ended his days at St. Helena. The Kaiser in his time will learn his lesson. This old world is not going backward. It is not going the way of the Kaiser. It is going the way of Clemenceau, Lloyd George, and Woodrow Wilson.

We must frankly face the fact that we cannot attain

success without great sacrifices, sacrifices of human life and of property. We may as well be prepared for them. The financial burden of war, in spite of anything we can do, is borne at the time war is waged. It cannot be shifted to future generations. Let us have no illusions about this. You cannot shift the burden. You merely create the credit relation of all to a few who lend their means and an obligation for repayment. The iron, the steel, the food, the clothing, and the ships are used and destroyed at the time and, for the most part, cannot be used again. If this were not so, then there would be no limit to the war a nation might wage. The ability of a people to wage war is measured by its ability to produce and to save. The government has called on you to do these things in the name of Liberty, and is calling again. You will not fail it.

Especially must we produce foods and feedstuffs and save them. The farmers will do their part. But an obligation more real than ever rests upon the towns and the cities to aid them by every constructive means, to aid them with finance and to aid them with labour. Last year, in spite of all the difficulties to be overcome—and they were many—the farmers planted the largest acreages in the history of the nation, produced record crops, and especially increased the numbers of the principal classes of live stock. I am confident that they will again overcome difficulties and generously supply, not only the needs of this nation but, to a considerable extent, of Europe. In this matter economic interest runs with patriotism.

That we have the physical resources to win this war, I entertain no doubt. That we have them in larger measure than any other nation in the world is a matter

of common knowledge. We have not yet fully realized
the enormous power of the country. If, in the 'sixties,
when we were a simple, crude, undeveloped nation doing
things, relatively speaking, on an "ox-cart" basis, with
the question yet undetermined whether we were to be one
nation or two, we could wage the mightiest war up to that
time and issue from it with unrivalled power, what can we
not do, with a united people and with immeasurably
greater resources, if our spirit is right and our purpose is
steadfast!

It is time for each individual to search his heart and to
purge his mind and purpose of selfish motives, and for
each class in society to think in terms of the nation rather
than in terms of its own interest. It is no time for any
class to hug to its bosom the delusion that it possesses a
monopoly of patriotism. Human nature is pretty evenly
distributed, and no little selfishness manifests itself in
every direction. I can conceive that each individual, no
matter what class of society he belongs to or what service
he renders, whether he be a manufacturer, a farmer, a
labourer, a lawyer, a scientist, a soldier, will take pains
to see that he attain for himself and his operations the
highest degree of efficiency and give the maximum service
or products to the nation at the lowest cost consistent with
efficient operation and effective standards of living; but it
is inconceivable to me that any citizen who dares to call
himself a patriot should aim to do less or to seek mere
selfish advantage. It is obviously the duty of each civilian
to reveal by his conduct the same standards of patriotism,
devotion, and sacrifice, if necessary, either of life or property, that we expect from the men whom we send to the
front directly to bear the brunt of battle.

[345]

There can be no slacking. If the free, democratic, law-abiding nations like Great Britain, Belgium, and France are destroyed, if Prussian militarism is permitted to dominate, then the Anglo-Saxon fight for free institutions and liberty, persisting from Runnymede to Yorktown, its fight against the absolute right of kings and barons, with its Magna Charta, its Bill of Rights, its Declaration of Independence, and the heroic fight of the French, of the Italians, of the Belgians, and of other free peoples, for liberty, will have been made in vain. The rights of the nation must be vindicated and its institutions preserved. Those who would keep the people of the world from going about their business in orderly and decent fashion must be taught a lesson once for all. Guarantees that there shall be no recurrence of such a world calamity as the present must be enforced. A finish must be made to things feudal, humanity safeguarded, and democracy impregnably intrenched. The lesson must be forced home that peoples shall no longer be put under subjection by force, that the only worthy and tolerable national aspiration is to have a clean national household from cellar to attic; and a durable and righteous peace must be secured in accordance with the recent history-making declaration of the President—a peace on the basis of reparation, justice, and security.

THE END

INDEX

INDEX

A. B. C. powers offer mediation in Mexican embroglio, 117.

Agricultural Advisory Committee of great service during the war, 343.

Agricultural Educational Extension Act, approved by the President, 204.

Agriculture, programme of the Department, 199; greatly increased production necessary on account of the war, 258; part played by the different organizations during the war, 329ff.

Alderman, E. A., letter on necessity of war with Germany, 247ff; is suggested by Secretary Houston as First Assistant Secretary of State, II, 69.

Ancona, protest to Austria against the sinking of, 153.

Anti-trust law should be explicitly defined, 110.

Appropriation Bill of 1920, brings out Congressional invasion of the executive field, II, 71; its veto recommended by Secretary Houston, 72, 75; its signing suggested by him, 76; is vetoed by President Wilson, 76; is signed by President Wilson after revision, 82.

Arabic, sunk in violation of German promises, 152.

Armaments, limitation of—*See* Article VIII.

Arming of merchantmen, discussed by the Cabinet, 233; President Wilson, failing in support of Congress, directs that arming be done, 241.

Armistice, German note discussed by Cabinet, 308; discussion of Austrian note, 319; acceptance of the Fourteen Points, 320; Congress addressed by President Wilson and informed of conditions, 325.

Army, preparations for enlargment, 158.

Army Appropriation Bill, passage of, 182.

Article I, Lodge ratification resolution limits its application, II, 42; Hitchcock reservation limits its application, 52.

Article VIII, Lodge ratification resolution limits its application, II, 45.

Article X, President Wilson explains that it does not limit Congress in matters of peace and war, II, 11, 15, 24; President Wilson calls it "the very backbone of the whole Covenant," 12; Senate Committee on Foreign Relations reports reservation opposing obliga-

tions under it, 18; defended by William H. Taft, 19; Lodge ratification resolution limits its application, 42; Hitchcock reservation limits its application, 52, 53; is opposed by Secretary Lansing, 68.

Article XV, President Wilson explains that it places domestic questions beyond League jurisdiction, II, 10, 27; Lodge ratification resolution limits its application, 43; Hitchcock reservation limits its application, 52.

Article XVI, Lodge ratification resolution limits its application, II, 45.

Austrian armistice note, discussed by Cabinet, 319.

Aviation, Naval Flying Corps created, 181.

Baker, Secretary Newton D., his position on severance of diplomatic relations with Germany, 229; advises raising of great army, and inauguration of universal training, 243; able conduct of his difficult task, 280; comments on President Wilson's collapse, II, 36.

Balfour, Rt. Hon. Arthur James, answer to President Wilson's peace note, 224; arrives in Washington at head of British Mission, 267; playing tennis with, 271, 274; at Washington's Tomb, 275; amazed at our war preparations, 277.

Baltimore Convention, the contest between Champ Clark and Woodrow Wilson, 7.

Ball, Senator-elect L. Heisler, signs Lodge's anti-league Round Robin, II, 2.

Banking, system of United States compared to those of Europe, 100.

Banking—*See also* Federal Reserve System.

Barrett, C. S., member National Agricultural Advisory Committee, 343.

Baruch, Bernard M., member Advisory Commission, Council of National Defence, 184.

Bernstorff, in the *Lusitania* controversy, 152; given his papers on severance of diplomatic relations, 231.

Bernhardi, comments on successful wars, II, 289.

Bethmann-Hollweg, T. von, denies responsibility to Parliament, II, 293.

Bismarck, Count Otto von, expresses theory of right of might, II, 289.

Bolshevism, President Wilson's fear of prop-

INDEX

Congress, 277; special services created, 278; under non-partisan management, 279.

Warren, Senator F. E., signs Lodge's anti-league Round Robin, II, 2.

Washington, George, on the compensation of government officers in relation to the expense of upholding their positions, 15.

Water-power legislation, urged in President Wilson's Second Annual Message, 122, 125.

Watson, Senator James E., signs Lodge's anti-league Round Robin, II, 2.

Wells, Rolla, telegram to National Democratic Committee at Baltimore Convention endorsing Wilson, 8; accepts Treasuryship of Campaign Committee, 9.

White, Chief Justice, applauds President Wilson's advice to Congress to declare state of war with Germany, 254.

Wickersham, George W., advocates ratification of the Treaty, II, 18.

Willard, Daniel, Chairman Advisory Commission Council of National Defence, 184; Chairman Council of National Defence, 184.

William II, claims to be responsible to God alone, II, 290, 339.

Williams, John Sharp, approves President Wilson's message to Congress advising declaration of war with Germany, 255.

Williams, John Skelton, at the hearings for deciding Federal Reserve cities, 108.

Wilson, Secretary of Agriculture, James, turns over the Department, 38.

Wilson, Oliver, member National Agricultural Advisory Committee, 343.

Wilson, Secretary William B., at the first Cabinet meeting, 35.

Wilson, Woodrow: at the Baltimore Convention, 7; early acquaintance with, 17; apprehensions as to his executive ability and capacity for team work, 18; talk with on tariff, taxation, and currency at Col. House's dinner, 18; his inauguration, 29; at the first meetings of the Cabinet, 33, 39; attitude toward political appointments, 40, 48; explains position toward Latin America, 43; to be his own Secretary of State, 44; his statement regarding Six-power Loan to China, 44; his tariff message, 47; resolves to deliver his messages to Congress in person, 48, 52; interested in establishment of stable government in China, 49; discusses the Japanese question, 51; brings up question of Panama Canal tolls at Cabinet meeting, 59; for recognition of China, 59; answer to Japan's protests against California exclusion laws, 65; opposed to recognition of Huerta, 69;

objects to proviso in Sundry Civil bill, 69; his statement on the lobby, 71; delivers message to Congress on the currency, 73, 80; and on the Mexican situation, 73; approves Underwood-Simmons Tariff Act, 74; in address before Southern Commercial Congress explains attitude toward Latin America, 76; patient and tolerant toward certain advisers, 88; signs Federal Reserve Act, 90; lays before Congress his views on the Trust question, 109; against interlocking directorates and great financial interests but for freedom of railroads, 110; reads before Congress his message on Panama tolls, 112; orders fleet to Mexican waters, 114; and taking of Vera Cruz, 116; death of his wife, 120; urges Congress to provide for internal taxes to offset revenues lost through war in Europe, 121; in his Second Annual Message urges water-power legislation, passage of the shipping bill, and preparation for national defence, 122; states he will veto the immigration bill, 127; proposes further warning to the Mexican factions, 133; treatment of the *Lusitania* question, 135ff; appears before Congress to advise it concerning situation with Germany, 155; against a large regular army, depending on a strengthened National Guard, 158; Preparedness measures, 159; on his change of mind, 161; correspondence with Secretary of War Garrison on events incident to the latter's resignation, 165ff; letter to Ass't-Sec'y Breckinridge accepting resignation, 179; asks Congress to provide revenues for defence programme, 185; renominated for the Presidency, 191; attitude toward hyphenated Americans, 193; approves Agricultural Educational Extension Act, 204; his peace note and its unfavourable reception, 217ff; his address to the Senate on the peace aftermath, 224; addresses Congress announcing severance of diplomatic relations with Germany, 231; attitude on arming of merchantmen, 234; characterization of filibuster group in the Senate, 240; his Inaugural Address devoted to foreign problems, 240; appears before Joint Session of Congress to advise that body to declare existence of a state of war with Germany, 253ff; his propaganda through psychology, 301ff; reply to Prince Maximilian's peace overtures, 306; his Mount Vernon Fourth of July address, 307; discussion of German note proposing armistice, 308ff; reply to the note, 317; discussion of Austrian note, 319; at Cabinet meeting advises of acceptance of the